THE ARTS OF CHINA

Michael Sullivan

THE ARTS OF CHINA

Third Edition

University of California Press

Berkeley • Los Angeles • London

University of California Press
Berkeley and Los Angeles, California

University of California Press, Ltd.
London, England

Library of Congress Cataloging in Publication Data

Sullivan, Michael, 1916–
    The arts of China.

    Bibliography: p.
    Includes index.
    1. Art, Chinese.   I. Title.
N7340.S92   1983   709'.51   82–16027
ISBN 0–520–04917–9
ISBN 0–520–04918–7 (pbk.)

Printed in the United States of America

to Khoan

Contents

List of Maps and Illustrations

Preface to the Third Edition

The publishers have once again kindly allowed me revisions and corrections to make this third edition as up-to-date as possible. My thanks are due to them, to those who have supplied me with new illustrations, and above all to the scholars and students of Chinese art whose work and whose comments on earlier editions have helped me to improve the book. I should particularly like to thank my students Ng Sokam and Linda Wu.

After careful consideration, I have decided for this edition to keep to the familiar Wade-Giles romanisation of Chinese names and words. It is still widely used and has the advantage, whatever its faults, of being easier for English-speaking readers to pronounce than the official *Pinyin*, which will be found in the Index.

MICHAEL SULLIVAN

Stanford, California
December, 1982

MAP 1 Modern China.

Chronological Table of Dynasties

HSIA			?–?
SHANG			C. 1750–1045 B.C.

CHOU	Western Chou
	Eastern Chou
	  'Spring and Autumn'
	    period
	  Warring States period
		1045–711
		770–256
		
		722–481
		480–222
			1045–256

CH'IN			221–207
HAN	Former (Western) Han Hsin Later (Eastern) Han	202 B.C.–A.D.9 9–23 25–220	202 B.C.–A.D. 220
THREE KINGDOMS	Shu (Han) Wei Wu	221–263 220–265 222–280	221–265
SOUTHERN (Six Dynasties) and	Chin Eastern Chin Liu Sung Southern Ch'i Liang Ch'en	265–316 317–420 420–479 479–502 502–557 557–587	265–581
NORTHERN DYNASTIES	Northern Wei (T'o-pa) Eastern Wei (T'o-pa) Western Wei (T'o-pa) Northern Ch'i Northern Chou (Hsien-pi)	386–535 534–543 535–554 550–577 557–581	
SUI			581–618
T'ANG			618–906
FIVE DYNASTIES	Later Liang Later T'ang (Turkic) Later Chin (Turkic) Later Han (Turkic) Later Chou	907–922 923–936 936–948 946–950 951–960	907–960
	Liao (Khitan Tartars) Hsi-hsia (Tangut Tibetan)	907–1125 990–1227	
SUNG	Northern Sung Southern Sung	960–1126 1127–1279	960–1279
	Chin (Jurchen Tartars)	1115–1234	
YÜAN (Mongols)			1260–1368
MING			1368–1644
CH'ING (Manchus)			1644–1912
REPUBLIC			1912–1949
PEOPLE'S REPUBLIC			1949–

Reign Periods of the Ming and Ch'ing Dynasties

MING 1368–1644

Hung-wu	1368–1398
Chien-wen	1399–1402
Yung-lo	1403–1424
Hung-hsi	1425
Hsüan-te	1426–1435
Cheng-t'ung	1436–1449
Ching-t'ai	1450–1457
T'ien-shun	1457–1464
Ch'eng-hua	1465–1487
Hung-chih	1488–1505
Cheng-te	1506–1521
Chia-ching	1522–1566
Lung-ch'ing	1567–1572
Wan-li	1573–1620
T'ai-ch'ang	1620
T'ien-ch'i	1621–1627
Ch'ung-chen	1628–1644

CH'ING 1644–1912

Shun-chih	1644–1661
K'ang-hsi	1662–1722
Yung-cheng	1723–1735
Ch'ien-lung	1736–1796
Chia-ch'ing	1796–1821
Tao-kuang	1821–1850
Hsien-feng	1851–1861
T'ung-chih	1862–1873
Kuang-hsü	1874–1908
Hsüan-t'ung	1909–1912

Before the Dawn of History

To admirers of Chinese art, the recent decades have been a time of bewilderment and frustration as they watched the Chinese apparently repudiating, even at times destroying, their cultural heritage. For years, as China carried out her gigantic social and political revolution, her doors were shut to almost all but her most uncritical admirers. While the lot of the masses improved beyond belief, art and the artist suffered, particularly during the ten terrible years from the Cultural Revolution to the death of Mao Tse-tung in 1976.

Yet even at the worst times, while artists and scholars were imprisoned or sent down to farm and factory, the archaeological work never ceased. Indeed, in the thirty years following the founding of the People's Republic in 1949, China has done more to excavate, protect, study, and display her cultural heritage than ever before in her history. If this was politically justified by Mao's insistence that the past must serve the present—and to do so it must be visible—it more truly reflects the sense of history that the Chinese have always felt and that not even the Cultural Revolution could destroy. For now, as always, the Chinese look upon their history as a deep reservoir from which they draw strength, not as a luxury but as something essential to the vitality of their culture.

Nor have the old legends been forgotten. One of these legends concerns the origins of the world.[1] In far-off times, it runs, the universe was an enormous egg. One day the egg split open; its upper half became the sky, its lower half the earth, and from it emerged P'an Ku, primordial man. Every day he grew ten feet taller, the sky ten feet higher, the earth ten feet thicker. After eighteen thousand years P'an Ku died. His head split and became the sun and moon, while his blood filled the rivers and seas. His hair became the forests and meadows, his perspiration the rain, his breath the wind, his voice the thunder—and his fleas our ancestors.

A people's legends of its origins generally give a clue as to what they think most important. This one is no exception, for it expresses an age-old Chinese viewpoint—namely, that man is not the culminating achievement of the creation, but a relatively insignificant part in the scheme of things; hardly more than an afterthought, in fact. By comparison with the beauty and splendour of the world itself, the mountains and valleys, the clouds and waterfalls, the trees and flowers, which are the visible manifestations of the workings of the *Tao*, he counts for very little. In no other civilisation did the forms and patterns of nature, and man's humble response to it, play so big a part. We can trace the germs of this attitude into the remote past, when in North China nature was a kinder master than she is now. Half a million years ago, in the time of Peking man, that region was comparatively warm and wet; elephants and rhinoceroses roamed a more luxuriant countryside than the barren hills and windswept plains of recent times. Within this till lately inhospitable area, forming the modern provinces of Honan, Hopei, Shensi, and Shansi, was born a uniquely Chinese feeling of oneness with nature which, in course of time, was to find its highest expression in philosophy, poetry, and painting. This sense of communion was not merely philosophical and artistic; it had a practical value as well. For the farmer's prosperity, and hence that of society as a whole, depended upon his knowing the seasons and attuning himself to the "will of heaven," as he called it. Agriculture in course of time became a ritual over which the emperor himself presided, and when at the spring sowing he ceremonially ploughed the first furrow, not only did he hope to ensure a good harvest thereby, but his office was itself further ennobled by this act of homage to the forces of nature.

This sense of "attunement" is fundamental in Chinese thinking. Man must attune himself not only to nature but also to his fellow men, in ever-widening circles starting from his family and friends. Thus, his highest ideal has always in the past been to discover the order of things and to act in accordance with it. As in the following pages the history of Chinese art unfolds, we will find that its characteristic and unique beauty lies in the fact that it is an expression of this very sense of attunement. Is that one reason why Westerners, often with no other interest in Chinese civilisation, collect and admire Chinese art with such enthusiasm? Do they sense, perhaps, that the forms which the Chinese artist and craftsman have created are *natural* forms—forms which seem to have evolved inevitably by the movement of the maker's hand, as an intuitive response to a natural rhythm? Chinese art does not demand of us, as does Indian art, the effort to bridge what often seems an unbridgeable gulf between extremes of physical form and metaphysical content; nor will we find in it that preoccupation with formal and intellectual considerations which so often makes Western art difficult for the Asian mind to accept. The forms of Chinese art are beautiful because they are in the widest and deepest sense harmonious, and we can appreciate them because we too feel their rhythms all around us in nature and instinctively respond to them. These rhythms, moreover, this sense of inner life expressed in line and contour, are present in Chinese art from its earliest beginnings.

Every lover of Chinese art today is familiar with the magnificent painted pottery of the Neolithic period, but it was not until 1921 that positive evidence was found that China had actually passed through a Stone Age at all. In that year the Swedish geologist J. Gunnar Andersson and his Chinese assistants made two discoveries of immense importance. The first was at Chou-k'ou-tien, southwest of Peking, where deep in a cleft in the hillside Andersson picked up a number of flint tools, indicating that it had been occupied by very early man. He himself did not excavate, but his find led to further excavations and to the eventual discovery by Dr. P'ei Wen-chung of fossil bones which, with the exception of late Java man, *Pithecanthropus erectus*, were the oldest human remains yet discovered. The bones were those of a hominid, *Sinanthropus pekinensis*, who lived in the middle Pleistocene period, about half a million years ago. The remains in the deep cleft, fifty metres thick, represent many thousands of years of occupation. Peking man had tools of quartz, flint, and limestone, made either from pebbles chipped to shape or from flakes struck off a large pebble. He was a cannibal who broke open the bones of his victims to suck out the marrow; he had fire, ate grain, and probably knew some very primitive form of speech. In 1964, in deposits on an open hillside in Lan-t'ien County, Shensi, palaeontologists discovered the cranium of a hominid believed, from related fossil remains, to be at least 100,000 years older than Peking man, and so roughly the same age as early Java man, *Pithecanthropus robustus*. Far older still are the fossil teeth of an ape-man discovered in 1965 in the Yüan-mou district in Yunnan dated by palaeomagnetism to 1.7 million years ago. The search for early man in China goes on.

Gradually, in the late Pleistocene, the evolution of early man in China gathered pace. In recent years, remains of *Homo sapiens* have been found in many areas. "Upper Cave Man" at Chou-k'ou-tien (c. 25,000 B.C.) had a wider range of stone tools than his ancestors, he probably wore hides sewn together, and his wife adorned herself with stone beads drilled and painted with hematite, the earliest known intentional decoration in the history of Chinese civilisation. Finely fashioned microliths (very small stone implements) have been found in many desert sites in Ning-hsia and the Ordos region, different types of blades and flakes being fashioned for different purposes. Further south, in the region of northern Honan that was to become the last seat of the Shang Dynasty, thousands of microliths were discovered in a habitation site in 1960; other rich remains have been found far to the southwest, in Szechwan, Yunnan, and Kweichow. Although as yet the dating of these scattered sites and their relationship to each other are by no means clear, their distribution suggests that the Upper Palaeolithic culture, shading imperceptibly into the Mesolithic, was spread very widely across ancient China.

The people of the Mesolithic era were hunters and fishermen. The "Neolithic Revolution" took place when the ancestors of the Chinese race settled down, began to build villages and to learn the

NEOLITHIC CULTURE

KANSU
YANGSHAO

Ch'i-shan•

LUNGSHAN

•ch'eng-tzu-yai

NUCLEAR
YANGSHAO

• Ta-wen-k'ou

Pan-shan• Chi'-chia-ping
• Ma-chia-yao Yang-shao •

Chengchow
• ch'ing-lien-kang

Pan-p'o •   P'ei-li-kang

CH'ING-LIEN-
KANG

Ho-mu-tu
•

SOUTHERN
NEOLITHIC
CULTURES

| 0 | 100 | 200 | 300 | 400 MI |

| 0 | 100 | 200 | 300 | 400 | 500 K.M. |

MAP 2 China in the Neolithic period.

arts of farming, horticulture, and pottery making. Each new discovery pushes the Neolithic revolution further back. At the time of this writing, the most important early sites are those of the "P'ei-li-kang culture." P'ei-li-kang is a village near Loyang. Most of the sites of this culture have been found in southern Hopei and northern Honan, making this area truly the cradle of Chinese civilisation. House floors, cemeteries, evidence of the domestication of animals have been found, while the kilns produced a crude pottery decorated with scratched designs. By carbon-14 dating archaeologists have put the P'ei-li-kang culture at around 6000 to 5000 B.C.

The next stage in the evolution of early Chinese civilisation has been known for over sixty years—ever since J. Gunnar Andersson, searching for minerals in Honan, discovered at the village of

Yang-shao simple burials furnished with the marvellous painted pottery that has given the name "Yangshao culture" to a major phase in Chinese prehistory lasting from about 5000 to 3000 B.C. In 1923 Andersson, noting the resemblance between the Yangshao pottery and that of the ancient Near East, went westwards to Kansu in search of linking sites and there found, at Pan-shan, graves with rather similar pottery. Since then, however, Chinese archaeologists have found so many "painted pottery" sites in different parts of north China that possible connections with western Asia are hardly discussed.

The most important discovery of the Yangshao culture occurred in 1953, when a group of Neolithic villages and a cemetery were unearthed at Pan-p'o, just east of Sian. The villages cover two and a half acres; four separate layers of houses have been found in a cultural deposit three metres thick, representing many centuries of occupation spanning the fifth millenium B.C. The earliest inhabitants lived in round wattle-and-daub huts with reed roofs and plaster floors and an oven in the centre, the design perhaps copied from an earlier tent or yurt. Their descendants built rectangular, round, or square houses with a framework of wooden planking, sunk a metre below ground-level and approached by a flight of steps. A further advance in the domestic architecture of late Stone Age China is marked by the three-room

1 Pan-p'o-ts'un, Shensi. Part of the Neolithic village after excavation; now a museum.

2 Pan-p'o-ts'un, Shensi. Neolithic houses, reconstructed. After Kwang-chih Chang.

houses excavated at Ta-ho-ts'un near Chengchow, the plaster walls of which were actually baked to give them a hard and durable surface.

The Pan-p'o potters made both a coarse grey or red pottery and a fine red ware burnished and then painted in black with geometric designs and occasionally with fishes and human faces (see Fig. 5). They seem not to have known the potter's wheel, but made their vessels by coiling long strips of clay. From clay they also made spindle whorls and even hairpins, but the finer objects such as needles, fishhooks, spoons, and arrowheads were made of bone. Part of the villages of Pan-p'o and Ta-ho-ts'un have been roofed over and preserved as museums of Chinese Neolithic culture.

The painted pottery found first by Andersson, and later in many other sites in Honan and Kansu, has not been matched in quality and beauty by any Neolithic wares discovered since. It consists chiefly of mortuary urns, wide and deep bowls, and tall vases, often with loop-handles set low on the body. Though the walls are thin, the forms are robust, their generous contours beautifully enhanced by the decoration in black pigment which was clearly executed with a crude form of brush. Some of the designs are geometric, consisting of parallel bands or lozenges containing concentric squares, crosses, or diamonds. The lower half of the body is always left undecorated; it may have been set in the sandy ground to prevent it from overturning. Many vessels are adorned with sweeping wavelike bands that gather into a kind of whirlpool; others make use of the stylised figures of men, frogs, fishes, and birds. Shards found at Ma-chia-yao in Kansu (c. 2500 B.C.) reveal a quite sophisticated brush technique, in one case depicting plants each of whose leaves ends in a sharp point with a flick of the brush—the same technique that was to be used by the Sung artist, three thousand years later, in painting bamboo. Naturalistic motifs, however, are rare, and the majority are decorated with geometric or stylised patterns whose significance is still a mystery.

Until recently it was thought that the painted pottery Yang-shao culture was more or less directly superseded by a totally different culture centered on Shantung, and represented by the burnished black pottery of Lung-shan. But under the impact of a succession of new discoveries, this rather simple picture has given way to a more complex and interesting one. First of all, the beautiful painted pottery from Ma-chia-yao and Pan-shan in Kansu (see Fig. 7, c. 2400 B.C.) is now known from carbon-14 analysis to be as much as two thousand years later in date than the painted pottery of the Yang-shao village of Pan-p'o, which has yielded a date as early as 4865 B.C. ± 110 years.[2] This seems to suggest a centrifugal movement of the nuclear Yang-shao outward from the Central Plain (Chung-yüan) and to disprove the old theory that the Chinese painted pottery was the product of a great eastward movement, if not of peoples, then of an essentially Western Asiatic culture. That there may have been some crossfertilisation with Western Asia is possible, particularly in the later Neolithic period, but in their lively, uplifted forms and, still more, in the dynamic linear movement of their brush decoration the Chinese painted vases reveal qualities that are uniquely Chinese.

Every year as new sites in eastern and southeastern China are discovered, the native origins of Chinese Neolithic culture are more firmly established. In 1973–74, for instance, at Ho-mu-tu in northern Kiangsu, remains of a village of about 5000 B.C., at least as early as Pan-p'o, were unearthed. The houses were built on timber posts over marshy land; the inhabitants cultivated rice, had pottery, knew the elephant and rhinoceros.[3] Another related phase in the eastern China Neolithic is seen at Ch'ing-lien-kang in northern Kiangsu, which produced the elegant bowl on this page, decorated with swirling patterns in red, white and black. As we move further northward up the coast, and later in time, we come to Ta-wen-k'ou in southern Shantung. The pottery jar from Ning-yang-hsien illustrated here is a product of the Ta-wen-k'ou culture, which, beginning perhaps as early as 4000 B.C., spread outward, even to influence the painted pottery tradition of Yang-

3 Bowl. Pottery decorated with scrolled ornament in red and white slip. Excavated at P'ei-hsien, Kiangsu. Ch'ing-lien-kang culture, late Neolithic period.

4 Jar. Pottery decorated with black and white slip. Excavated in Ning-yang-hsien, Shantung. Lung-shan culture, late Neolithic period.

5 Bowl. Pottery decorated with masks and nets(?) in black slip. Excavated at Pan-p'o-ts'un, Shensi. Early Yang-shao culture, Neolithic period.

6 Stemcup. Black pottery. Excavated at Wei-fang, Shantung. Lung-shan culture, late Neolithic period.

shao. Many Chinese scholars think that the marks scratched on the Ta-wen-k'ou pottery, dateable around 2500–2000 B.C., represent the first true writing in China and are the ancestors of the bronze and oracle-bone script of the Shang Dynasty described in the next chapter.

By about 2400 B.C. the Ta-wen-k'ou culture was shading imperceptibly into the "Black Pottery culture" first found by Dr. Wu Chin-ting in 1928 in Lung-shan in Shantung. Most famous among the Lung-shan wares is a delicate pottery made of dark grey clay burnished black and of incredible fragility, being sometimes as little as half a millimetre thick. The shapes are elegant, while the decoration, consisting chiefly of raised bands, grooves, and milled rings, gives it a somewhat metallic, machine-made look. It must have been extremely difficult to make, let alone use, for in the succeeding Bronze Age the tradition died out completely. Recent discoveries at Wei-fang in Shantung reveal that the Black Pottery culture also produced a white pottery of remarkable vigour and originality, illustrated in Fig. 8 by the extraordinary pitcher, called a *k'uei*, which seems to imitate a vessel made of hides bound with thongs.

While the painted and black wares are certainly the most spectacular, they represent only a small fraction of all the utensils pro-

duced by the Chinese Neolithic potter. There was much plain red
ware and even more coarse grey ware representing an all-pervading continuation of the earliest ceramic tradition in China. To the
art lover, these grey wares are often of interest more for their legacy than for any intrinsic merit they may possess, for later we will
find some of these shapes, notably the *ting* and *li* tripods and the
hsien steamer (a pot with perforated base standing on a *li*), adopted
in the Bronze Age as ritual vessels used in the ancestral sacrifices of
the Shang Dynasty; while the technique of impressing designs in
the wet clay, which later developed, particularly in eastern China,
into a sophisticated language of stamped motifs, also played its
part in the decoration of the bronzes.

As we move westward again from Shantung into Honan, we
find black Lung-shan pottery in strata overlying the earlier Yang-
shao and representing a still later stage in the development of the
Neolithic culture of the Central Plain. In some of the latest Black

7 Funerary urn. Pottery decorated with
red and black slip. Excavated at Pan-
shan, Kansu. Yang-shao culture,
Neolithic period.

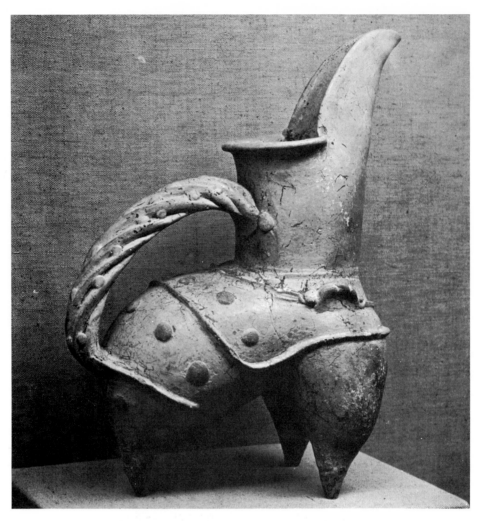

8 Pitcher. Greyish-white pottery. Excavated at Wei-fang, Shantung. Lung-shan culture, late Neolithic period.

Pottery sites, such as Ch'i-chia-p'ing in Kansu, dated by carbon-14 to around 2000–1750 B.C., simple artifacts of pure copper begin to appear, heralding the dawn of the great Bronze Age culture that will be described in Chapter 2.

Though often beautifully made and finished, most of the stone implements of late Neolithic times were utilitarian objects such as hoes, scrapers, and axes, one of the latter being the ancestor of the *ko*-type dagger axe of the Shang Dynasty (p. 27). The finest of these implements were made of polished jade, a stone which because of its hardness, fine texture, and purity of colour was destined to become an object of special veneration in Chinese cultural history. Among Neolithic jades are bracelets (*huan*), penannular rings (*chüeh*), and half-rings (*huang*), a flat disc with a hole in the centre (*pi*) and a ring or short tube squared on the outside (*tsung*). In later historic times these shapes acquired a ritual or ceremonial function, the *pi* and *tsung*, for example, symbolising respectively heaven and earth; but there is no means at present of knowing whether they already had this, or indeed any, symbolic meaning in the late Stone Age.

It is natural that in a history of art we should chronicle the early stages of civilisation in that most indestructible of crafts—pottery. Just who the people were who made it is not yet certain. There were many tribes in prehistoric China, some communicating with each other, others not, some advanced, others backward. Hundreds of Neolithic sites have been excavated all over China, and although many problems remain unsolved, a picture is beginning to form of how Chinese society was emerging, and of how local customs and craft traditions were beginning to develop.

For all the regional differences, it seems that by the end of the Neolithic period, which should be put in the most advanced areas at about 2000 B.C., the Chinese were leading an organised social life, centred on the farm and the village and bound together by ritual; that they practiced high standards of craftsmanship, were preoccupied with death, made ritual use of jade, and had mastered the flexible brush as an instrument of artistic expression. This primitive culture lingered on in southern and western China long after the coming of bronze had opened up a new and incomparably richer chapter in Chinese history.

9 *Hsien* steamer. Excavated at Chengchow, Honan. Second millennium B.C.

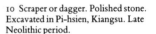

10 Scraper or dagger. Polished stone. Excavated in Pi-hsien, Kiangsu. Late Neolithic period.

11 Ritual vessel, *chüeh*. Bronze. From Yen-shih, Honan. Early Shang Dynasty.

2
The Shang Dynasty

For centuries, farmers living in the village of Hsiao-t'un near An-yang in Honan have been picking up peculiar bones which they found lying in the fields after rain or while they were ploughing. Some were polished and shone like glass; most had rows of oval notches in their backs and T-shaped cracks; a few had marks on them that looked like primitive writing. The farmers would take these bones to apothecaries in Anyang and neighbouring towns, who often ground off the marks before selling them as "dragon bones," a potent ingredient in restoratives. In 1899 some of the inscribed bones fell into the hands of the noted scholar and collector Liu Ngo, who recognised the writing as an older form of the archaic script already known on the ritual bronzes of the Chou Dynasty. Soon other scholars, notably Lo Chen-yü and Wang Kuo-wei, took up the study of what were, in fact, fragments of the archives of the royal house of Shang, the existence of which had hitherto not been proved, though Chinese historians had never doubted it.

The bones were traced to Anyang. The farmers began to dig deeper, and before long there began to appear on the antique market in Peking and Shanghai magnificent bronze vessels, jades, and other objects, whose exact place of origin was kept secret. For nearly thirty years the farmers and dealers' agents, working at night or during the idle winter months, continued their indiscriminate pillaging of Shang tombs. Finally, in 1928, the Chinese National Research Institute (Academia Sinica) began at Anyang an important series of excavations which were to provide the first definite archaeological evidence that the Shang Dynasty had actually existed and was not, as some Western writers had come to suspect, a pious fabrication of the backward-looking Chinese. By 1935 more than three hundred graves had been discovered, ten of which, of enormous size, were undoubtedly royal tombs.

These discoveries posed more problems than they solved. Who were the Shang people and where did they come from? How was it that their earliest remains revealed a culture of such sophistication, particularly in their bronze techniques? If the Shang had existed, then perhaps remains would be found of the even earlier Hsia Dynasty.

The Chinese traditionally believe that they are descended from Huang Ti, the Yellow Emperor, who lived for a hundred years. He succeeded Fu Hsi, who first drew the magical diagram *pa kua* (the "eight trigrams") from which the art of writing is descended. Shen Nung, the Divine Farmer, invented agriculture and discovered the use of medicinal herbs. Then came Yao and the filial Shun, the ideal rulers, and finally Yü the Great, who founded the Hsia Dynasty. In these legendary figures the Chinese personified all that they held most sacred: agriculture, good government, filial piety, and the art of writing. Now it is believed that all these personages were invented or took on these roles at a much later date. Yü, Yao, and Shun appeared first in late Chou literature. Huang Ti was probably invented by the Taoists. As for the Hsia, before the rise of Shang there were, as we saw in Chapter 1, many primitive communities, and one of those conquered by the first Shang ruler may have been called Hsia. Such communities form a connecting link between the late Neolithic and the full flowering of the Bronze Age.

Until 1950 our knowledge of Shang culture was derived almost wholly from the remains of the Shang at Anyang, founded by King P'an-keng around 1400 B.C. and finally conquered by the

12 Ritual vessel, *ting*. Bronze. Excavated at Chengchow, Honan. Middle Shang period.

MAP 3 Ancient China with major
Shang and Chou Dynasty sites.

armies of the Chou very probably in 1045 B.C. At Anyang the
bronze culture was at its height; the metalworkers were producing sacrificial vessels of a quality that has been equalled nowhere in
the world—the culmination, clearly, of centuries of development. The oracle bones gave the names of eighteen kings before
P'an-keng and, according to tradition, the Shang had moved their
capital five times before finally settling at Anyang. If traces of
these earlier capitals could be found, the gap between the late Neolithic and the mature bronze culture of Anyang might be closed.

This is in fact just what is happening. Artefacts of pure copper
have been found in sites of the Kansu painted pottery culture of
about 3000 B.C. and in the Lung-shan Black Pottery site of San-li-

ho in Shantung (about 2100 B.C.), while true bronze objects, made from a copper-tin alloy, have been unearthed in Ma-ch'ang and Ch'ia-chia sites in Kansu dateable between 2300 and 2000 B.C. The late Yang-shao and Lung-shan cultures, therefore, hitherto assigned entirely to the late Stone Age, can now be seen as the era of the discovery and early evolution of metal-working in China, although metal objects are still very rare.

In the 1950s Chinese archaeologists began to search for the beginnings of a true Bronze Age civilisation in the area of northern Honan and southern Shansi traditionally known as the "Waste of Hsia." Their work was rewarded with the discovery of over a hundred sites, of which the richest is at Erh-li-t'ou, between Loyang and Yen-shih. There they discovered the remains of a town, with a palace (?) on a terrace, bronze workshops, vessels, weapons, and other artefacts, some inlaid with turquoise, and objects of jade. They divided the "Erh-li-t'ou culture period," as it is now called, into four stages, covering the period roughly from 1900 to 1600 B.C. From the third stage comes the primitive but elegant vessel for heating and pouring wine called a *chüeh* (illustrated on p. 11), one of the earliest ritual vessels yet discovered in China, and ancestor of the remarkable bronzes of the mature Shang Dynasty.

Archaeologists are now debating whether all four phases of the Erh-li-t'ou culture should be assigned to the Hsia Dynasty, or only the first two, in which case this vessel would be very early Shang. But until written evidence is found, it will not be possible to assign any site to the Hsia Dynasty with certainty.

13 Ritual vessel, *ting*. Bronze.
Excavated at P'an-lung-ch'eng, Hupei.
Middle Shang period.

By about 1500 B.C. the Bronze Age culture was widely spread over northern, central, and eastern China, as our map shows. Spectacular sites of this pre-Anyang stage have been discovered at Chengchow. The lowest strata at Chengchow are typical Lung-shan Neolithic, but the next stages, Lower and Upper Erh-li-kang, show a dramatic change. Remains of a city wall more than a mile square and sixty feet across at the base have been uncovered, together with what were probably sacrificial halls, houses, bronze foundries, pottery kilns, and a bone workshop. Large graves were furnished with ritual bronze vessels, jade, and ivory, while the pottery included both glazed stoneware and the fine white ware first found at Anyang. It is possible, though by no means proved, that Chengchow was one of the early Shang capitals, although precisely which one has not been definitely established.

To the same stage of Shang civilisation belongs P'an-lung-ch'eng in the Yangtse valley. There in 1974 were discovered the remains of a large palace and richly furnished tombs, whence comes the noble ritual tripod vessel, called a *ting*, illustrated here. At the time of writing it is not known whether this supposed palace was the seat of a Shang feudal chief or district governor, or of an independent ruler—although some bronzes are inscribed, they do not yield this kind of information—but the presence of so important a city so far to the south is a clear indication of the extent and grandeur of Bronze Age civilisation by the middle of the second millennium B.C.

All that we have seen of Bronze Age culture so far was but a preparation for the climax of the Shang at Anyang, a region which the succeeding Chou conquerors called Yin. Over half a century of excavation there has given us a detailed picture of the city and of its social and economic life. Chinese historians today, following orthodox Marxist doctrine, describe Shang and Chou as pre-feudal slave societies, and indeed the contents of the royal tombs at Anyang alone are enough to show that, under the Shang, slaves were many and brutally treated. But it seems that elements of feudalism were already present, for the inscriptions on the oracle bones indicate that successful generals, sons, and even wives of the Shang rulers were enfeoffed, while small neighbouring states paid regular tribute. Prominent among the officials was the *chen-jen*, who, as a scribe, composed and probably wrote the inscriptions on the oracle bones, and, as a diviner, interpreted the cracks that appeared in them when a hot metal rod was applied to one of the holes bored into the back.

These inscriptions were generally engraved, though a few were written with brush and ink. Over three thousand characters have been identified, about half of which have been deciphered; they were written in vertical columns, moving either to the left or to the right, apparently according to the dictates of symmetry. In the early stages at Chengchow the oracle bones were mainly scapulae of pig, ox, or sheep; in the final phase at Anyang tortoise shells were used almost exclusively, fastened together with thongs passed through holes at each end, as is shown in the pictograph for a book, *ts'e*: 冊 . The inscriptions on the bones are either declarations of fact or of the ruler's intentions, or questions about the future that could be answered with a simple yes or no. They relate chiefly to agriculture, war, and hunting, the weather, journeys, and the all-important sacrifices by means of which the ruler attuned himself to the will of heaven. They reveal that the Shang people had some knowledge of astronomy, knew precisely the length of the year, had invented the intercalary month and divided the day into periods. Their religious belief centred in a supreme deity, Ti, who controlled the rain, wind, and human affairs, and in lesser deities of the heavenly bodies, of the soil, of rivers, mountains, and special places (the *genii loci*). Special respect was paid to the ancestral spirits, who lived with Ti and could affect the destinies of men for good or ill, but whose benevolent concern in the affairs of their descendants could be ensured by sacrificial rites.

14 Reconstruction of a house at Hsiao-t'un, Anyang. Late Shang Dynasty. After Shih Ch'ang-ju and Kwang-chih Chang.

The Shang people built chiefly in wood and tamped earth. Remains have been found of several large buildings; one of them, over ninety feet long, was raised on a high plinth, its presumably thatched roof supported on rows of wooden pillars, of which the stone socles remain. Another was laid out axially with steps in the centre of the south side, and but for its roof would not have looked so very different from any large building in North China today. Some of the more important buildings were adorned with formalised animal heads carved in stone, and their beams were painted with designs similar to those on the ritual bronzes. The most popular method of construction—presumably because it was cheap and provided good protection against the piercing cold of the North China winter—was the *pan-chu* ("plank building") technique, in which the earth was tamped between vertical boards with a pole: the smaller the diameter of the pole, the stronger the wall.

In spite of sixty years of excavation, a mystery still hangs about Anyang. One of the first things the excavators noticed was that it did not have the defensive wall that surrounded every major Chinese city until modern times; moreover, the buildings, unlike those at Chengchow and P'an-lung-ch'eng, are aligned north/south and strung out in no apparent order. Perhaps Anyang was not a capital city at all, but merely the centre of the royal tombs, sacrificial halls, bronze workshops, and the dwellings of the officials and priests, artisans, and humble folk who served them. If so, where was the administrative capital of late Shang? Perhaps it was still at Chengchow, or at a site somewhere near Anyang that has still to be identified. Yet even if it was not at Anyang itself, this complex of halls, tombs, workshops, and dwellings was supremely important in the cultural history of early China.

The Chinese belief that the spirit of the departed must be provided with all that he or she possessed (or indeed, would have liked to possess) in his earthly life led to immolation and human sacrifice on a gigantic scale. Later the more frightful practises were abandoned, but until the Ming Dynasty the custom persisted of placing in the tomb pottery models not only of furniture, farms, and houses, but also of servants, guards, and domestic animals. At the same time, the corpse was decked out with the richest clothing, jewellery, and jades that his family or the state could afford. Collectors are even known to have been buried with their favourite paintings. However much one may deplore this custom, it has ensured the preservation of many beautiful things that would otherwise have been irretrievably lost.

The Shang tombs throw a lurid light upon early Chinese civilisation. Some of them were of enormous size and furnished with bronze vessels, jade objects, and pottery. One royal personage, apparently an animal lover, had his pets, including an elephant, buried near him in separate graves. The tomb excavated at Wu-kuan-ts'un contained the remains of a canopy of painted leather,

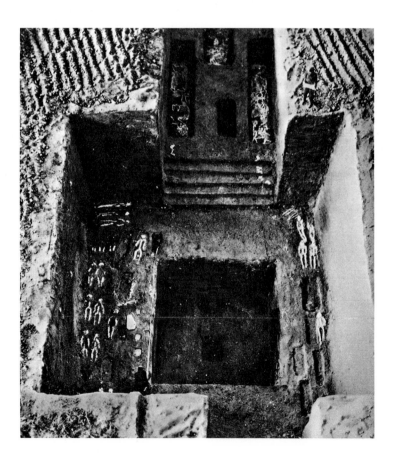

15 Replica of excavated tomb at Wu-kuan-ts'un, Anyang. Late Shang Dynasty.

16 Carriage burial, showing bronze
fittings in place, Anyang. Late Shang
Dynasty.

17 Ritual vessel, *tsun*, in the shape ot an
elephant. Bronze. Isolated find near
Changsha, Hunan. Late Shang period.

18 Ox-head. Marble. Excavated at
Hou-chia-chuang, Anyang. Late Shang
Dynasty.

woodbark, and bamboo; in the approaching ramps and main
chamber lay the complete skeletons of no fewer than twenty-two
men (one beneath the tomb chamber) and twenty-four women,
while the skulls of a further fifty men were buried in adjacent pits.
In some cases the bodies show no signs of violence—the result,
perhaps, of voluntary self-immolation by relations or retainers of
the dead man—while in others, decapitation suggests that the victims may have been slaves, criminals, or prisoners-of-war. Elsewhere at Anyang, light carriages with their horses and driver were
buried in specially prepared pits, with channels dug out for the
wheels. The wood has of course perished, but impressions in the
earth have made it possible to reconstruct the carriage itself, and
thus to determine the position and function of many of its beautiful bronze fittings. Mass immolation was not practised officially
by the Chou, though it appears to have been revived from time to
time, on a more modest scale, by later rulers.

One of the biggest surprises at Anyang was the discovery of
Shang marble sculpture in the round, a notable example of which
is the head of an ox illustrated here. Previously, nothing of the sort
earlier than the Han Dynasty was known, and even today only a
handful of Chou stone carvings have been unearthed and those so
small as hardly to deserve the name of sculpture. Other figures include tigers, buffalo, birds, tortoises, and a kneeling captive (or

sacrificial victim) with his hands tied behind his back. A few of the larger pieces have slots in the back, suggesting that they might have been part of the structure and decoration of a building, perhaps a sacrificial hall; for there is a close similarity in style between many of these figures and those depicted on the ritual bronzes. They are carved foursquare out of the block, rigidly frontal, and have something of the formality and compactness of Egyptian art. Their impressiveness (although none is more than a metre or so in maximum dimension) derives from their solid, monumental feeling of weight and from the engraved geometric and zoomorphic designs which play over their surface, rather than from the tension over the skin itself which enlivens Egyptian sculpture.

SHANG POTTERY

Ceramics formed the backbone of early Chinese art, indispensable, ubiquitous, reflecting the needs and tastes of the highest and the lowest, lending its forms and decoration to the metalworker and, less often, borrowing from him. In the Shang, the crudest is a grey earthenware, cord-marked, incised or decorated with repeated stamped motifs ranging from squares and coils—the ancestor of the *thunder pattern* (*lei-wen*)—to simple versions of the zoomorphic masks that appear on the bronzes. Pottery decorated by stamping or carving geometric designs in the wet clay has been found in a number of Neolithic sites in the southeast, notably in Fukien (Kuang-tse) and Kwangsi (Ch'ing-chiang). In South China, this technique persisted into the Han Dynasty and was carried thence to Southeast Asia—if, indeed, it had not originated there. It is very seldom found in the Neolithic pottery of North China, and its appearance on vessels at Chengchow and Anyang suggests that by the Shang Dynasty the culture of the southern peoples was already beginning to make its influence felt.

19 Urn. Carved white pottery. From Anyang. Late Shang Dynasty.

The beautiful white Shang pottery is unique in the history of Chinese ceramics. So fine is it that it has been taken for porcelain, but it is in fact a very brittle ware made from almost pure kaolin, finished on the wheel, and fired at about 1000° C. Many writers have remarked how closely its decoration echoes that of the bronzes, but there is no proof that this style in fact originated in bronze. As we have seen, southeastern China had already evolved a technique for stamping designs in the wet clay, which in turn influenced bronze design; the white stoneware urn in the Freer Gallery illustrated here is indeed very close in design and decoration to a bronze vessel in the Hellström collection. The Chengchow finds suggest that some of the motifs decorating both the white ware and the bronzes originated in the earlier stamped grey pottery; the techniques and designs used in woodcarving suggest another possible source. Some of the grey and buff ware found in Shang sites in Honan and Hupeh is glazed. While in some cases the glaze was produced accidentally when wood ash fell on the heated pottery in the kiln, in others it was a deliberately applied ash glaze. These Shang glazed wares, which are now being found over a wide area of northern, central and eastern China, mark the begin-

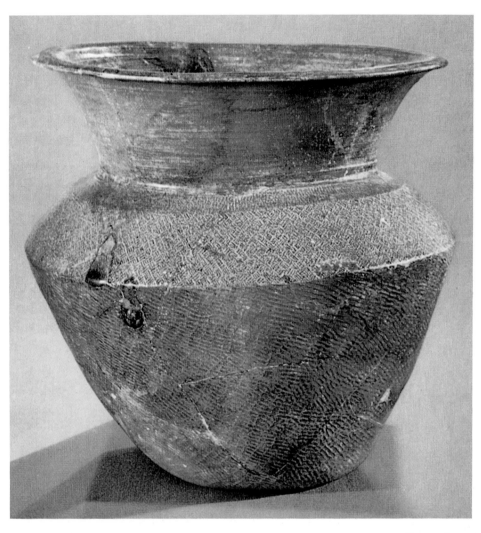

20 *Tsun* vase. Stoneware decorated with impressed design under yellowish-brown ash glaze. Excavated at Chengchow, Honan. Middle Shang period.

ning of a tradition that culminates, two thousand years later, in the Yüeh wares and celadons of Chekiang and Kiangsu.

According to tradition, when the great emperor Yü of the Hsia divided the empire, he ordered nine *ting* tripods to be cast in metal, brought as tribute from each of the nine provinces, and decorated with representations of the remarkable things characteristic of each region. These tripods were credited with magical powers; they could ward off noxious influences, for example, and cook food without fire. From dynasty to dynasty they were handed down as the palladia of empire, but at the end of the Chou they were lost. The unsuccessful efforts of the first Ch'in emperor, Shih-huang-ti, to recover one of them from a riverbed are mocked in several delightfully humorous Han reliefs, though one of the Han emperors tried to accomplish the same thing by means of sacrifices with no better success. But so strong was the tradition of

THE RITUAL BRONZES

21

21 *Ya-hsing*, enclosing an ideograph for offering wine.

22 Sectional clay moulds for bronze-casting. After Shih Ch'ang-ju and Kwang-chih Chang.

the nine tripods that as late as the T'ang Dynasty the "empress" Wu caused a set to be cast in order to bolster up her dubious claim to the throne.

Long before any archaeological evidence of the Shang Dynasty had been unearthed, the ritual bronzes bore witness to the power and vitality of this remote epoch in Chinese history. Bronze vessels have been treasured by Chinese connoisseurs for centuries: that great collector and savant, the Sung emperor Hui-tsung (1101–1125), is even said to have sent agents to the Anyang region to search out specimens for his collection. These vessels, which, as Hansford aptly observed, formed a kind of "communion plate," were made for the offerings of food and wine to ancestral spirits that formed the core of the sacrificial rites performed by the ruler and the aristocracy. Some of them bear very short inscriptions, generally consisting of two or three characters forming a clan name. Often this inscription is enclosed within a square device known as the *ya-hsing*, from its resemblance to the character *ya*. A number of theories as to its meaning have been advanced. The recent discovery at Anyang of bronze seals leaving an impression of precisely this shape suggests that it was in some way connected with the clan name.

Chemical analysis shows that the bronze vessels were composed of 5–30 percent tin, 2–3 percent lead, the rest (apart from impurities) being copper. In course of time many of them have acquired a beautiful patina, much valued by connoisseurs, which ranges from malachite green and kingfisher blue to yellow or even red, according to the composition of the metal and the conditions under which the vessel was buried. Forgers have gone to enormous trouble to imitate these effects, and a case is recorded of one family of which each generation buried fakes in specially treated soil, to be dug up and sold by the next generation but one. It was long thought that the Shang and Chou bronzes were made by the

23 Ritual vessel, *fang* (square) *ting*. Bronze. From the tomb of Fu Hao, Anyang. Shang Dynasty.

TING   LI   YEN (HSIEN)   TUI   TOU

KUI   FU

CHÜEH   CHIAO   CHIA   HO   TSUN

KU   CHIH   YU   HSI-KUANG   YI

NIAO-TSUN   HU   LEI   P'AN   CHIEN   YI   YÜ

24 Major types of Shang and Chou bronze vessels. After Kwang-chih Chang.

cire-perdue method; for how, it was argued, could such exquisite detail have been modelled except in wax? However, while the technique was probably in use before the Han period, large numbers of outer and inner clay moulds and crucibles have been found at Anyang and Chengchow, and there is now no question that the vessels were cast in sectional moulds assembled around a solid central core and that legs and handles were cast separately and soldered on. Many vessels still show ridges or rough places where two mould sections were imperfectly joined.

There are at least thirty main types of ritual vessels, which range in size from a few inches in height to a gigantic *ting* unearthed at Anyang in 1939 which was cast by a Shang king in memory of his mother; it is over four feet high and weighs 800 kilograms. They can most simply be grouped according to their use in the sacrifices. For cooking food (of which the essence only was extracted by the spirits, the participants later eating what they left behind), the chief vessels were the hollow-legged *li* tripod and the *hsien* steamer. Both of these types, as we have seen, were common in Neolithic pottery and may then already have had a more-than-utilitarian function in some primitive rite. The *ting*, which has three or four straight legs, is a variant of the *li*, and like it generally has fairly large handles or "ears" to enable it to be lifted off the fire. Vessels made for serving food included the two-handled *kuei* and the *yü* (basin). Among those for fluids (chiefly wine) were the *hu* (a vase or jar with a cover), the *yu* (similar, but with a swing or chain handle and sometimes fitted with a spout), the *chih* (a cup with a bulbous body and spreading lip), the *ho* (kettle), the tall and elegant trumpet-mouthed *ku* for pouring libations, and its fatter variant, the *tsun* (both derived from pottery prototypes), the *chia* and the *chio* for pouring and probably also for heating wine, and the

25 Ritual vessel, *yu*. Bronze. Late Shang Dynasty.

kuang, for mixing wine, shaped like a gravy boat, generally with a cover and provided with a ladle. Other vessels such as the *i* and *p'an* were presumably made for ritual ablutions.

During the fifteen hundred years that bronze-casting was a major art form in China, the art went through a series of changes in style, reflecting ever greater sophistication in technique and decoration, which make it possible to date vessels within a century or less. Bronzes of the pre-Anyang phase typified by those found at Chengchow and P'an-lung-ch'eng are often thinly cast and rather ungainly in shape. They are decorated with *t'ao-t'ieh* masks and dragonlike creatures with bosses resembling eyes, all either rendered in thin thread relief (Style I) or in a band of ornament that looks as if it had been crudely carved in the clay model before casting (Style II). The next stage (Style III), found both at Chengchow and at Anyang, is much more refined and accomplished, with dense, fluent curvilinear designs that often cover almost the whole surface of the vessel. In Style IV the decoration (*t'ao-t'ieh*, cicada, dragon, and so on) is separated from the background of fine curling scrolls by being modelled in clear flat planes. Finally, in Style V, the main zoomorphic motifs rise in bold relief, and the background spirals may disappear altogether.

When Professor Max Loehr first identified these five styles in 1953 he suggested that they followed each other in an orderly sequence, but subsequent excavations have shown that this was not so. Styles I and II were contemporary in pre-Anyang bronzes, while Styles III, IV, and V all appear in the rich collection of vessels discovered in 1976 in the tomb of Fu Hao, consort of the third Anyang-period king Wu Ting, so all three must belong to the early Anyang stage. What happened to Shang bronze style after that was essentially an elaboration and refining of these three later styles. The zoomorphic motifs which adorn the Shang bronzes and give them their intense vitality may seem to be innumerable but are for the most part variations and combinations of the same few elements—notably the tiger, water buffalo, elephant, hare, deer, owl, parrot, fish, cicada, and, possibly, the silkworm. Occasionally, in a frieze around an otherwise plain vessel, these creatures may be represented naturalistically, but far more often they are so stylised as to be barely recognisable; their bodies dissolve, their limbs break down or take on a life of their own, sprouting other creatures. The *k'uei* dragon, for example, may appear with gaping jaws, with a beak, with a trunk, wings, or horns, or he may form the eyebrow of that most impressive and mysterious of all mythical creatures, the *t'ao-t'ieh*.

This formidable mask, which often appears to be split open on either side of a flange and laid out flat on the belly of the vessel, is the dominating element in the decoration of Shang bronzes. Sung antiquarians named it *t'ao-t'ieh* in deference to a passage in a third-century B.C. text, the *Lü Shih Ch'un-ch'iu*, which runs, "On the *ting* of the Chou there is applied the *t'ao-t'ieh*: having a head but no body he ate people, but before he had swallowed them, harm came to his body." Thus, by the end of Chou, the *t'ao-t'ieh* was

26 Ritual vessel, *chia*. Bronze. Phase I, Middle Shang period.

27 Ritual vessel, *li-ho*. Bronze. Phase II, Middle Shang period.

28 Ritual vessel, *p'ou*. Bronze. Phase III, Shang Dynasty, early Anyang period.

29 Ritual vessel, *kuang*. Bronze. Phase IV, Late Shang period.

30 Ritual vessel, *chia*. Bronze. Phase V, Late Shang period.

31 Ritual vessel, *ku*. Bronze. Phase V, Late Shang period.

considered a monster; later it came to be called "the glutton" and was interpreted as a warning against overeating. Modern scholars have claimed that it represents a tiger or a bull; sometimes it has the characteristics of the one, sometimes of the other. Mizuno has drawn attention to a passage in the *Ch'un-ch'iu Tso-chuan* describing the *t'ao-t'ieh* as one of the four devils driven away by the emperor Shun, and subsequently made defenders of the land from evil spirits.[1] Like the grotesque characters in the Tibetan "devil dance," the more terrifying the *t'ao-t'ieh*, the greater his protective power.

Two examples will show how effectively the various elements can be combined and integrated with the shape of the vessel itself. The lid of the *kuang* shown on this page terminates in a tiger's head at one end and an owl's at the other; the tiger's legs can clearly be seen on the front of the vessel, the owl's wing at the back. Between them a serpent coils up onto the lid, ending in a dragon's head at the crown of the dorsal flange. The main decoration of the magnificent *chia* in Kansas City (Fig. 30) consists of *t'ao-t'ieh* masks divided down the centre by a low flange and standing out against a background of spirals, called *lei-wen* by Chinese antiquarians from their supposed resemblance to the archaic form of the character *lei* ("thunder"). However, like the endless spirals painted on the Yang-shao pottery, their meaning, if any, is lost. The *t'ao-t'ieh* has large "eyebrows" or horns; a frieze of long-tailed birds fills the upper zone, while under the lip is a continuous band of "rising blades" containing the formalised bodies of the cicada, a common symbol of regeneration in Chinese art. The vessel is crowned with a squatting heraldic beast and two large knobs for lifting it off the fire with tongs, while the tapering legs are decorated with a complex system of antithetical *k'uei* dragons.

Several distinct bronze styles appear to have existed simultaneously.[2] Some vessels are plain, some richly ornamented, while some confine the decoration to a band below the lip; the *kuei* may have *t'ao-t'ieh* on its body, or vertical fluting like a Georgian teapot, while its handles, like those on many Shang bronzes, are vigorously modelled in the form of elephants, bulls, tigers, or more fabulous composite creatures. That this mastery of the craft was not confined to Anyang is shown by the magnificent *tsun* illustrated here, which was excavated in 1957 at Funan in Anhui. At first it was thought that it could not have been made locally but must have been imported from Anyang, but now we realise that Shang culture reached far beyond the Central Plain and that this richly conceived vessel, whose decoration is more flowing and "plastic" that that of the typical late Anyang bronzes, must represent a vigorous local tradition far to the southeast. Occasionally, the effect is too bizarre and extravagant to be altogether pleasing, but in the finest vessels the main decorative elements play over the surface like a dominant theme in music against a subtle ground bass of *lei-wen*; indeed, to pursue the analogy further, these motifs seem to interpenetrate one another like the parts in a fugue and at the same time to pulsate with a powerful rhythm. Already in the sweeping decoration of the Yang-shao painted pottery we saw a hint of that uniquely Chinese faculty of conveying formal energy through the medium of dynamic linear rhythms; here in the bronzes that faculty is even more powerfully evident, while many centuries later it will find its supreme expression in the language of the brush.

The bronze weapons used by the Shang people show several aspects of this many-faceted culture. Most purely Chinese was a form of dagger-axe known as the *ko*, with pointed blade and a tang which was passed through a hole in the shaft and lashed to it, or, more rarely, shaped like a collar to fit around the shaft. The *ko* probably originates in a Neolithic weapon and seems to have had a ritual significance, for some of the most beautiful Shang specimens have blades of jade, while the handle is often inlaid with a mosaic of turquoise. The *ch'i* axe, which also originated in a stone tool, has a broad, curving blade like that of a mediaeval executioner's axe, while its flanged tang is generally decorated with *t'ao-t'ieh* and other motifs. A fine example of a *ch'i* axe, excavated in 1976 at Yi-tu in Shantung, is illustrated here. On either side of the terrifying mask is a cartouche of *ya-hsing* shape, containing the figure of a man offering wine on an altar from a vessel with a ladle. Less

32 Ritual vessel, *tsun*. Bronze. Excavated at Funan, Anhui. Late Shang period.

33 Dagger-axe, *ko*. Bronze with jade blade. From Anyang. Late Shang period.

34 Axe, *ch'i*. Bronze. From Yi-tu, Shantung.

35 Knife with ibex head. Bronze. From Anyang. Late Shang period.

exclusively Chinese are the bronze daggers and knives, simple forms of which have been found at Chengchow. At Anyang they become more elaborate, the handle often terminating in a ring or in the head of a horse, ram, deer, or elk. These have their counterpart in the "animal style" of the Ordos Desert, Inner Mongolia, and southern Siberia.

The problem as to whether China or central Asia was the source of this style has long been debated. Much turns upon the date of the southern Siberian sites such as Karasuk where it also appears, and until this is established the question of priority cannot be finally settled. It seems that an animal style existed simultaneously in western Asia (Luristan), Siberia (Karasuk), and China roughly between 1500 and 1000 B.C., and that China drew upon this style from her western neighbours and at the same time contributed from her own increasingly rich repertoire of animal forms. Elements of the animal style appear also in the bronze fittings made for furniture, weapons, and chariots. Excavations at Anyang have made it possible to reconstruct the Shang chariot and to assign to their correct place such objects as hubcaps, jingles, pole ends, awning-fittings, and the V-shaped sheaths for horses' yokes.

The origin of the decoration on the bronzes represents a difficult problem. The most striking element in it is the profusion of animal motifs, not one of which appears in Chinese Neolithic art. The Shang people had cultural affinities with the steppe and forest folk of Siberia and, more remotely, with the peoples of Alaska, British Columbia, and Central America. The similarities between certain Shang designs and those, for example, in the art of the West Coast Indians of North America are too close to be accidental. Li Chi has suggested that the richly decorated, square-sectioned bronze vessels with straight sides are a translation into metal of a northern woodcarving art, and there is much evidence for the stylistic similarity between the decor of these bronzes and the art of the northern nomadic peoples. On the other hand, the art of carving formalised animal masks on wood or gourd is native to Southeast Asia and the Archipelago and is still practised today. Also surviving in Southeast Asia till modern times is the technique of stamping designs in the wet clay, which may have contributed the repeated circles, spirals, and volutes to bronze ornament. But even if some elements are not native to China, taken together they add up to a decorative language that is powerfully and characteristically Chinese.

Whatever the origins of this language, we must not think of it as confined solely to the sacrificial bronzes. Could we but transport ourselves to the home of some rich Anyang nobleman we would see *t'ao-t'ieh* and beaked dragons, cicadas and tigers, painted on the beams of his house and applied to hangings of leather and matting about his rooms, and, very probably, woven into his silk robes. That this is likely we know from the contents of the tombs, and it tends to reinforce the view that these motifs are not tied to the form or function of any individual bronze vessel but belong to the whole repertoire—part decorative, part symbolic, part magical—of Shang art.

Already in certain Neolithic sites we have encountered jade, selected, it appears, for objects of more than purely utilitarian purpose by virtue of its hardness, strength, and purity. In the Shang Dynasty, the craft of jade-carving progresses a step further, and we must briefly consider the sources of this stone, the technique of carving it, and the unique place it occupies in early Chinese culture. Although early Chinese texts speak of jade from several places in China, for many centuries the chief source has been the riverbeds of the Khotan region in central Asia, and Western scholars came to the conclusion that jade did not exist in its true state in China proper. Recent discoveries, however, seem to lend some support to the ancient texts, for a jadeitic stone used today by Peking jadesmiths has been traced to Nanyang in Honan and Lant'ien in Shensi. However, the true jade (chen yü) prized throughout history by the Chinese is nephrite, a crystalline stone as hard as steel and of peculiar toughness. In theory it is pure white, but even small amounts of impurities will produce a wide range of colours from green and blue to brown, red, grey, yellow, and even black. In the eighteenth century, Chinese jade carvers discovered in Burma a source of another mineral, jadeite, whose brilliant apple and emerald greens have made it deservedly popular for jewellery both in China and abroad. Because of its unique qualities, jade has since ancient times been regarded by the Chinese with special reverence. In his great dictionary the *Shuo-wen Chieh-tzu*, the Han scholar Hsü Shen described it in words now well known to every student of Chinese art: "Jade is the fairest of stones. It is endowed with five virtues. Charity is typified by its lustre, bright yet warm; rectitude by its translucency, revealing the colour and markings within; wisdom by the purity and penetrating quality of its note when the stone is struck; courage, in that it may be broken, but cannot be bent; equity, in that it has sharp angles, which yet injure none."[3] While this definition applies essentially to true jade, the word yü may include not only nephrite and jadeite but other fine stones such as serpentine, tremolite, hornblende, and even marble.

The hardness and toughness of jade make it very difficult to carve. To work it one must use an abrasive. Hansford has demonstrated that it is possible, given time, to drill a hole in a slab of jade using only a bamboo bow drill and builder's sand. It has recently been suggested that metal tools were already employed at Anyang, and there is evidence that the Shang lapidary may also have used a drill-point harder than modern carborundum. Some small pieces carved in the round have been found in Shang sites, but the vast majority consist of weapons, ritual and decorative objects carved from thin slabs seldom more than half an inch thick. The jades from Chengchow include long, beautifully shaped knives and axe blades (ko), circles, sections of discs, a figure of a tortoise,

JADE

36 Stone and jade figurines. From the tomb of Fu Hao, Anyang. Shang Dynasty.

37 Axe-blade. Jade. From Anyang. Late Shang period.

38 Chime carved with tiger design. Stone. From tomb at Wu-kuan-ts'un, Anyang. Late Shang period.

and flat plaques in the shape of birds and other creatures pierced at each end for use as clothing ornaments or pendants.

The finds at Anyang have been incomparably richer in beauty, workmanship, and range of types than those at Chengchow. They include plaques in the shape of birds, fishes, silkworms, and tigers; *pi* discs, *tsung* tubes, *yüan* rings, and other ritual objects; beads, knives, and ceremonial axes. Among the rarest newly discovered pieces are the small kneeling figures of servants or slaves from the tomb of Fu Hao, which are of particular value for the evidence they offer of dress and hair styles in the early Anyang period. The largest find at Anyang—although it is of marble rather than true jade—was a chime found lying on the floor of the grave pit at Wu-kuan-ts'un. Cut from a thin slab, pierced for suspension, and decorated with a tiger in raised thread relief, this impressive object bears witness to the importance of music in the rituals of the Shang court.

Not all carving was done in such intractable materials as jade and marble. Some of the most beautiful of all Shang designs were carved in bone and ivory. Elephants roamed North China in prehistoric times and probably were still to be found north of the Yangtse in the Shang Dynasty. We know that at least one Shang emperor kept one as a pet, possibly sent as tribute from Yüeh, while a plentiful supply of ivory could be had from China's southern neighbours. On plaques of ivory and bone a few inches square, made presumably as ornaments for chariots, furniture, or boxes, were carved *t'ao-t'ieh* and other designs of extraordinary intricacy and beauty, sometimes inlaid with turquoise. Like the bronzes, these bone and ivory carvings show striking similarities with the art of the West Coast Indians of North America. For years scholars have toyed with the fascinating possibilities that these similarities have opened up, but as yet no archaeological connecting links have been found to account for them.

39 Carved bone handle. Excavated at Anyang.

3
The Chou Dynasty

During the last years of the decline of Shang, the vassal state of Chou on her western frontier had grown so powerful that its ruler Wen was virtually in control of two-thirds of the Shang territories. Finally, very probably in 1045 B.C., Wen's son Wu, the Martial King, captured Anyang, and the last Shang ruler committed suicide. Under Wu's young successor, Ch'eng Wang, a powerful regent known to history as the Duke of Chou (Chou Kung) consolidated the empire, set up feudal states, and parcelled out the Shang domains among other vassals, though he took care to permit the descendants of Shang to rule in the little state of Sung so that they could keep up the hereditary sacrifices to their ancestral spirits. Chou Kung was chief architect of the dynasty that was to have the longest rule in China's history, and even though its later centuries were clouded by incessant civil wars in which the royal house was crushed and finally engulfed, the Chou Dynasty gave to China some of her most characteristic and enduring institutions.

There was no abrupt break with Shang traditions; rather were many of them developed and perfected. Feudalism, court ritual, and ancestor worship became more elaborate and effective instruments in welding the state together, so effective indeed that from the time of confusion at the end of the dynasty many conservatives, Confucius among them, came to look back upon the reigns of Wen, Wu, and Duke Chou as a golden age. Religious life was still centred in worship of Shang Ti, though the concept of "heaven" (T'ien) now began to appear and eventually replaced the cruder notions embodied in Shang Ti. Bronze inscriptions and early texts indicate the beginnings of a moral code centred in adherence to the will of heaven and in respect for te ("virtue"), both of which would become fundamental in the teachings of Confucius. The Chou court became the focus of an elaborate ritual in which music, art, poetry, and pageantry all combined under the direction of the "master of ceremonies" (pin-hsiang) to give moral and aesthetic dignity to the concept of the state. The king held audiences at dawn and dusk (a custom that survived until 1912); orders for the day were written on bamboo slips, read out by the court historian, and then handed out to officials for execution. From the time of Mu Wang (947–928) onward it became the custom to preserve these orders by casting them on the bronze ritual vessels. These inscriptions, which became longer as time went on, are one of the main sources for the study of early Chou history, the other chief documents being the *Book of Songs* (*Shih-ching*), an anthology of ancient court odes, ballads, and love songs said to have been compiled by Confucius, and the authentic chapters of the *Classic of History* (*Shu-ching*), which tell of the fall of Shang and the early years of the Chou. These documents bear witness to that sense of history which is one of the most striking features of Chinese civilisation, and, as a corollary, to the almost sacred place held in Chinese life by the written word.

The first phase of Chou history ended in 771 B.C. with the death of Yu Wang and the shift of the capital eastward from Shensi to Loyang. By this time the feudal states were growing more and more powerful, and P'ing Wang, the first ruler of Eastern Chou, was helped to power by two of them—Chin and Cheng. Before long the Chou state was declining still further, till eventually it became a mere shadow of its former self, kept artificially alive by the powerful states that surrounded it solely in order to maintain the prestige of the royal house, from which the "mandate of heaven" had not yet been withdrawn. The period from 722 to 481 is often known as the *Ch'un-ch'iu* ("spring and autumn"), because the events of the greater part of it are recorded in the *Spring and Autumn Annals* of the state of Lu, while for the rest we have the stories in another classic, the *Tso-chuan*. The feudal chiefs spent their time, it appears, in making aggressive and defensive alliances with other states, in keeping the northern barbarians at bay, and in honouring the shrunken Chou, which survived, a pale shadow of its former glory, till its destruction in 256 B.C. at the hands of Ch'in.

CHOU CITIES

At the moment, more is known about Shang architecture than about that of the early Chou, for which we have to rely largely upon the evidence of the written word. One of the chief sources for the study of Chou institutions is the *Chou-li*, a manual of ritual and government compiled, it is believed, in the Former Han Dynasty. Its authors, looking back through the mists of time to the remote golden age, present a somewhat idealised picture of Chou ritual and life; but the *Chou-li* is not without significance, for its descriptions were taken as canonical by later dynasts who strove always to follow the ancient institutions and forms as the *Chou-li* presented them. Writing of the ancient Chou city, the *Chou-li* says: "The architects who laid out a capital made it a square nine *li* [about three miles] on a side, each side having three gateways. Within the capital there were nine lengthwise and nine crosswise avenues, each nine chariot tracks wide. On the left was the ancestral temple, on the right the Altar of the Soil; in front lay the Court of State, at the rear the market-place."

For many years it was not known where the seat of early Chou power lay. Then in the late seventies the remains of an ancient Chou city with palace buildings were found at Ch'i-shan, about a

40 Hoard of bronze vessels excavated at Chuang-po, Fu-feng, Shensi. Western Chou period.

hundred kilometres west of Sian. The Chou continued to rule from Ch'i-shan for some years after the conquest. Closer to Sian on either side of the Feng River, archaeologists have for thirty years been unearthing rich remains from Chou tombs, and hoards of bronze vessels most probably buried when the capital was hurriedly moved to Loyang in 771 B.C.

Later in the Chou, as the independent feudal states proliferated, the number of cities grew. Some were very large. The capital of the state of Ch'i in Shantung, for instance, was a mile from east to west and two and a half miles from north to south, surrounded by a wall of tamped earth over thirty feet high. The capital of Yen in Hopei was even larger. These late Chou cities and their attendant princely cemeteries form an almost inexhaustible mine of treasures for the archaeologist and art historian.

The Book of Songs contains several vivid descriptions of ancestral halls and palaces. Here is part of one of them, translated by Arthur Waley:

ARCHITECTURE
AND SCULPTURE

To give continuance to foremothers and forefathers
We build a house, many hundred cubits of wall;
To South and east its doors.
Here shall we live, here rest,
Here laugh, here talk.
We bind the frames, creak, creak;
We hammer the mud, tap, tap,
That it may be a place where wind and rain cannot enter,
Nor birds and rats get in,
But where our lord may dwell.
As a halberd, even so plumed,
As an arrow, even so sharp,
As a bird, even so soaring,
As wings, even so flying
Are the halls to which our lord ascends.
Well levelled is the courtyard,
Firm are the pillars,

Cheerful are the rooms by day,
Softly gloaming by night,
A place where our lord can be at peace.
Below, the rush-mats; over them the bamboo-mats.
Comfortably he sleeps,
He sleeps and wakes
And interprets his dreams. [1]

Such ballads give us a picture of large buildings with rammed earth walls standing on a high platform, of strong timber pillars supporting a roof whose eaves, though not yet curving, spread like wings, of floors covered with thick matting like the Japanese *tatami*, of warmth, light, and comfort. While the most monumental buildings were the ancestral halls, the palaces and private houses were often large, and some already had several successive courtyards as they do today. Chou texts are full of warnings against those who build too extravagantly, and above all against the usurper of royal prerogatives. Confucius, for example, rebuked a contemporary who kept a tortoise (presumably for divination) in a pavilion adorned with the hill pattern on its capitals and the duckweed pattern on its kingposts, insignia reserved exclusively for the king. By comparison, the authors of these texts extol the simplicity of ancient times, when a virtuous ruler roofed his ancestral shrine with thatch, when King Ho-lu of Wu never "sat on double mats. His apartments were not lofty . . . his palaces had no belvederes, and his boats and carriages were plain."

The most conspicuous of Chou buildings, apart from palaces and ancestral halls, must have been the *Ming-t'ang* ("bright hall"), a ritual edifice of which detailed but conflicting accounts are given in early texts, and the towers (*t'ai*) constructed of timber on a high platform of rammed earth. Passages in the *Tso-chuan* show that the princes used them as fortresses, for feasting, or simply as lookouts. Perhaps they survived in the tall storage and lookout towers that were, till recently, a feature of villages and farms in south China.

No trace of the kind of decorative stone sculpture that adorned Shang interiors has yet been discovered in Chou sites. But the Chou craftsmen were certainly capable of modelling a figure in the round and endowing it with extraordinary vitality, even when, as in the famous pair of tigers in the Freer Gallery (one of which is shown here) its limbs and features are stylised. Indeed, here the rhythmic movement of the semi-abstract decoration over the surface gives these creatures a curious animation different from, but no less intense than, that which a more naturalistic treatment would have achieved. Although they have been tentatively dated as early as the tenth century B.C., the coarseness of the modelling and the overall baroque decoration seem to herald the style of the middle Chou period.

THE RITUAL BRONZES

In the earliest Western Chou ritual bronzes, the Shang tradition is carried on with little change, one of the more significant differences being in the inscriptions. In the Shang, these had been simple dedications for offerings to the spirits. Under the Chou, their religious function decayed as they became a means of communicating to the clan ancestor, and recording for posterity, some honour or achievement of the living aristocrat, and thereby proclaiming his prestige and power. Sometimes running to several hundred characters in length, they are valuable historical documents in themselves. A typical short early Chou inscription on a *kuei* in the Alfred Pillsbury Collection shows the function of the vessel quite clearly: "The King attacked Ch'i-yü and went out and attacked Nao-hei. When he came back, he made *liao*-sacrifice [burnt offering] in Tsung-chou and presented to me, Kuo Pao X, ten double strings of cowries. I presume in response to extol the King's grace, and so I have made my accomplished dead father's *kuei* vessel. May for a myriad years sons and grandsons forever treasure and use it."[2]

42 Ritual vessel, *lei*. Bronze. From a hoard discovered in K'o-tso-hsien, Liaoning. Western Chou period.

For perhaps a century after the Chou conquest, Shang bronze styles survived, particularly in the Loyang region of northern Honan, though increasingly modified by the taste of the Chou court. Gradually, popular Shang shapes such as the *ku*, *chüeh*, *kuang*, and *yu* disappeared, and the *p'an*, a shallow basin, became more common, perhaps reflecting less wine-swilling and more clean hands in the Chou rituals, while the *ting* had now become a wide shallow bowl on three cabriole legs.

Bronzes of this period tend to be more coarsely modelled, shapes sagging and heavier, flanges large and spiky, the vessels more treasured by Chinese connoisseurs for their inscriptions than for any beauty of form. The animals that featured so prominently in Shang decor, notably the *t'ao-t'ieh*, have dissolved into broad bands, meanders, and scale patterns. The flight of the animals was due not to any inevitable stylistic evolution but to a change in the religious outlook of the ruling class. The Shang had believed that animals real or imaginary were both clan ancestors and messengers of the gods. The Chou people, once they had forgotten Shang traditions, saw birds and animals not as protective spirits but as fierce creatures, even as enemies to be fought against or conquered by earthly heroes such as Yi the Archer, who shot out of the sky the nine sun-birds that were scorching the earth.

The stylistic change was given a further impetus in the eighth and seventh centuries by foreign ideas and techniques brought

43 Ritual vessel, *fang*-(square)*i*. Bronze. Long dedicatory inscription of the court annalist Ling.

44 Ritual vessel, *yi*. Bronze. Late Western Chou period, about eighth century B.C.

45 Ritual vessel, *kuei*. Bronze. Dated by inscription to 825 B.C. Western Chou period.

46 Ritual vessel, *hu*. Bronze. Dated by inscription to 862 or 853 B.C.: "It was in the 26th year, 10th moon, first quarter, on the day *chi-mao*, when Fan Chü Shang had this bridal *hu* cast as a bridal gift for his first child Meng Fei Kuai. May sons and grandsons forever treasure and use it."

47 Ritual vessel, *hu*. Bronze. Early Eastern Chou period, about seventh century B.C.

back by the Chou kings from their northern campaigns, and by the rise of the feudal states, which were beginning to develop artistic styles of their own. The most striking new feature the northern contact introduced is the art of interlacing animal forms into intricate patterns. This first appears in Chinese art in the bronzes excavated from seventh-century graves at Hsin-cheng and Shang-ts'un-ling in Honan. A more highly developed example is the *hu*, unearthed at Hsin-cheng in Honan and dateable around 650 B.C., which is illustrated here. It stands on two tigers; two more tigers with huge horns and twisting bodies curl up the sides to form handles, while smaller tigers play at their feet. The body is covered with an overall pattern of flat, ropelike, interlaced dragons, the lid surrounded with flaring leaf-shaped flanges. Gone is the wonderfully integrated quality of the early bronzes, which achieved so perfect a fusion of form and decoration. Gone too is the coarse but imposing strength of the early middle Chou. These Hsin-cheng bronzes represent a restless period of transition before the flowering of the refined art of the Warring States.

Reliable archaeological evidence on the jade of the early and middle Chou is scanty but constantly increasing with new finds. Before the Second World War, archaeologists working at Hsin-ts'un in Hsün-hsien (Honan) discovered a number of jade objects which were for the most part rather crude versions of Shang types, with the relief carving often confined to shallow incisions on a flat surface. Since 1950, excavations have tended to confirm the impression that there was a decline in the craft in the early Western Chou. But the Chou jades excavated under controlled conditions still represent a minute proportion of the total number; this, combined with the likelihood that the traditional forms must have persisted for long periods without change, and that when buried, jades may already have been treasured antiques, makes the dating of individual pieces extremely difficult.[3]

There is less doubt, fortunately, about the meaning and function of the ritual and funerary jades. According to the *Chou-li* (and there is no reason to doubt its reliability) certain shapes were appropriate to particular ranks. The king in audience, for example, held a *chen-kuei*, a broad, flat, perforated sceptre; a duke held a *huan* (ridged sceptre); a prince a *hsin* (elongated sceptre); an earl a *kung* (curved sceptre); while the lower ranks of viscount and baron held *pi* discs decorated with the little bosses known as the "grain pattern." Proclamations were issued with jade objects to indicate the royal authority—as, for instance, the *ya-chang* (a long knife) for mobilising the imperial garrison, a *hu* (tiger) in two halves for transmitting military secrets, a *yen-kuei* (sceptre with concave butt) for protecting official envoys, and so on. Equally specific were the jades used to protect the body at burial, numbers of which have been found in their original positions in the grave. Generally, the corpse lay on his back (a change from Shang practice). On his chest was placed a *pi* disc, symbol of heaven; beneath

JADE

48 Ritual and funerary jades: 1. *kuei*;
2. *pi*; 3. *tsung*; 4. *ya-chang*;
5. *yen-kuei*; 6. *huang*; 7. *chang*; 8. *han*.

49 Ritual tube, *tsung*. Jade. Chou Dynasty.

his body a *tsung*, symbol of earth; to the east of the body was placed a *kuei* sceptre, to the west a tiger, to the north (at his feet) a *huang* (half-circle), to the south a *chang* (a short stubby *kuei*); the seven orifices of the body were sealed with jade plugs, while a flat plaque, *han*, generally in the shape of a cicada, was placed in the mouth. Thus was the body protected from all harm without, and sealed lest any evil influences should escape from within.

An extreme instance of the belief in the preserving power of jade was the jade burial suit, long known from references in early literature but never seen (except in fragments) until the accidental discovery of the tombs of a Han prince and princess at Man-ch'eng, Hopei, in 1968 (see p. 78). The corpses of Lui Sheng (died 113 B.C.) and of his wife Tou Wan were completely encased in head mask, jacket, and trousers, each made of over two thousand thin jade plaques sewn together with gold thread. Each suit, it has been calculated, would have taken an expert jadesmith ten years to make.

In addition to mortuary jades, the early Chou lapidaries carved many kinds of pendants and ornaments, as in the Shang Dynasty, but as these were to be far more beautiful and refined in the late Chou period, we will defer discussion of them to Chapter 4.

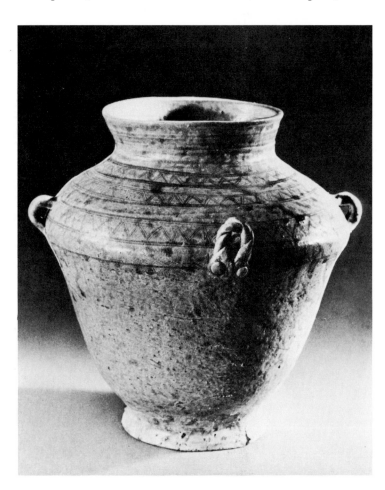

50 Jar. Stoneware covered with greenish-yellow glaze. From a tomb at Pei-yao-ts'un, Loyang, Honan. Western Chou period.

By comparison with the bronzes, the pottery of Western and early Eastern Chou is sober stuff. Many of the finest pieces are crude imitations of bronze vessels, though generally only the shape is copied, such bronzelike decoration as there is being confined to bulls' heads or *t'ao-t'ieh* masks attached to the sides. Although a few specimens of plain red ware have been found, most Western Chou pottery consists of a coarse grey ware, the most popular purely ceramic shape being a round-bottomed, wide-mouthed storage jar which is often cord-marked.

But recent discoveries show that in addition to this mass of un-glazed wares a much more sophisticated ceramic art was beginning to develop. The Chinese language only distinguishes two types of ware: *t'ao* (pottery) and *tz'u* (which includes both stone-ware and porcelain). Some of the Western Chou wares are certainly *tz'u*, if not what we would call porcelain, a particularly fine example being the glazed jar illustrated here, which was unearthed in 1972 from an early Western Chou burial at Pei-yao-ts'un in Honan. The important tomb of the reign of Mu Wang at P'u-tu-ts'un near Sian contained rather similar vessels decorated with horizontal grooves and covered with a thin bluish-green felspathic glaze quite different from the blackish or yellowish Shang glazes. Other glazed wares, dateable by bronze inscriptions to the eleventh and tenth centuries B.C., have been found in graves in Honan, Kiangsu, and Anhui. They may all be considered as ancestors of the great family of celadons of later dynasties.

4

The Period of the Warring States

A map of China in the sixth century B.C. would show a tiny and impotent state of Chou, somewhat like modern Canberra, surrounded by powerful principalities constantly forming and breaking alliances and attacking each other, condescending to consult the royal house only on matters of legitimacy and inheritance. In the north, Chin kept the desert hordes at bay until it was destroyed in 403 and parcelled out among the three states of Chao, Han, and Wei: at one time these three states formed an alliance with Yen and Ch'i in the northeast against the power of the semi-barbarian Ch'in, now looming dangerously on the western horizon. The smaller states of Sung and Lu, which occupied the lower Yellow River Valley, were not militarily powerful, though they are famous in Chinese history as the home of the great philosophers. In the region of modern Kiangsu and Chekiang, Wu and Yüeh were emerging into the full light of Chinese culture, while a huge area of central China was under the domination of the southward-looking and only partly Sinicised state of Ch'u. Gradually Ch'u and Ch'in grew stronger. In 473, Wu fell to Yüeh, then Yüeh to Ch'u. Ch'in was even more successful. In 256 she obliterated the pathetic remnant of the great state of Chou; thirty-three years later she defeated her great rival Ch'u, simultaneously turning on the remaining states of Wei, Chao, and Yen. In 221 B.C. she defeated Ch'i, and all China lay prostrate at her feet.

As often happens in history, these centuries of ever-increasing political chaos were accompanied by social and economic reform, intellectual ferment, and great achivement in the arts. Iron tools and weapons were coming into use. Now for the first time private individuals could own land, and trade was developing, much aided by the invention of currency—bronze "spade" money in central China, knife-shaped coins in the north and east. This was the age of the Hundred Schools, when roving philosophers known as *Shui-k'e* ("persuading guests") offered their council to any ruler who would listen to them. The most enlightened patronage was that offered by King Hsüan of Ch'i, who welcomed brilliant scholars and philosophers of every school to his court.

MAP 4 China in the Warring States period.

But this was exceptional. Confucius, the greatest of them, was ill-used in the state of Lu; for in those chaotic times few rulers saw any immediate advantage in the Sage's emphasis upon the moral and social virtues, upon *jen* ("human-heartedness") or upon the value of knowledge and self-cultivation. Wanting power at home and victory over their enemies abroad, they were often more attracted by the Machiavellian doctrines of Lord Shang and the Legalists, which were to find their ultimate justification in the rise of the totalitarian state of Ch'in.

Against the social commitment of Confucius and his follower Mencius on the one hand and the amoral doctrines of the Legalists on the other, the Taoists offered a third solution—a submission not to society or the state but to the universal principle, *Tao*. Lao Tzu taught that discipline and control only distort or repress one's natural instinct to flow with the stream of existence. In part, this was a reaction against the rigidity of the other schools, but it was also a way of escape from the hazards and uncertainties of the times into the world of the imagination. It was, in fact, through Taoism, with its intuitive awareness of things that cannot be measured or learned out of books, that the Chinese poets and painters were to rise to the highest imaginative flights. The state of Ch'u was the heart of this new liberating movement. The great mystical philosopher-poet Chuang Tzu (c. 350–275) belonged in fact to the neighbouring state of Sung, but, as Fung Yu-lan has observed, his thought is closer to that of Ch'u, while Ch'ü Yüan and Sung Yü, who in their rhapsodic poems known as *sao* poured out a flood of such passionate feeling, were both natives of Ch'u. It is perhaps no accident that not only the finest poetry of this period but also the earliest surviving paintings on silk should have been produced within its boundaries.[1]

During the early Warring States period, however, the Chung-yüan of southern Shensi and northern Honan was still the heart of Chinese civilisation, protected by the defensive walls which were being constructed at intervals along China's northern frontiers. The most ancient section of wall was built about 353 B.C. across modern Shensi, not only to keep the marauding nomads out but, equally, to keep the Chinese in and to attempt to prevent that de-Sinicisation which in the Six Dynasties was to accompany the foreign occupation of large areas of North China.

Until recently, archaeologists had given much less attention to the remains of the Chou Dynasty than had been devoted to the Shang. Before the Second World War, only one important late Chou site had been scientifically excavated, at Hsin-cheng in Honan, where were found tombs containing bronzes that span the years from the baroque extravagances of middle Chou to the simpler forms and more intricate decoration of the early Warring States. At the same time, the local farmers living between Loyang

51 Chariot burial. Lui-li-ko, Hui-hsien, Honan. Warring States period.

52 Mythical animal. Bronze inlaid with silver. From a royal tomb of the state of Chung-shan near Shih-chia-chuang, Hopei. Warring States, late third century B.C.

and Chengchow had for some years been robbing tombs at Chin-ts'un. Bronzes believed to have come from these tombs range in style from late, and rather subdued, versions of the Hsin-cheng manner to magnificent examples of the mature style of the fourth and third centuries B.C.

By the 1980s, many excavations had revealed the extravagance of the feudal courts. The burying of no fewer than nineteen carriages with their horses in a Wei State royal grave at Liu-li-ko, Hui-hsien, shows that the old Shang custom still survived, soon to be superseded by the interring of models in pottery, bronze, or wood.

The Chin-ts'un and Hui-hsien finds lay in the territory of a powerful state, but not all the finest bronzes have been unearthed from such sites. A royal tomb of the hitherto almost unknown state of Chung-shan, opened south of Peking in 1978, yielded huge bronze standards of a kind never seen before and intricately inlaid bronze creatures, one of which is illustrated here; while some of the most remarkable finds of recent years have come from tombs of the tiny state of Tseng, which led a precarious existence in Central China till it was swallowed up by Ch'u in 473 B.C.—but not before one of its rulers had been buried with the largest and finest set of bronze bells ever discovered in China. Such finds show that the feudal rulers, however weak, used their bronzes not merely as symbols of power but to display their wealth and high culture to their neighbours and rivals. Perhaps the lack of this inter-state competition when China was united under the Ch'in and Han dynasties may help to account for the greater plainness and uniformity of Han bronzes.

CHANGES IN
BRONZE STYLE

Already in the seventh century a change was beginning to become apparent in the bronze style. The huge extravagance of the middle Chou decor seems to have exhausted itself. Ungainly excrescences are shorn off, and the surface is smoothed away to produce an unbroken, almost severe silhouette. The decoration becomes even more strictly confined and is often sunk below the surface, or inlaid in gold or silver. Hints of archaism appear in the emphasis upon the *ting* tripod and in the discreet application of *t'ao-t'ieh* masks, which now make their reappearance as the clasps for ring-handles. But this stylistic revolution was not accomplished all at once. In vessels unearthed in 1923 far to the north at Li-yü in Shansi, but now known to have been cast at Hou-ma in the south-west corner of the province, capital of the state of Chin from 584 to 450 B.C., the pattern of flat interlocking bands of dragons looks forward to the intricate decoration of the mature late Warring States style; but in their robust forms, in the tiger masks that top their legs and the realistic birds and other creatures that adorn their lids, these vessels recall the vigour of an earlier age.

This decrescendo from the coarse vigour of the middle Chou style continues in the later bronzes from Hsin-cheng and in the new style associated with Chin-ts'un and Hou-ma. The typical broad, three-legged *ting* from these northern sites, of which the best known is Li-yü, for example, is decorated with bands of interlocked dragons separated by plaitlike fillets. There is a tendency to imitate other materials such as a leather water flask, the strap-work and texture of the animal's pelt being clearly suggested by what Karlgren called "teeming hooks," which may be seen filling the background on the top of the bell illustrated on p. 46. But on the most beautiful of these flasks, such as the *pien-hu* ("flat vessel")

53 Ritual vessel, *ting*, with reversible cover, "Li-yü style." Bronze. Early Eastern Chou period, sixth to fifth century B.C.

54 Flask, *pien-hu*. Bronze inlaid with silver. Warring States period, late fourth to early third century B.C.

55 Ritual vessel, *ting*. Bronze inlaid with silver. Probably from Chin-ts'un, Loyang. Late Warring States period, fourth to third century B.C.

shown here, the symmetrical decoration consists of bars, angles, and volutes, inlaid in silver and probably derived from lacquer painting, that give the vessel a quite extraordinary liveliness and elegance. This vessel is typical of the finest inlaid bronzes unearthed from the later phases at Chin-ts'un. The simple shapes often recall pottery; except for the masks and ring-handles the surface is flat, giving full play to the inlaid decoration, which is sometimes geometric, sometimes sweeps in great curves over the contour of the vessel. Gold had been used at Anyang, but now the goldsmith's art comes into its own, and in form, decoration, and craftsmanship the finest of the inlaid Warring States bronzes from the Loyang region are unsurpassed.

With the decline of the old ruling caste and the emergence of a wealthy upper-middle class less schooled in the traditional rites, the metalworker's art was diverted, so to speak, from "communion plate" to "family plate." A rich man would give his daughter inlaid vessels as part of her dowry, while for himself he could adorn his furniture and carriages with bronze fittings inlaid with gold, silver, and malachite, and when he died, take them with him into the next world. If anyone criticised him for his extravagance, he might well quote in self-defence this advice from the philosophical and economic treatise *Kuan Tzu*: "Lengthen the mourning period so as to occupy people's time, and elaborate the funeral so as to spend their money. . . . To have large pits for burial is to provide work for poor people; to have magnificent tombs is to provide work for artisans. To have inner and outer coffins is to encourage carpenters, and to have many pieces for the enshrouding is to encourage seamstresses."

The value of music as a moral force in society was recognised by Confucius as it was by his contemporary Pythagoras. Solemn dances accompanied the sacrifices at the feudal courts, as an aid to right thinking and harmonious action, so it is not surprising that some of the finest bronzes of the Eastern Chou and Warring States should be the bells made in sets of up to sixteen. The long-handled *nao* bells already in use in the Shang were set mouth-upward in a wooden frame; turned mouth-downward and hung diagonally on the frame they became the *chung*, fully developed under the Chou. The *po* illustrated here appears in middle Chou, reaching its greatest refinement in the Warring States, when its projecting bosses, now reduced to serpent coils, alternate with bands of delicate interlacing on either side of a central panel for a dedicatory inscription that may be inlaid in gold.

Elliptical in section, the ancient Chinese bells are unique in the world in producing two different notes, depending upon whether they are struck at the rim or near the centre. The most complete set of musical instruments yet discovered occupied two sides of the "music room" in the tomb of the Marquis I of the petty state of Tseng (433 B.C.). It contained sixty-five two-tone bells, thirty-two stone chimes, zithers, pipes, a drum, and in a separate room the remains of twenty-one girls. Clearly by this time music was

56 Harness plaques. Bronze.

57 Bell, *po*. Bronze. Warring States period.

45

58 Bell, *po*. Bronze. Detail of
decoration on top.

59 Rack of bronze bells from the tomb
of the Marquis Yi of Tseng, Sui-hsien,
Hupei. Detail. Warring States period.

60 Striking the bells. From a rubbing of
a third-century A.D. stone relief in the
tomb at I-nan, Shantung, illustrated on
p. 61.

no longer purely ritual (if indeed it ever had been) but had become
a prominent feature of the entertainment of the feudal courts.

While the aristocracy of metropolitan China were indulging in
music, dancing, and other delights in the comfort and security of
their great houses, those in less fortunate areas were fighting a desperate battle against the savage tribes who harried the northern
frontiers. Mounted on horseback and using the compound bow,
the nomads were more than a match for the Chinese troops, who
were finally forced to abandon the chariot and copy both their
methods and their weapons of war. Their influence on the
Chinese did not end with warfare. Their arts were few but vigorous. For centuries they and their western neighbours of the central
Asiatic Steppe had been decorating their knives, daggers, and harnesses with animal carvings—first in wood, and later in bronze
cast for them, it is believed, by slaves and prisoners of war. This
animal style, as it is called, was totally unlike the abstract yet fanciful style of the Chinese bronzes. Sometimes the modelling is realistic, but more often it is formalised crudely and without the typical Chinese elegance of line. With barbaric vigour the nomads of
the Ordos Desert and the wild regions to the north and west of it
fashioned elk and reindeer, oxen and horses; they liked also to depict with compact savagery a tiger or eagle leaping on the back of

61 Ritual vessel, *hu*. Inlaid bronze with hunting scenes (inlay missing). Warring States period.

some terrified game beast—a scene they often witnessed, and the representation of which probably was intended to bring success to their own hunting expeditions. Hints of this animal style appeared, as we have seen, on some of the knives at Anyang. During the late Chou and Han, when the impact on China of the Hsien-yün, the Hsiung-nu, and other northern tribes was at its height, its influence can be seen in the design of some of the inlaid bronzes, on which hunting scenes with fights with fierce beasts are modelled with a curiously un-Chinese angularity and harshness of form, although the shape of the vessel itself and its geometric decoration are purely Chinese.

The widest variety of animal designs is found on the bronze garment or belt hook. Many of these hooks are indeed purely Chinese in style, being carried out in the exquisite inlaid technique of Chin-ts'un and Shouchou. Court dancers wore them, as we know from the *Chao Hun*:

Two rows of eight, in perfect time, perform a dance of Cheng;
Their *hsi-pi* buckles of Chin workmanship glitter like bright suns.[2]

The beautiful specimen illustrated here is fashioned in gilt bronze, inlaid with a dragon in jade and multicoloured balls of glass.

62 Belt-hook. Gilt bronze inlaid with jade and glass. Late Warring States period.

Some, representing the creatures of the steppes singly or in mortal combat, are almost purely "Ordos." Yet others are in a mixed style: a garment hook recently excavated at Hui-hsien, for example, is decorated with three penannular jade rings in a setting formed of two intertwined dragons in silver overlaid with gold. The dragons are Chinese, but the sweeping angular planes in which they are modelled come from the northern steppes.

CERAMICS

No such barbarian influences appear in the pottery of North China at this time: the nomads, indeed, had little use for pottery and no facilities for making it. The grey tradition continues, but the coarse cord-marked wares of the early Chou are left behind. Shapes become more elegant, often imitating bronze—the most popular forms being the *tsun*, the three-legged *ting*, the tall covered *tou* ("stem-cup") and an egg-shaped, covered *tui* on three feet. Generally they are heavy and plain, but some of those found at Chin-ts'un bear animals and hunting scenes stamped or incised with great verve in the wet clay before firing. Sometimes the potter even attempted to imitate the original metal by giving his vessel a lustrous black surface or, more rarely, clothed it in tinfoil.

During the early 1940s, a group of miniature pottery vessels and figurines, said to have come from late Chou tombs in the Hui-hsien region, began to appear on the Peking antique market. Very heavily potted and beautifully finished, the vessels included miniature *hu*, covered *ting* and *p'an*, and a garment hook and mirror, on the burnished black surface of which the inlaid geometric decoration of the Chin-ts'un bronzes was imitated in red pigment. These are indications that many, if not all, of these pieces are modern forgeries, possibly inspired by the similar, though artistically inferior, pottery figurines discovered in a tomb at Ch'ang-chih in south Shansi, and by miniature pottery vessels unearthed in 1959 in a Warring States tomb at Ch'ang-p'ing near Peking, three of which are illustrated on this page.[3]

63 Miniature vessels. Pottery painted in red and black. Excavated at Ch'ang-p'ing. Late Warring States period.

THE ARTS OF CH'U

While what might be called the classical tradition was developing in the Honan-Shensi region, a quite different style of art was maturing in the large area of central China dominated by the state of Ch'u. It is not known precisely how widely her boundaries extended (particularly in a southward direction), but they included the city of Shou-chou on the Huai River in modern Anhui, while the influence of the art of Ch'u can be traced in the bronzes of Hui-hsien, Honan, and even northern Hopei. Until Ch'in rose menacing in the west, Ch'u had been secure, and in the lush valleys of the Yangtse and its tributaries had developed a rich culture in which poetry and the visual arts flourished exceedingly. So vigorous, indeed, was Ch'u culture that even after Ch'in sacked the last Ch'u capital, Shou-chou, in 223 B.C., it survived with no significant change into the Western Han, which is why discussion of Ch'u art is shared between this chapter and the next.

In the late sixth century B.C., Shou-chou was still under the state of Ts'ai. A grave of this period recently excavated in the district

64 Covered bowl. Grey stoneware with olive-green glaze. Probably from Shou-chou, Anhui. Late Warring States period.

contained bronzes most of which were rather restrained versions of the Hsin-cheng style, and the art of Shou-chou, even after its absorption into the expanding state of Ch'u, always retained some of its northern flavour. It must also have been an important ceramic centre at this time, if we are to judge by the beauty and vigour of the pottery excavated there. The body is of grey stoneware with incised decoration under a thin olive-green glaze, the immediate predecessor of the Yüeh-type wares of the Han Dynasty and the ancestor of the celadons of the Sung.

It is only in recent years that archaeological excavation of Ch'u sites, notably at the capital near Chiang-ling and at Changsha and Hsin-yang, has revealed both the wealth and the essentially southern character of Ch'u art. Indeed, it is interesting to speculate on the course that Chinese culture would have taken if the victory in 223 B.C. had gone, not to the Ch'in savages from the western marches, but to this relatively sophisticated and enlightened people.

Since the replanning of Changsha started in 1950, many large tombs have been brought to light. The coffin—or, rather, multi-layered coffins, such as the *Kuan Tzu* recommended as giving employment to worthy artisans—was placed at the bottom of a deep shaft and often surrounded by a layer of charcoal and a much thicker layer of white clay, which has in some mysterious way preserved the contents in spite of the fact that many of the tombs have been waterlogged for more than two thousand years. The space between the outer coffin and the chamber wall is often crammed with funerary furniture (*ming-ch'i*). Sometimes the body lay on a long wooden plank carved with exquisite pierced scroll patterns, while about it were set discs of jade, stone, and

65 Sketch of reconstructed tomb, showing lining of pit, tomb chamber, and triple coffin. Ma-wang-tui, Changsha, Hunan. Western Han Dynasty.

66 Painted figurines from tombs at Changsha, Hunan. Wood. Late Warring States or early Han period. After Kwang-chih Chang.

glass (excavations have yielded glass beads as early as Western Chou), bronze weapons and vessels, pottery and lacquer ware. The filter of white clay and charcoal has even preserved fragments of silk and linen, documents written with a brush on slips of bamboo, beautifully painted shields of lacquered leather, and musical instruments.

Here for the first time we find large numbers of wooden figurines of attendants and slaves. Confucius is said to have condemned this practice as he thought it would lead people on, or back, to burying the living with the dead. He thought straw figures were safer. In the succeeding Han Dynasty, pottery cast in moulds was found to be both cheaper and more enduring than wood, and perhaps more acceptable to Confucians. The Changsha figures, carved and painted, give useful information about late Chou costume. More spectacular are the cult objects, consisting of grotesque monster heads, sometimes sprouting antlers and a long tongue, and the drum or gong stands formed of birds standing back-to-back on tigers or entwined serpents, decorated in yellow, red, and black lacquer. The gong stand illustrated on page 51, found in 1957 in a tomb in the Ch'u city of Hsin-yang in Honan, reflects its contacts with the south: similar stands are engraved on a number of bronze vessels from Ch'u sites, while bronze drums found in the Dông-s'on region of northern Vietnam also bear snake and bird designs believed to be connected with rain magic.

PICTORIAL ARTS

Miraculously preserved in the Ch'u graves were the two oldest paintings on silk yet discovered in China, one of which is illustrated here. Swiftly sketched with deft strokes of the brush, it shows a woman in full-skirted dress tied with a sash at the waist, standing in profile attended by a phoenix and by a dragon whose reptilian origin is clearly suggested. Other and far larger silk paintings, recently found in Han tombs at Changsha, are discussed in Chapter 5. A bamboo brush with rabbit's-fur tip has also been found at Changsha, together with other writing and painting materials. Some of the most beautiful painting, however, appears on the lacquer ware of Ch'u and Shu (Szechwan). The craft had first developed in North China during the Shang Dynasty, but now it reached a new level of refinement. Lacquer is the pure sap of the lac tree (*Rhus vernificera*), with colour added. It was applied in thin layers over a core of wood or woven bamboo; more rarely a fabric base was used, producing vessels of incredible lightness and delicacy. In late Chou and Han tombs in central China, large quantities of lacquer bowls, dishes, toilet boxes, trays, and tables have been found. They are beautifully decorated in black on a red ground, or red on glossy black, with swirling volutes that may transform themselves into tigers, phoenixes, or dragons sporting amid clouds.

Also to be classed with the pictorial arts are the lively scenes cast in the body of bronze vessels and inlaid, generally with silver. On the *hu* illustrated in figure 71 we can see an attack on a city wall, a fight between longboats, men shooting wild geese with arrows on the end of long cords, feasting, mulberry picking and other domestic activities, all carried out in silhouette with great vitality, elegance, and humour. It is instructive to compare these essentially southern scenes with the fiercely northern combats illustrated on the *hu* in figure 61.

67 Cult object or guardian in the form of a horned, long-tongued creature eating a snake. Carved and lacquered wood. Excavated in Hsin-yang, Honan. Late Warring States period.

68 Drawing of drum or gong stand. Lacquered wood. From Hsin-yang, Honan. Late Warring States period.

69 Woman with dragon and phoenix. Painting on silk. From Changsha, Hunan. Late Warring States period.

70 Bowl. Painted lacquer. Late Warring States period.

71 Designs on an inlaid bronze *hu*. Late Warring States period.

BRONZE MIRRORS

Large numbers of bronze mirrors have been found both in the north and within the confines of Ch'u state. At first, and always to some degree, their purpose was not to reflect one's face only but one's very heart and soul. An entry in the *Tso-chuan* under the year 658 B.C. says of a certain individual: "Heaven has robbed him of his mirror"—i.e., made him blind to his own faults. The mirror too is that in which all knowledge is reflected—as it was to the mediaeval encylopaedist St. Vincent of Beauvais—"The heart of the sage is quiet," wrote Chuang Tzu, "it is a mirror of Heaven and Earth, a mirror of all things." The mirror also holds and reflects the rays of the sun, warding off evil and lighting the eternal darkness of the tomb.

Bronze mirrors were made at Anyang during the Shang Dynasty, while mirrors almost as crude have been found in tombs of the early Eastern Chou. The craft improved remarkably, like all else, during the Warring States. Of the many new types I can only mention a few. Mirrors from the Loyang region have stylised

72 Rubbing of back of a mirror. Excavated from Kuo State Cemetery at Shang-ts'un-ling, Honan. "Spring and Autumn" period, early Eastern Chou.

73 Mirror, Loyang type. Bronze. Late Warring States period, third century B.C.

74 Mirror, Shou-chou type. Bronze. Late Warring States period, third century B.C.

dragon-like creatures that whirl round the central boss (to which a tassel was attached) against a background of geometric designs picked out in minute granulations. The swirling coils of the dragons relate to lacquer painting, while the backgrounds seem to be copied from textile designs. By contrast, many of the mirrors from the State of Ch'u have concentric rings of interlaced snakes or large staggered 山 -shaped motifs resembling the later form of the character for the mountain, *shan*, set against an intricate "comma" pattern. This rich inventory of Warring States mirror designs was inherited and only gradually modified by the craftsmen of the Western Han.

This power to unite in one object the most intricate refinement of detail with a dynamic rhythm and boldness of silhouette is present also in the carved jades of the late Chou period, which must surely be among the great achievements of the Chinese craftsman. Now jade was no longer reserved for worship of heaven and earth or for the use of the dead; it became at last a source of delight for the living. Indeed, as the ritual objects such as the *pi* and *tsung* lost their original symbolic power they too became ornaments, while jade was now used for sword fittings, hairpins, pendants, garment hooks—in fact, wherever its qualities could show to best advantage. Until recently very few jades had been found in controlled excavations, and dating on purely stylistic grounds is often, in view of the Chinese love of copying the antique, extremely unreliable. But the jade objects found in scores of Warring States tombs since 1950 confirm the impression that at this time the quality of carving rises to new heights; the stones are chosen for their rich, unctuous texture; the cutting is flawless and the finish beautiful. A chain of four discs in the British Museum, connected by links and carved from a single pebble less than nine inches long, is a technical tour-de-force which suggests that the iron drill and cutting disc were already in use. Few of the *pi* of the period are left plain; their surface is generally decorated with a row of spirals, either engraved or raised to form the popular "grain pattern," and sometimes confined within an outer geometric border. Flat plaques in the form of dragons, tigers, birds, and fishes combine an arresting silhouette with a surface treatment of extraordinary delicacy. One of the most beautiful early Chinese jades yet discovered is the celebrated disc in Kansas City, ornamented with heraldic dragons, two on the outer rim, a third crawling around a small inner disc in the center.

As we survey the inlaid bronzes of Chin-ts'un, the mirrors of Shou-chou, the marvellous lacquer ware of Changsha, the jades and the minor arts, we become aware that the period between 500 and 200 B.C. was one of the great epochs in the history of Chinese art, for it was at this time that the ancient symbolic creatures such as the *t'ao-t'ieh* were domesticated, as it were, and refined into a vocabulary of decorative art that was to provide an inexhaustible reservoir of designs for the craftsmen of later dynasties.

JADE

75 Chain of four discs with linking collars, carved from a single piece of jade. Late Warring States period.

76 Two concentric *huan* discs with dragons. Jade. Late Warring States period.

5

The Ch'in and Han Dynasties

By 221 B.C. the inexorable steamroller of the Ch'in armies had crushed the remnants of the ancient feudal order. Now all China was united under the iron rule of King Cheng, who set up his capital in Hsien-yang and proclaimed himself Ch'in Shih-huang-ti—first emperor of the Ch'in Dynasty. Aided by his Legalist minister Li Ssu, he proceeded to consolidate the new state. He strengthened the northern frontiers against the Huns and, at the cost of a million lives, linked the sections of wall built by the previous kings of Chao and Yen into a continuous rampart 1,400 miles long. The boundaries of the empire were greatly extended, bringing South China and Tonkin for the first time under Chinese rule. The feudal aristocracy were dispossessed and forcibly moved in tens of thousands to Shensi; rigid standardisation of the written language, of weights and measures, and of wagon axles (important in the soft loess roads of North China) was enforced, and over it all Shih-huang-ti set a centralised bureaucracy controlled by the watchful eye of censors. All that recalled the ancient glory of Chou was to be obliterated from men's minds; copies of the classical texts were burned, and the death penalty was imposed on anyone found reading or even discussing the *Book of Songs* or the *Classic of History*. Many scholars were martyred for attempting to protest. But while these brutal measures imposed an intolerable burden on the educated minority, they unified the scattered tribes and principalities, and now for the first time we can speak of China as a political and cultural entity. This unity survived and was consolidated on more humane lines in the Han Dynasty, so that the Chinese of today still look back on this epoch with pride and call themselves "men of Han."

The megalomania of the first emperor drove him to build at Hsien-yang vast palaces the like of which had never been seen before. One series, ranged along the riverside, copied the apartments of each of the kings whom he had defeated. The climax was the O-p'ang, or O-fang, Kung; he never lived to complete it, and it was destroyed in the holocaust which, as so often in Chinese history, marked the fall of his dynasty. The emperor lived in constant

MAP 5 China in the Han Dynasty.

fear of assassination, and the roads connecting his many palaces
were protected by high walls. So great was his dread of even a natural death that he was forever seeking through Taoist practitioners
the secret of immortality. In his search for the elixir, tradition has
it that he sent a company of aristocratic boys and girls across the
Eastern Sea to where the fabulous Mount P'eng-lai rises amid the
waves, ever receding as one approaches it. They never returned,
and it was later thought that they might have reached the shores of
Japan.

   Shih-huang-ti died in 210 B.C. The reign of his son Hu Hai was
short and bitter. His assassination in 207 was the climax of a rebellion led by Hsiang Yü, a general of Ch'u, and Liu Pang, who had
started his life as a bandit. In 206 the Ch'in capital was sacked;
Hsiang Yü proclaimed himself King of Ch'u, while Liu Pang took
the crown of Han. For four years the two rival kings fought for supremacy, till finally in 202, when defeat seemed inevitable, Hsiang

Yü committed suicide and Liu Pang, after the customary refusals, accepted the title of Emperor of the Han with the reign name Kao-tsu. He established his capital at Ch'ang-an, and there inaugurated one of the longest dynasties in Chinese history.

So sharp was the popular reaction against the despotism of the Ch'in that the Former, or Western, Han rulers were content to adopt a policy of laissez-faire in domestic matters and even restored the old feudal order in a limited way. At first there was chaos and disunion, but Wen Ti (179–157) brought the scattered empire together and began to revive classical learning and to restore to court life some of the dignity and order that had attended it under the Chou. The early Han emperors were constantly either fighting or bribing the Hsiung-nu, who had taken advantage of the fall of Ch'in to drive their arch-enemy the Yüeh-chih westward across the deserts of central Asia and invade North China. Finally, in 138 B.C. the Emperor Wu (140–87) sent out a mission under General Chang Ch'ien to make contact with the Yüeh-chih and form an alliance with them against the Hsiung-nu. The Yüeh-chih were no longer interested in their old and now distant enemy and the mission failed; but Chang Ch'ien spent twelve years in the western regions, where he found Chinese silk and bamboo brought there, he was told, by way of India. He returned to Ch'ang-an with a report which must have stirred the public imagination as did the travels of Marco Polo or Vasco da Gama. Henceforth, China's eyes were turned westward. Further expeditions, sent into distant Ferghana to obtain the famous "blood-sweating" horses for the imperial stables, opened up a trade route which was to carry Chinese silk and lacquer to Rome, Egypt, and Bactria. Travellers told of great snowcapped ranges reaching to the clouds, of fierce nomadic tribes, and of the excitement of hunting wild game among the mountains. Somewhere beyond the horizon lay Mount K'un-lun, the axis of the world and home of Hsi Wang Mu, Queen Mother of the West, and the counterpart of the foam-washed P'eng-lai on which dwelt Tung Wang Kung, the immortal King of the East.

During these first two centuries of the Han, the popular mind, from the emperor down, was filled with fantastic lore, much of which is preserved in pseudo-classical texts such as the *Huai Nan Tzu* and *Shan-hai-ching* (*Classic of Hills and Seas*), which are useful sources for the interpretation of the more fabulous themes in Han art. With the unification of the empire, many of these cults and superstitions found their way to the capital, where were to be found shamans, magicians, and oracles from all over China. Meanwhile, the Taoists were roaming the hillsides in search of the magical *ling-chih* ("spirit fungus"), which, if properly gathered and prepared, would guarantee one immortality, or at least a span of a few hundred years. Yet, at the same time, Confucian ceremonies had been reintroduced at court, scholars and encyclopaedists had reinstated the classical texts, and Wu Ti, in spite of his private leanings toward Taoism, deliberately gave Confucian scholars precedence in his entourage.

77 The hunt among mountains. Detail of decoration of a bronze tube inlaid with gold and silver. Han Dynasty.

It is these diverse elements in Han culture—native and foreign, Confucian and Taoist, courtly and popular—that give to Han art both its vigour and the immense variety of its styles and subject matter.

When Wu Ti died, China was at one of the highest points of power in her history. The empire was secure; her arms were feared across the northern steppes, Chinese colonies were flourishing in Tonkin, Liaoning, Korea, and central Asia. But Wu Ti's successors were weak and the administration crippled by palace intrigues and the power of the eunuchs, a new force in Chinese politics. In A.D. 9, a usurper named Wang Mang seized the throne and under the cloak of Confucian orthodoxy embarked upon a series of radical reforms which, had he been served by an honest and loyal administration, might have achieved a revolution in Chinese social and economic life. But by antagonising the privileged class, Wang Mang ensured his own downfall. He was murdered by a merchant and his brief Hsin Dynasty came to an end in A.D. 25. The Han house was restored and at once began the task of reconstruction. From their capital at Loyang, the Later, or Eastern, Han reached out once more into central Asia, consolidated their hold on Annam and Tonkin and for the first time made contact with Japan. By the end of the century, so great was their prestige that for a time even the distant Yüeh-chih, now established as the Kushan Dynasty in Afghanistan and northwest India, sent embassies to Ch'ang-an.

The Kushan brought Indian culture and religion into central Asia. This region became a melting pot of Indian, Persian, and provincial Roman art and culture, which in turn travelled eastward to China by way of the oases to north and south of the Tarim Basin. Buddhism may have been known by repute at least in the Former Han—the mythical Mount K'un-lun was very likely a Chinese version of the Buddhist Meru, or the Hindu Kailas, the axis of the universe—but now it began to take root in Chinese soil. The well-known story of the Emperor Ming, who in A.D. 67 dreamed of a "golden man" (i.e., a Buddhist image) in the far west and sent emissaries to fetch it, is a late fabrication, but already two years earlier the Prince of Ch'u had held a feast for monks (*śrāmana*) and lay brethren, which indicates that at least one monastic community was in existence in central China by that date, while there are references to Buddhism in the *Hsi-ching-fu* (*Rhapsody on the Western Capital*) (Ch'ang-an) by Chang Heng (78–139). Early evidence for Buddhism, which some scholars accept as of late Eastern Han date, exists also in the form of motifs on bronze mirrors and in crude rock-cut reliefs long known at Chia-ting in Szechwan and more recently found at the other side of China, in northern Kiangsu.

78 Seated Buddha in *abhaya-mudrā*. Rubbing of a relief in a shaft tomb at Chiating, Szechwan. Late Han period(?).

Until the time of troubles that accompanied the downfall of the Han, however, Buddhism was merely one among many popular cults. Officially, Confucianism still reigned supreme, and the Later Han saw the enormous expansion of a scholarly and official class nurtured in the Confucian doctrines. Many of these men had been trained in the Imperial Academy, founded by Wu Ti in 136 B.C. From its graduates, selected by competitive examination in the classics, were drawn recruits for that remarkable civil service which was to rule China for the next two thousand years. Unswerving loyalty to the emperor, respect for scholarship, and a rigid conservatism which sought for every measure the sanction of antiquity—these became the guiding principles of Chinese social and political life. Such ideals, however, offer no stimulus to the imagination, and it was not until Confucianism was enriched by Buddhist metaphysics in the Sung Dynasty that it became a source of highest inspiration to painters and poets.

Already in the Former Han, those who possessed skills useful to the emperor were organised under a bureau known as the Yellow Gate (*huang-men*), which was based on the somewhat idealised picture of Chou institutions set out in the *Chou-li*. The highest ranks in this professional hierarchy were known as *tai-chao*, officials in attendance on the emperor. These included not only painters, Confucian scholars, and astrologers, but also jugglers, wrestlers, and fire-swallowers, who might be called upon at any time to display their various skills in the imperial presence. The lower ranks of artists and artisans, those who made and decorated furniture and utensils for court use, for example, were known as *hua-kung*. This organisation was not confined to the court, however; each commandery—in theory—had its own agency (*kung-kuan*) for the production and decoration of such things as ritual vessels, robes, weapons, and lacquer ware, for which latter Ch'u and Shu (Szechwan) were especially famous. Gradually, however, this system was relaxed. Under the Later Han, the emergence of the scholar-official class, the decline of the rigid Confucian order at court, and the corresponding rise of Taoist individualism all combined to reduce the importance and activity of these largely anonymous professionals. By the end of the dynasty there had come into being a gulf between the intellectual aristocracy on the one hand and the unlettered craftsmen on the other which was to have a profound influence on the character of later Chinese art.

The wonders of Ch'ang-an and Loyang are vividly described in the *fu* rhapsodies on the Han capitals by Chang Heng and Ssu-ma Hsiang-ju, and though their beauties may have been somewhat exaggerated, some idea of the scale of the palace and government buildings can be gauged from the fact that the audience hall of the Wei-yang Palace at Ch'ang-an was over 400 feet long—considerably longer than the T'ai-ho-tien, its counterpart in latter-day Peking. To the west of the capital, Han Wu Ti built a pleasure palace, linked to the Wei-yang Palace within the city by a covered two storey gallery ten miles long. At Loyang the palace lay in the centre of the city with a park behind it, built up with artificial lakes and hills into a fairy landscape in which the emperor could indulge his Taoist fancies. Other parks further from the capital and likewise landscaped on a colossal scale were stocked with all manner of game birds and beasts—some brought as tribute from remote corners of the empire. From time to time a vast imperial hunt, or rather slaughter, was organised, followed by lavish feasting and entertainments. The *fu* poems describe these extraordinary spectacles, in which, by some Leonardesque device, P'eng-lai and K'un-lun, with wild animals fighting on their slopes, might be made to appear out of a cloud of smoke while attendants in galleries overhead crashed great boulders together to simulate thunder. These hunts among mountains, and the wild, extravagant orgies that followed them, were to become favourite subjects in Han art.

The palace gateways were marked by pairs of tall watchtowers (*ch'üeh*), while within the palace precincts stood multistoreyed pavilions (*lou*) or towers (*t'ai*) which were used for entertainment, for admiring the view, or simply for storage. When Loyang burned in A.D. 185, the Cloud Tower (*Yün-t'ai*) went up in flames, and with it a huge collection of paintings, books, records, and objets d'art—to say nothing of the portraits of thirty-two distinguished generals which Wu Ti had had painted on the walls of the tower itself. This is the first recorded occasion when the art treasures accumulated through a whole dynasty were destroyed in a few hours, a disaster that was repeated again and again in Chinese history. Palaces, mansions, ancestral halls were built of timber, their straight-tiled roofs supported by a simple system of brackets resting on wooden pillars. Their timberwork was picked out in rich colours and their inner walls, like those of the Yün-t'ai, were often decorated with wall paintings.

These great mansions come vividly before our eyes as we read such poems as the *Chao Hun*, a passionate appeal addressed by an

ARCHITECTURE

79 Gateway to a palace or mansion. Rubbing from brick relief. From Szechwan. Han Dynasty.

unknown Han author to the soul of a king which, in his illness, has left his body and gone wandering to the edge of the world. To lure it back, the poet describes the delights that await it in the palace:

"O soul, come back! Return to your old abode.
All the quarters of the world are full of harm and evil.
Hear while I describe for you your quiet and reposeful home.
High halls and deep chambers, with railings and tiered balconies;
Stepped terraces, storeyed pavilions, whose tops look on the high mountains;
Lattice doors with scarlet interstices, and carving on the square lintels;
Draughtless rooms for winter; galleries cool in summer;
Streams and gullies wind in and out, purling prettily;
A warm breeze bends the melilotus and sets the tall orchids swaying.
Crossing the hall into the apartments, the ceilings and floors are vermilion,
The chambers of polished stone, with kingfisher hangings on jasper hooks;
Bedspreads of kingfisher seeded with pearls, all dazzling in brightness;
Arras of fine silk covers the walls; damask canopies stretch overhead,
Braids and ribbons, brocades and satins, fastened with rings of precious stone,
Many a rare and precious thing is to be seen in the furnishings of the chamber.
Bright candles of orchid-perfumed fat light up flower-like faces that await you;
Twice eight handmaids to serve your bed, each night alternating in duty,
The lovely daughters of noble families, far excelling common maidens . . .
O soul, come back!"[1]

80 Horse and cavalryman. Life-size pottery figures from tomb-pit of Ch'in Shih-huang-ti, Lin-t'ung, Shensi. Ch'in Dynasty.

81 Isometric sketch of a stone tomb at
I-nan, Shantung. Third century A.D.

Much of our knowledge of Han architecture is derived from the
reliefs and engravings on the stone slabs lining tombs and tomb
shrines. In crude perspective, they show two-storeyed gateways
flanked with towers and often surmounted by a strutting phoenix,
symbol of peace and of the south. The reliefs from the Wu family
shrines in Shantung show a two-storeyed house in whose kitchens
on the ground floor a banquet is in preparation, while the host en-
tertains his guests on the *piano nobile* above. The humbler dwellings—farmhouses, granaries, even pigsties and watchmen's
huts—survive in the rough and lively pottery models made to be
placed in the tombs.

Never in Chinese history, indeed, was so much care lavished on
the tomb and its contents as in the Han Dynasty. Huge numbers
have survived and every day more are revealed. They are interesting not only for their contents but also for their structure, which
varies considerably in different areas and provides us with almost
the only surviving remains of Han architecture. They are not, of
course, representative of Han building as a whole, nearly all of
which was carried out in timber; the more adventurous techniques of the dome and vault in brick or stone were reserved almost exclusively for the permanent mansions of the dead. In the
Chinese colonies in Korea and Manchuria, tombs were square or
rectangular with flat roofs of stone slabs supported on stone pillars, or shaped like clusters of beehives with corbelled brick
vaults. Tombs in Shantung were also of stone, sunk in the ground,
while before them stood stone shrines, *tz'u*, for offerings to the
spirits of the departed. An elaborate example of a Shantung tomb,
discovered at I-nan, is laid out as if for a living occupant, with re-
ception halls, bedrooms, and kitchen. In Szechwan most of the
tombs are small barrel-vaulted structures built of bricks on the inner face of which a lively scene was stamped in relief, though at
Chiating deep tomb shafts were cut into the cliffs in groups with a
common vestibule carved out to suggest a timber building. The
tombs of the Ch'u people of central China, whose culture under-
went a considerable revival during the Han, were either deep pits
containing layered timber coffins, or rectangular chambers sometimes vaulted in brick.

Elaborate as some of these tombs were, they were nothing compared to the tombs of the Ch'in and Han emperors, whose stone passages and vaults were enclosed in the heart of an artificial hill approached by a "spirit way" lined with guardian figures carved in stone and guarded by booby traps. It has long been thought that all the tombs of the Han royal house were desecrated at the fall of the dynasty. But the accidental finding of the concealed rock-cut tombs of Han Wu Ti's elder brother Liu Sheng and his wife Tou Wan, clad in the jade suits described in Chapter 3, suggests that this was not the case and that, hidden Tutankhamenlike in the cliffs and valleys of North China, there may be more great tombs still intact, awaiting discovery.

SCULPTURE AND THE
DECORATIVE ARTS

It is in the Ch'in and Han Dynasties that we encounter the earliest monumental sculpture in stone, surprisingly late in the history of one of the major civilisations, and suggestive, possibly, of the effect of contact with western Asia. Near Hsien-yang in Shensi is a mound believed to be the grave of General Ho Ch'ü-ping, who died in 117 B.C. after a brief and brilliant career of campaigning against the Hsiung-nu. Before the tomb, a life-size stone figure of a horse stands with majestic indifference over a fallen barbarian soldier who is attempting to kill him with his bow. The modelling is massive but shallow, giving the impression more of two reliefs back-to-back than of carving in the round, and indeed in its heavy,

82 Horse trampling on a barbarian archer. Stone sculpture which formerly stood before the reputed tomb of Ho Ch'ü-ping (died 117 B.C.). Hsing-p'ing, Shensi. Western Han Dynasty.

flat, and somewhat coarse treatment this piece is from the technical point of view more reminiscent of the Sasanian rock-cut reliefs at Taq-i Bustan in Iran than of anything in early Chinese art. Many writers have pointed out how appropriate such a monument would be to a Chinese general whose victories over the Western nomads were due to the very horses China had acquired from the enemy and used so effectively against them.

Clearly, however, the Chinese sculptor had not yet mastered the art of carving in the round on a big scale. Indeed, carving is not the technique in which he feels happiest. He is more at home in clay modelling and in the human figures and animals cast from clay moulds in bronze by the *cire-perdue* process. The vessel in the form of a rhinoceros (see Fig. 84) was once inlaid all over the body with an intricate pattern of scrolls, and only the glassy eye remains; but even with the inlay gone this marvellous piece, found buried in a field to the west of Sian in 1963, shows how successfully the craftsman of Ch'in or early Han was able to combine surface decoration with a lively realism. During the Han Dynasty this gift for modelling in clay found expression chiefly in the tomb figurines discussed below. These have their spectacular forerunners in the extraordinary clay figures found in 1975 in a pit to the east of the tomb of Ch'in Shih-huang-ti. This one pit alone—originally, it seems, a huge subterranean shed—contained about six thousand life-size figures of men and horses, with their chariots, while other similar but smaller pits lie nearby. Each figure is individually fashioned. The legs are solid, the hollow body, head, and arms being formed of an inner core of coiled strips of clay over which a "skin" of finer clay was smeared, with the features stuck on or worked with a tool. The civilian officials and armour-clad soldiers bearing shining bronze swords were painted, and some bear the seals of the craftsman and foreman in charge. Unprecedented in number and size, they may well have been inspired by earlier straw figures such as Confucius had recommended as a humane alternative to immolation. To the west of the tomb another smaller pit was discovered in 1980, in which lay chariots, horses, and charioteers one-third life-size, of bronze picked out in gold and silver. Taken together with the tomb of the first emperor himself, this must be one of the most remarkable archaeological sites ever discovered.

Modelling in clay is the first stage in bronze-casting, and some of the most striking relics of Han art are the bronze figures and animals found in tombs. A particularly beautiful example in gilt bronze is the kneeling servant girl (Fig. 85) from the tomb of Liu Sheng's wife Tou Wan, holding a lamp of which the chimney is her sleeve and arm; while arresting in a more dynamic way is the bronze horse (Fig. 86) from an Eastern Han tomb discovered in Kansu in 1969. He is poised as if flying, and one of his hooves rests lightly on a swallow with wings outstretched, suggesting in a beautiful and imaginative way the almost divine power which the Chinese at this time believed the horse to possess.

83 Warrior. Painted terracotta. From the tomb pit of Ch'in Shih-huang-ti, Lin-t'ung, Shensi. Ch'in Dynasty, about 210 B.C.

84 Rhinoceros. Bronze inlaid with
gold. Found in Hsing-p'ing district,
Shensi. About third century B.C.

85 Lamp held by kneeling servant-girl.
Gilt bronze. From the tomb of Tou Wan
(died c. 113 B.C.), Man-ch'eng, Hopei.
Western Han Dynasty.

86 Pacing horse poised on a swallow with wings outstretched. Bronze. From a tomb at Lei-t'ai, Kansu. Eastern Han Dynasty, second century A.D.

While the idea of executing stone sculpture in relief may possibly have been derived from western Asia, it had been thoroughly assimilated by the Later Han. Stone reliefs have been found in almost every part of China. The most truly sculptural are the animals and figures carved on a pair of funerary pillars standing before the tomb of an official named Shen who was buried in Ch'ü-hsien in Szechwan during the second century A.D. The pillars themselves are timber towers translated into stone. In high relief between the beam ends is a monster like a gargoyle; at the corners crouching Atlantean figures—perhaps representing barbarian prisoners—support the beams, while above on each main face stand a beautifully modelled deer and rider. The only figures in flat relief are the directional symbols: on the east the dragon, on the west the tiger, to the north the "dark warrior" (snake and tortoise), to the south the phoenix.

Nearly all of what passes for relief sculpture in the Han period, however, is not really sculpture at all so much as engraving in the

87 Top of memorial pillar (*ch'üeh*) for a member of the Shen family. Stone. Ch'ü-hsien, Szechwan. Han Dynasty.

flat surface of a stone slab or flat relief with the background cut back and striated to give a contrasting texture. These slabs preserve the subject matter—and something even of the composition—of the lost mural paintings of the Han Dynasty. They not only give a vivid picture of daily life in this far-off time but also show clear regional differences in style, so that we can without much difficulty identify the elegant dignity of some of the Shantung reliefs, the luxuriance of the stones from Nanyang in Honan, the cruder vigour of the reliefs from distant Szechwan. After the Han Dynasty, China becomes ever more a single cultural entity, and these regional styles will largely disappear.

The stone shrines standing before the tombs were often decorated with engraved designs, the best-known series being those at the Hsiao-t'ang-shan (Hill of the Hall of Filial Piety) near Fei-ch'eng in Shantung, and the slabs from four now-demolished shrines of the Wu family near Chia-hsiang in southwestern Shantung, which are dated by their inscriptions between A.D. 145 and 168. They give a vivid impression of the syncretic nature of Han art, in which Confucian ideals, historical events (real and legendary), and Taoist mythology and folklore are all brought together. On the shallow end gables of two of the shrines to east and west we find Tung Wang Kung and Hsi Wang Mu, respectively; below, the legendary meetings of Confucius and Lao Tzu, or ancient kings, filial sons, and virtuous women. The attempted assassination of Ch'in Shih-huang-ti, and his effort to raise one of the tripods of the emperor Yü, are favourite themes. The central recess and most of the remaining space is devoted to a banqueting scene, of which we can only show a detail. This depicts on the left the cult hero Yi, shooting out of the *Fu-sang* tree the nine extra suns (here symbolised as crows) that were scorching the earth, while to the right the guests bow to their host and a feast takes place upstairs.

88 The archer Yi, the *Fu-sang* tree, and a mansion. Detail of rubbing from a stone relief in the tomb shrine of Wu Liang, Chia-hsiang, Shantung. Eastern Han Dynasty.

We see the ponderous officials in their voluminous robes, the short, deep-chested horses of central Asian stock who trot with high-stepping precision, while the air above them is filled with swirling clouds and loud with the clamour of a fantastic assortment of winged creatures come to do honour to the dead. In this fabulous setting, the soul of the deceased can pass easily from the world of men to the world of the spirits.

PAINTING

There can be little doubt that both the style and the subject matter of the tomb reliefs owe much to the great cycles of wall paintings in halls and palaces, almost all trace of which has disappeared. Only a few miles away from the Wu family tombs lay the Ling-kuang Palace built by a brother of Han Wu Ti. The fame of its wall paintings is celebrated in a poem by Wang Yen-shou, written a few years before the Wu shrines were erected, which exactly describes the subject matter of their reliefs:

> Upon the great walls
> Flickering in a dim semblance glint and hover
> The Spirits of the Dead.
> And here all Heaven and Earth is painted, all living things
> After their tribes, and all wild marryings
> Of sort with sort; strange spirits of the sea,
> Gods of the hills. To all their thousand guises
> Had the painter formed
> His reds and blues, and all the wonders of life
> Had he shaped truthfully and coloured after their kinds.[2]

These paintings live only in the imagination, for the buildings that housed them have long since crumbled to dust. But an increasing number of painted tombs are coming to light which give an impression of Han wall-painting at a rather humbler level. Many depict with lively naturalism the daily life of a country estate not unlike the self-contained villa estates of late Roman Britain; but the paintings are difficult to reproduce satisfactorily, and published copies are deceptive. We find the same naturalism in moulded brick reliefs from tombs at Kuang-han in Szechwan. One depicts the salt mines, with pipelines of bamboo carrying the brine over the hills to the evaporating pans, methods still in use in Szechwan in the twentieth century. Another, divided horizontally, shows in the lower half men harvesting and threshing in the rice fields, while another brings their lunch; above, two hunters kneel at a lake shore, shooting up at the rising ducks with arrows trailing long cords. The border of the lake winds back, seeming almost to lose itself in the mist, while behind the hunters stand two bare trees. On the surface of the water are fishes and lotus flowers, and ducks swimming away as fast as they can go. This delightful scene shows that in the later Han, craftsmen in Szechwan were beginning to solve the problem of continuous recession in depth. Another way to solve it was simply to omit the landscape altogether. In the lively scene on the wall of a tomb in Liao-yang, with horsemen and carriages coming to the funeral feast, there is

89 Shooting birds on a lake shore, and harvesting. Moulded pottery tile. From Kuang-han, Szechwan. Han.

no ground, no hint of any setting, and yet we seem to be looking down from above on an open plain across which they dash with tremendous speed. This painting shows that the lateral movement from right to left, and the sense of a space that seems to extend far beyond the picture area, both characteristic of later scroll painting, were already mastered by painters before the end of the Han Dynasty.

Landscape, however, must have played a very subordinate part in the great fresco cycles that decorated the palaces and ancestral halls. The themes were most often Confucian, as illustrated by a passage from the *Han shu* (*History of the Han Dynasty*): "The mother of Jih Ti in teaching her sons had very high standards: the Emperor [Wu Ti] heard of it and was pleased. When she fell ill and died, he ordered her portrait to be painted on [the walls of] the Kan-ch'üan Palace. . . . Every time Jih Ti saw the portrait he did obeisance to it and wept before he passed on." Other passages in the *Han shu* bear witness to the Taoist predilections of the Han emperors. Wu Ti, for example, had a tower in the Kan-chüan Palace where were depicted "the demons and deities of Heaven, Earth, and the Supreme Unity. Sacrificial utensils were set out, by which the divine beings were to be addressed."

Didactic too, if in a more human and amusing way, are the figures painted on a celebrated series of tiles from the gable of a tomb-shrine now in the Boston Museum of Fine Arts. One scene depicts an animal combat; another may represent, as Sickman has suggested, an incident in the life of the virtuous Princess Chiang, of the ninth century B.C., who took off her jewels and demanded to be incarcerated in the jail for court ladies as a protest against the emperor's dissipation—a threat which soon brought him to his senses. The figures, drawn in long sweeping lines with a sensitive, pliant brush, stand and move with wonderful ease and grace; the men discuss the affair in dignified agitation while the women, el-

90 Guests arriving for the funeral feast. Detail of a wall painting. From a tomb in Liao-yang, northeastern China. Eastern Han Dynasty.

egant and playful, seem to find the whole incident rather amusing. Happy the man whose tomb was adorned with such charming figures!

The power of the Chinese craftsman to impart life and movement to his subjects is vividly shown in the decoration of the lacquer objects for which Szechwan province was especially famous. That the output of her factories—especially those of Shu and Kuanghan—must have been considerable we know from the first century A.D. *Discourses on Salt and Iron*, whose author protests that the wealthy classes were spending five million copper cash annually on lacquer alone. A number of Szechwan lacquer bowls, cups, and boxes, bearing dates between 85 B.C. and A.D. 71, have been found in tombs in the vicinity of Pyongyang in North Korea.

Most famous, though undated, is the "painted basket" (actually a box) found in a tomb at Lo-lang. Around the top, under the fitted lid, are ninety-four figures of filial sons, virtuous and wicked rulers and ancient worthies. All are sitting on the floor, but monotony is avoided by the skill and inventiveness with which they

LACQUER

91 Gentlemen in conversation. Detail of a painted pottery tile. Eastern Han Dynasty.

turn to one side or the other, gesticulate or engage in lively conversation. Even in this crowded space we find the same sense of individuality, of interval and psychological relationship between the figures as we encountered on the Boston tiles. Other lacquer objects such as bowls and trays, of which many beautiful examples have been preserved in the waterlogged soil of Changsha, are adorned with sweeping scrolls and volutes evolved out of the decor of the lacquers and inlaid bronzes of the Warring States. Now, however, these whirls erupt into flamelike tongues. The presence of a flying phoenix turns these tongues into clouds; when set about with tigers, deer, and hunters they are magically transformed into hills; sometimes the transformation is aided by vertical striations suggesting grass, or by little trees which grow from the volutes. There is no attempt to depict a real landscape; rather has the craftsman taken the sweeping volute as the essential form common to all things in nature and by means of a few accessories transformed it into clouds, waves, or mountains without robbing it of any of its rhythmic force. Because its forms follow the natural sweep and movement of the artist's hand, they express the rhythms of nature itself.

92 Paragons of filial piety. Lacquer painting on basketwork box. From Lo-lang, Korea. Eastern Han Dynasty.

From the kind of pictorial art that I have been describing we may imagine what the finest Han paintings must have been like. They were probably painted on silk or hemp cloth, for paper, a Chinese invention, was still in the early stages of its development at this time. Fragments of a hemp-fibre paper wrapping a mirror have been found in an early Western Han tomb near Sian; while in A.D. 105, the eunuch Ts'ai Lun, in charge of the Imperial Workshop (*Shang-fang*), presented to the throne what must have been a

93 Detail of a funerary banner, *fei i*. From Tomb No. 1 at Ma-wang-tui, Changsha, Hunan. Western Han Dynasty.

much improved paper made from vegetable fibres. Paper, however, was probably not used by artists for some time, and paintings continued to be executed on rolls of silk. Figure subjects included illustrations to the classics and histories and more fanciful works such as the *Huai Nan Tzu* and *Shan-hai-ching*, while for landscape there were illustrations to the *fu* rhapsodies describing the capitals, palaces, and royal hunting parks.

It has long been thought that the hanging scroll was introduced with Buddhism from India, because the earliest known pictures in this form were the Buddhist banners of the T'ang Dynasty discovered at Tunhuang. However, in the tombs of the wife of the Marquis of Tai and of her son at Ma-wang-tui in the suburbs of Changsha have been found two T-shaped banners, draped over the swathed corpse in the coffin, that are a thousand years older than all known Chinese hanging scrolls and leave no doubt that the format is native to China. Called "flying garments" in the inventory placed in the tomb itself, because they were believed to bear the soul of the dead aloft into the sky, they depict beings of the nether world, the world of men, and the heavens, and include a portrait of the deceased and a sacrificial scene. These tombs were also hung with large silk paintings of courtly and domestic pursuits, feasting and dancing, and a remarkably accurate map of the presumed domain of the Marquis, embracing much of modern Hunan and Kwangtung.

94 Covered square-section jar, *fang-hu*. Lacquered wood. From a tomb at Ma-wang-tui, Changsha, Hunan. Western Han Dynasty.

95 Funerary banner from which the detail in figure 93 is taken. Line drawing. From Tomb No. 1, Ma-wang-tui, Changsha, Hunan. Western Han Dynasty.

With the fall of the Chou, the traditional rituals were forgotten, and consequently Han bronzes, while many were no doubt used in domestic rites of various sorts, are generally more utilitarian or decorative than those of Shang and Chou. Shapes are simple and functional, the commonest being the deep dish and the wine jar (*hu*), which were often decorated with inlaid designs in gold or silver. One object with definite ritual associations is the *Po-shan hsiang-lu*, a censer in the shape of a fairy mountain often covered with animals, hunters, and trees modelled in relief. Its base is lapped by the waves of the Eastern Sea, while a hole behind each little peak emits the incense smoke symbolising the cloud-vapour (*yün-ch'i*) which is the exhalation of the fairy mountain—and, indeed, of all mountains, for according to traditional Chinese belief, all nature is alive and "breathing." The beautiful hill-censer inlaid with gold illustrated here was found in the Western Han tomb of Liu Sheng, the jade-clad brother of the emperor Wu.

China's neighbours to the southwest were in a far more primitive stage of development than the nomads of the north and northwest. Over the years, at Shih-chai-shan in southern Yunnan, there have been found the remains of a bronze culture of late Chou and early Han date very different from that of China proper. More than a score of tombs containing bronze weapons and ritual objects, gold and jade ornaments have been opened. Most extraordinary are the bronze drums and drum-shaped containers filled with cowrie shells, the top of one of which is illustrated in Figure 97. The figures who crowd it are evidently taking part in some sacrificial rite. Prominent are the ceremonial drums, some of which

BRONZE

96 Fairy mountain incense burner, *Po-shan hsiang-lu*. Bronze inlaid with gold. From the tomb of Liu Sheng (died 113 B.C.) at Man-ch'eng, Hopei. Western Han Dynasty.

97 Drum-shaped container for cowrie shells, with modelled sacrificial scene. Bronze. From Shih-chai-shan, Yunnan. Second to first century B.C.

seem to be of enormous size, while a set of smaller drums stands on a platform under a wagon roof of a type still to be found in Southeast Asia and Sumatra today.

From Chinese sources we know that these are the tombs of the rulers of a non-Chinese tribe, or group of tribes, which they called Tien and which flourished in remote independence well into the Han Dynasty. The realistic modelling on the tops of the Shih-chai-shan "drums" has a counterpart in the Chinese tomb figurines of the Han Dynasty; but in its technique and decoration, Shih-chai-shan bronze art seems to be more closely related to the simple bronze crafts of China's western minorities and to the more sophisticated culture of northern Vietnam known as Dông-s'on.

In Han tombs there have been found great quantities of bronze objects, including harnesses and carriage fittings, swords and knives, utensils and belt buckles, many of which are inlaid with gold or silver, turquoise or jade. Even the trigger mechanism of a crossbow was often so cunningly inlaid as to make it an object of beauty. Some of these show the powerful impact of the animal style of the Ordos region, which in turn was influenced by that curious mixture of stylisation and realism characteristic of the art of the northern steppes.

98 Carriage fittings. Bronze inlaid with silver. Han Dynasty.

BRONZE MIRRORS

The bronze mirrors of the Han Dynasty continue the traditions developed at Loyang and Shou-chou during the Warring States. The Shou-chou coiled dragon design becomes more complex and crowded, the dragon's body being drawn in double or triple lines, while the background is generally crosshatched. Another group, also chiefly from Shou-chou, has an overall design of spirals on which a scalloped, many-pointed device is sometimes superimposed; its significance may be astronomical. Most interesting and most pregnant with symbolic meaning are the so-called TLV mirrors, of which the finest were produced in the Loyang region from the Wang Mang interregnum (A.D. 9–25) to about A.D. 100, although the design was already being used on mirror backs in the second century B.C.

99 TLV-type cosmological mirror.
Bronze. Han Dynasty.

A typical TLV mirror has a large central boss surrounded by a square panel with twelve smaller bosses separating the characters of the twelve earthly branches. The Ts, Ls, and Vs protrude into a circular zone adorned with animals, which, taken together with the fifth, central zone, symbolise the five elements, a system of cosmology first set down by Tsou Yen (c. 350–270 B.C.) and very popular in Han times. According to this system, the great ultimate (*t'ai-chi*) produces the positive–negative dualism of *yang* and *yin*, the interaction of which in turn gives birth to the five elements (*wu-hsing*) from which all events and objects are derived. The way in which the five elements relate to each other and are symbolised is as follows:

element	function	colour	direction	season	symbol
WATER	puts out fire	black	north	winter	"black warrior" (snake and tortoise)
FIRE	melts metal	red	south	summer	bird (phoenix)
METAL	destroys wood	white	west	autumn	tiger
WOOD	overcomes earth	green	east	spring	dragon
EARTH	absorbs water	yellow	centre		*tsung*

On the TLV mirror, the central circle within a square represents the earth symbol, *tsung*, while the four directions, seasons, and

75

colours are symbolised by their animals in the appropriate quarters. Many bear inscriptions which clearly set out the meaning and purpose of the design, such as this one on a mirror in the Museum of Far Eastern Antiquities, Stockholm:

> The Imperial mirror of the *Shang-fang* [imperial workshop] is truly without blemish; a skilled artisan has engraved it and achieved a decoration; to the left the Dragon and to the right the Tiger eliminate what is baleful; the Red Bird and Black Warrior conform to the *yin* and *yang* forces; may your sons and grandsons be complete in number and be in the centre; on it are Immortals such as are customary [on mirrors]; may you long preserve your two parents; may your joy and wealth be splendid; may your longevity outstrip that of metal and stone; may you be like a prince or a king.[3]

100 Immortals playing *liu-po*. Rubbing from a stone relief in a tomb at Hsinchin, Szechwan. Han Dynasty.

The TLV design was primarily an auspicious cosmological diagram combining celestial and terrestrial symbols. Its terrestrial elements made up the board for playing *liu-po*, a popular game in Han times that is represented on a number of Han reliefs and in clay models. The object of this game, which Professor Yang Liensheng has reconstructed from ancient texts, is to capture your opponent's men or drive them into the "benders" (presumably the Ls on the outer edge) in order to attain the centre, or, as Cammann has put it: "to establish an axis for symbolic control of the Universe." In Han mythology *liu-po* was a favourite game of Tung Wang Kung and of ambitious human heroes who sought to pitch their skill against that of the gods and, by defeating them, to acquire magic powers. To judge by the mirror designs, the game seems to have gone out of fashion toward the end of the Han Dynasty. The mirror backs of Late Han and the Three Kingdoms produced in the Shao-hsing district of present-day Chekiang often preserve the directional symbolism but now become crowded with figures fully modelled in relief; for the most part these are Taoist fairies and immortals, but after A.D. 300, Buddhist themes begin to appear as well.

101 Mirror with Taoist motifs. Bronze. Late Eastern Han period, second to third century A.D.

JADE   The advances in jade carving techniques made in the Warring States were continued under the Han. Now the lapidary could hollow out quite large pebbles in the form of toilet boxes and bowls such as the *yü-shang* ("winged cup"), a small oval bowl for eating and drinking, with flanges on the long sides. Winged cups have been found in sets standing on a tray and were made not only in jade but in silver, bronze, and pottery and lacquer. This new technical freedom made the lapidary more adventurous, inspiring him to carve, in three dimensions, figurines and animals—of which one of the most beautiful specimens is the famous horse in the Victoria and Albert Museum. He no longer rejects the flawed stone but, rather, begins to exploit the discolorations: the brown stain, for instance, becomes a dragon on a white cloud. Jade has by this time begun to lose its ritual significance; it now becomes instead the delight of the scholar and the gentleman, for whom its ancient associations and beauty of colour and texture will become a source of the profoundest intellectual and sensual pleasure. Henceforward he will be able to enjoy his pendants and garment hooks, his seals and the other playthings on his desk, in the confident knowledge that in them aesthetic and moral beauty are united. This, however, can hardly be said of the jade burial suits described on page 38, which were made at enormous cost in human travail for members of the Han imperial family. After the fall of the Han there was a reaction against this sort of extravagance; jade shrouds, for instance, were banned in 222 A.D., and most Six Dynasties graves are more simply furnished.

102 "Winged cup," *yü-shang*. Jade. Late Chou Dynasty.

103 Head and shoulders of a horse. Jade. Han Dynasty.

104 Burial suit. Jade plaques sewn together with gold thread. From the tomb of Liu Sheng (died 113 B.C.) at Man-ch'eng, Hopei. Western Han Dynasty.

TEXTILES

Under the Han Dynasty, the customs and amenities which in Shang and Chou had been confined to a minute privileged aristocracy in a small region now spread over a much wider area and a much larger segment of society. At the same time, Chinese handicrafts have been found far beyond its own frontiers—in Indo-china and Siberia, Korea and Afghanistan. The ruins of a Chinese-style palace recently discovered in southern Siberia contained Chinese bronze fittings, coins, tiles, and pottery house models, the latter presumably made locally by Chinese potters. Chinese archaeologists have suggested that this might have been the palace of the daughter of Madame Wen-chi, who had been married to a chieftain of the Hsiung-nu in A.D. 195 but eventually was forced to return to China, leaving her devoted husband and children behind.

Chinese textiles, too, reached the limits of the civilised world. The Greek word *Seres* ("the Silk People") was probably first used not of the Chinese themselves—of whom the Greeks had no direct knowledge—but of the western Asiatic tribes who traded in this precious commodity. Direct intercourse with China came only after Chang Ch'ien's expedition and the establishment of the Silk Road across central Asia. This great caravan route, leaving China at the Jade Gate in modern Kansu, crossed central Asia to the north or south of the Taklamakan Desert, reuniting in the region of Kashgar whence one branch led westward across Persia to the Mediterranean world while the other struck south into Gan-

dhāra and India. Chinese stuffs have been found in the Crimea, in
Afghanistan, Palmyra, and Egypt, while in Rome in the time of
Augustus there was a special market for imported Chinese silk, in
Vicus Tuscus. According to legend, it was the consort of the Yellow Emperor who first taught the Chinese people the cultivation
of the mulberry on which the silkworms feed, the spinning,
dyeing, and weaving of the threads; and so important has the industry been to China that, until the Revolution of 1911, the empress sacrificed to the spirit of the consort of the Yellow Emperor
every year in her own temple in Peking.

Evidence of the art of weaving was found in the Neolithic village of Pan-p'o in Shensi; the Shang people at Anyang had tailored
clothing of silk and hemp, while a number of passages in the *Book
of Songs* refer to coloured woven silk. Silk panels with painted designs have been found in late Chou graves at Changsha, while
equally important finds of early Chinese textiles were made in
central Asia, notably in the waterlogged tumulus graves at Noin-
Ula, in southern Siberia, excavated by the Koslov expedition in
1924/25, and in the sand-buried sites of Turfan and Khotan, explored first by Sir Aurel Stein in the early years of the twentieth
century and, more recently, by Chinese archaeologists. The grave
in Changsha that yielded the silk banner shown here was also
crammed with rolls of silk. The techniques included moiré, damask, gauze, quilting, and embroidery, and the designs were chiefly
of three kinds: pictorial, generally representing animal combats

105 Figured silk fabric. From Noin-
Ula, Mongolia. Han Dynasty.

106 Woven silk textile. From Tomb
No. 1 at Ma-wang-tui, Changsha,
Hunan. Western Han Dynasty.

107 Silk panel from Noin-Ula. Line
drawing. Han Dynasty.

such as appear also on the Ordos bronzes; diapered, with geomet-
rical motifs repeated over the whole surface; and composed of
those endless rhythmic cloud volutes which we have already encountered on the inlaid bronzes, set about with horsemen, deer, tigers, and more fabulous creatures. The silk panel from Noin-Ula
illustrated here is a kind of Taoist landscape composed of giant
spirit-fungi (*ling-chih*) alternating with rocky crags topped by
phoenixes and adorned with formalised trees, executed in a mixed
Chinese-Western style which suggests that Chinese weavers were
already designing for the export market.

Han ceramics vary enormously in quality, from unglazed and roughly modelled earthenware to a high-fired, glazed stoneware verging on porcelain. Most of the grave goods were made of coarse pottery generally covered with a lead glaze which easily oxidises, producing that silvery-green iridescence which is so attractive a feature of this class of Han wares. The technique of lead-glazing was known in the Mediterranean world before the Han, and if not discovered independently may have been introduced by way of central Asia. The finest of these lead-glazed wares are the jars (*hu*) for grain or wine. Their shapes are simple and robust, the imitation of bronze being aided by a very precise finish and the application of *t'ao-t'ieh* masks in relief, while incised lines or geometric motifs around the shoulder enhance the beauty of their form. Sometimes they are decorated with a frieze, depicting, in relief under the glaze, a hunt among mountains, in which all manner of creatures real and imaginary chase each other around and around—as on those extraordinary full-scale models of Mount

108 Jar, *hu*. Stoneware decorated with relief designs under a dark-green glaze. Han Dynasty.

109 The hunt among mountains. Relief on the shoulder of a pottery *hu*. Line drawing after Palmgren. Han Dynasty.

110 Watchtower. Pottery with green glaze. Eastern Han Dynasty.

111 Dog. Pottery covered with reddish-brown glaze. From Changsha, Hunan. Han Dynasty.

P'eng-lai which were made to appear at the hunting feasts of the Han emperors. These reliefs, in which we often find towering ranges of hills, may well preserve the designs of Han scroll paintings on silk.

In Han times, many people believed that on quitting this world one could take with him to heaven his family, servants, personal possessions, domestic animals, and even his house. As these could not actually accompany him, models (*ming-ch'i*, literally, bright, or spirit, utensils) were placed in the tomb, and the custom persisted long after the fall of the Han.[4] Thus, we find in the Han tombs a retinue of servants and guards, farmhands, musicians, and jugglers such as its occupant probably never enjoyed in his lifetime. There were barns with fowl modelled in relief on the top. There were watchtowers in several storeys, their wooden beams and transoms either indicated by incisions in the clay or painted red. The house and barns of the South China tombs are raised on stilts, like those in Southeast Asia today. Farm animals are modelled with uncanny realism; watchdogs from Szechwan graves are squat and menacing; those from Changsha, with heads erect and muzzles quivering, so alert one can almost hear them sniffing. These figurines are a useful source of information on the daily life, beliefs, and economy of Han China. The delightful tableau excavated in 1969 from a Western Han tomb at Tsinan, Shantung, depicts the kind of entertainment with music, tumblers, and dancers that was often represented on the walls of tombs and tomb shrines. They illustrate, too, the extent of China's foreign contacts at this time. The pottery stand for a bronze "coin-tree" found in a grave in Szechwan, for example, is decorated with a frieze of elephants in relief, modelled with a lively naturalism that has no counterpart in other Han reliefs but at once calls to mind the animals of the four quarters carved on the capital of the Aśokan column at Sarnath.

Some of the Han figurines were individually modelled, but the majority of the smaller pieces were mass-produced in moulds: though the forms are reduced to essentials, none of their vitality or character is lost. At Changsha, where the clay was often poor and glazes apt to flake off, the *ming-ch'i* were generally made of painted wood, which, like the silk and lacquer found in the Changsha tombs, has miraculously survived the ravages of time.

Of quite a different kind was the fine-quality felspathic stoneware, which was made in a number of centres in Chekiang. This ancestor of the Sung celadons has a hard body and thin glaze ranging in colour from grey to olive-green to brown. It is often called Yüeh ware, because the type-site is at Chiu-yen near Shao-hsing, the old name of which is Yüeh-chou. Recent Chinese writers confine the term *Yüeh ware* to the porcellaneous celadon made for the court of Wu-Yüeh in the tenth century A.D., calling all earlier celadons "old Yüeh" or simply *ch'ing tz'u*, "green porcelain." However, in translation this is misleading, as some of it can hardly be called green, and none of it is true porcelain. In this book, therefore, the term *Yüeh ware* is retained to cover the whole huge family of pre-Sung Chekiang celadons.[5]

112 Tray with figures of musicians, dancers, acrobats, and spectators. Painted pottery. From a tomb at Tsinan, Shantung. Western Han Dynasty.

113 Stand for a lamp or "coin-tree." Pottery. From a tomb at Nei-chiang, Szechwan. Eastern Han Dynasty.

83

114 Basin, Yüeh ware. Stoneware with
modelled and incised decoration under a
grey-green glaze. Third or fourth
century A.D.

The Chiu-yen kilns were in operation at least from the second
century A.D.; those at Te-ch'ing, north of Hangchow, perhaps a
little later. Many of their products, found in dated tombs in the
Nanking region, are imitations of bronze vessels, even to the
loop-handles and *t'ao-t'ieh* masks that adorn them. Some are
stamped with geometric or diaper designs under the glaze, preserving an ancient tradition of central and southern China which
spread not only northward but also into the Nan-hai, the penin-
sula and islands of Southeast Asia. Gradually, however, true ceramic forms began to emerge, aided by a rich, luminous, and even
luscious glaze. The Chiu-yen kilns seem to have closed down in
the sixth century, after which the Yüeh tradition was carried on in
many parts of Chekiang, the chief factories being around the
shores of Shang-lin-hu in Yü-yao-hsien, where the remains of
more than twenty celadon kilns have so far been discovered.

6

The Three Kingdoms and the Six Dynasties

During the four hundred years between the fall of the Han Dynasty and the rise of the T'ang, China went through a period of political, social, and intellectual ferment comparable to that of modern Europe. No fewer than thirty dynasties and lesser kingdoms passed across the scene before the Sui reunited the empire in 581. At the fall of the Han Dynasty in A.D. 220, China was divided into the Three Kingdoms of Wu, Wei, and Shu; in 280 it was once more reunited, under a Wei general who had usurped the throne in 265 and renamed the dynasty Chin. Beyond the northern frontiers, the Hsiung-nu and the Hsien-pi were watching with interest the incessant civil wars to which the now shrunken empire was victim. When, soon after A.D. 300, two rival princes rashly appealed to them for aid, they promptly advanced into China. In 311 the Hsiung-nu captured Loyang, massacred twenty thousand of its inhabitants and took the emperor prisoner; they then moved on to Ch'ang-an, which they put to the sack, while the Chin court fled in panic to Nanking. The Hsiung-nu and Hsien-pi were not the only tribes to take advantage of China's weakness in order to invade the north; sixteen petty barbarian kingdoms were to rise and fall before the Toba Wei, a Turkish tribe, brought the whole of North China under their rule in 439. They established their capital near Ta-t'ung in northern Shansi, abandoned their nomadic way of life and adopted Chinese dress, eventually becoming so Sinicized that the use of the Toba language was forbidden altogether. At the same time, they energetically defended their northern borders against other and more barbarous tribes and pushed their cavalry as far as Kucha in the Tarim Basin, thus reopening the trade route into central Asia.

The invasions had split China into two countries, with two cultures. While the north sank into barbarism, tens of thousands of Chinese refugees migrated to the south. Nanking now became the cultural and political centre of "free China," to which merchants and Buddhist missionaries came from Southeast Asia and India. Yet this region too was in a perpetual state of turmoil and unrest, in which enormous quantities of art treasures were destroyed.

A

B

MAP 6 China during the Three
Kingdoms and Six Dynasties period.
A. A.D. 220–280. *B*. About A.D. 520.

Four more dynasties—the Liu Sung, Southern Ch'i, Liang, and Ch'en—ruled from Nanking before the split between north and south was healed. The Confucian order was undermined, and the southern Buddhist temples and monasteries now grew to such vast proportions—particularly under Liang Wu Ti (502–550)—that they constituted a serious threat to the political and economic stability of the realm. With the eclipse of the Confucian bureaucracy, it was often the great landed families who exerted the most influence on politics and the arts, outliving the dynasties themselves.

Many intellectuals in the south sought escape from the chaos of the times in Taoism, music, calligraphy, and the delights of pure talk (ch'ing-t'an). Taoism came into its own in the third and fourth centuries, for it seemed to answer the yearnings of men of feeling and imagination for a vision of the eternal in which they could forget the chaos of the present. This conglomeration of folklore, nature worship, and metaphysics was rooted in the native soil of China. It had first become a cult in the Later Han when Chang Tao-ling, a mystic and magician from Szechwan who called himself the T'ien-shih ("heavenly master"), gathered round him a group of followers with whom he roamed the countryside in search of the elixir of life. Sometimes he would take them to the top of the Cloud Terrace Mountain (Yün-t'ai-shan) and there invent ordeals to test their magic powers. By the Chin Dynasty, the movement that had originated as a private revolt against the established order had grown into a full-fledged church, with a canon of scriptures, a hierarchy, temples, and all the trappings of a formal religion copied from the Buddhists.

On a higher level, however, the Taoists were the intellectual avant-garde. The reaction against Confucianism had produced a thaw in the rigidly traditional view of art and literature, and now the imagination took flight once more in poetry more inspired than any since the elegies of Ch'u. Typical of the age is the poet T'ao Yüan-ming (365–427) who, though forced several times to take office to support his family, retired whenever he could to his country cottage where he grew his own vegetables, drank excessively, and read books, though he said he did not mind if he failed to understand them completely. This was not merely escape from political and social chaos; it was escape also into the world of the imagination.

It was in these turbulent years that the Chinese painter and poet first discovered himself. Lu Chi's *Wen fu* (*Rhymeprose on Literature*), written in A.D. 300, is a penetrating, even passionate, rhapsody on that ordeal which T. S. Eliot called the "intolerable wrestle with words and meanings" and on the mysterious sources of poetic inspiration.[1] In the traditional Confucian view, art had served a primarily moral and didactic purpose in society. Now that position was abandoned, and new critical standards were evolved, culminating in Hsiao T'ung's preface of A.D. 530 to his

TAOISM

AESTHETICS

anthology *Wen-hsüan,* in which he wrote that his selection of prose and poetry had been guided not by moral considerations but by aesthetic merit alone. This sophisticated position was not reached at once, however. Literary criticism in the third and fourth centuries had taken the form of *p'in-tsao*—a mere classification (often in nine grades) according to merits and faults, first applied to statesmen and other public figures, then to poets. The great painter Ku K'ai-chih used it in discussing artists of Wei and Chin (if indeed the surviving text is from his hand). It was employed more methodically by Hsieh Ho in his famous *Ku hua p'in lu* (*Ancient Painters' Classified Record*), written in the second quarter of the sixth century, in which the author grades forty-three painters of former times into six classes, a useful but undistinguished contribution to art history. What has made this brief work so significant for the whole history of Chinese painting is its preface, which sets out the six principles (*liu fa*) by which paintings, and painters, are to be judged.

Much—perhaps too much—has been written about the six principles. But they cannot be passed over, for they have, with some variation or rearrangement, remained the pivot around which all subsequent art criticism in China has revolved. They are:

1. *Ch'i yün sheng tung*: Spirit Harmony—Life's Motion (Arthur Waley); Animation through spirit consonance (Alexander Soper).
2. *Ku fa yung pi*: bone-means use brush (Waley); structural method in the use of the brush (Soper).
3. *Ying wu hsiang hsing*: fidelity to the object in portraying forms (Soper).
4. *Sui lei fu ts'ai*: conformity to kind in applying colours (Soper).
5. *Chin ying wei chih*: proper planning in placing [of elements] (Soper).
6. *Ch'uan i mu hsieh*: that by copying, the ancient models should be perpetuated (Sakanishi).

The third, fourth, and fifth laws are self-explanatory; they reflect the kind of technical problems that painting encountered in its early development. The sixth involves on the one hand the need to train one's hand and acquire an extensive formal repertoire, and on the other a reverence for the tradition itself, of which every painter felt himself to be in a sense a custodian. Making exact copies of ancient, worn masterpieces was a way of preserving them, and, at a later date, working "in the manner of" great painters of the past, while adding something of oneself, was a way of putting new life into the tradition.

The experience of the painter—what Cézanne called, in a celebrated phrase, "une sensation forte devant la nature"—is enshrined in the phrase *ch'i yün,* Soper's "spirit consonance." *Ch'i* is that cosmic spirit (literally, breath or vapour) that vitalises all things, that gives life and growth to the trees, movement to the water, energy to man, and is exhaled by the mountains as clouds and mist. It is the task of the artist to attune himself to this cosmic spirit and let it infuse him with energy so that in a moment of inspiration—and no word could be more appropriate—he may become the vehicle for its expression. William Acker once asked a famous calligrapher why he dug his ink-stained fingers so deep into the hairs of his huge brush when he was writing; the calligrapher replied that only thus could he feel the *ch'i* flow down his arm, through the brush and onto the paper. The *ch'i* is a cosmic energy that, as Acker puts it, "flows about in ever-changing streams and eddies, here deep, there shallow, here concentrated, there dispersed."[2] It infuses all things, for there is no distinction between the animate and the inanimate. Seen in this light, the third, fourth, and fifth principles involve more than mere visual accuracy; for, as the living forms of nature are the visible manifestations of the workings of the *ch'i*, only by representing them faithfully can the artist express his awareness of this cosmic principle in action.

The quality in a painting through which awareness of the inner vital spirit is expressed is the second of Hsieh Ho's principles, *ku* (the "bone"), the structural strength of the brush-stroke itself, whether in painting or calligraphy. The sudden flowering of calligraphy at the end of the Han Dynasty as an art form in its own right was partly due to the popularity of the *ts'ao-shu* ("draft script"), the cursive style which freed the scholar from the formal angularity of the typical Han *li-shu* ("official" or "clerical script") and enabled him to express himself in a style more personal, more charged with energy and grace, than any other writing that man has devised. It is no accident that many of the greatest calligraphers of this period, including Wang Hsi-chih and his son Hsien-chih, were Taoists. Both the techniques and the aesthetic of this subtle art had a considerable influence upon the development of Chinese painting during the three centuries following the fall of the Han.

The Taoist ideal in action is illustrated in the life and work of Tsung Ping, a distinguished Buddhist scholar and painter of the early fifth century, who spent his life wandering amid the beautiful hills of the south with his equally romantic wife, and who, when he was too old to wander any more, recreated the landscapes that he loved on the walls of his studio. A short *Preface on Landscape Painting* (*Hua shan-shui hsü*), one of the earliest surviving writings on this new art form, is attributed to him. In it he maintains that landscape-painting is a high art because landscapes "both have material existence and reach out into the realm of the spirit." He declares that he would like to be a Taoist mystic, meditating upon the void. He has tried it and is ashamed to confess that he failed; but, he asks, is not the art of the landscape painter, who can reproduce the very forms and colours that inspire the Taoist adept, even more wonderful? He is innocently amazed at the power of the artist to bring down a vast panorama of mountains within the compass of a few inches of silk. Visual accuracy he holds to be essential, for if the landscape is well and convincingly executed, if the forms and colours in the picture correspond to those in nature,

115 Anonymous. Copy after Wang Hsi-chih (c. 303–361): Beginning of the letter "Hsing-jang. . . ." *Hsing-shu* style. Ink on paper. T'ang Dynasty.

then "that correspondence will stir the spirit, and when the spirit soars, truth will be attained. . . . What more," he asks, "could be added to this?"

Another brief essay, attributed to Wang Wei, a scholar, musician, and man of letters who died in 443 at the age of twenty-eight, starts by pointing out that paintings must correspond to the *pa kua* (the "eight trigrams"), meaning that just as the *pa kua* is a symbolic diagram of the workings of the universe, so must landscape-painting be a symbolic language through which the painter may express not a relative, particularised aspect of nature seen at a given moment from a given viewpoint but a general truth, beyond time and place. Though he too is full of wonder at the artist's mysterious power of pictorial compression, he insists that painting is more than the exercise of skill: "The spirit must also exercise control over it; for this is the essence of painting." The landscapes of Wang Wei, Tsung Ping, and their contemporaries were all lost centuries ago, but the ideals that are enshrined in these and other writings of this critical formative period have been the inspiration of Chinese painters up to the present day.

116 After Ku K'ai-chih (c. 344–406). Illustration to *The Fairy of the Lo River*. Detail of a handscroll. Ink and colour on silk. About twelfth century.

KU K'AI-CHIH AND THE BIRTH OF LANDSCAPE PAINTING

The life and work of Ku K'ai-chih (c. 344–406), more perhaps than that of any other creative personality of this time, seem to embody the forces that inspired men in these turbulent years. Himself wildly unconventional and yet a friend of the great at court, a calligrapher and painter of Taoist landscapes who yet was seldom far from the hurly-burly of intrigue in the capital, he moved unharmed among the rival politicians and warlords, protecting himself by the aura of idiocy which the Taoists held to be the only true wisdom. His biography tells us that he was famous for his portraits, in which he captured not merely the appearance but the very spirit of his subject.[3] A fascinating essay attributed to him describes how he would go about painting the Cloud Terrace Mountain and the ordeal to which Chang Tao-ling subjected one of his disciples on the top of a precipice. The text shows that he

conceived of the mountain in strictly Taoist terms, bracketed east
and west by the green dragon and the white tiger, its central peak
ringed with clouds and surmounted by the strutting phoenix,
symbol of the south. We do not know whether he ever painted this
picture or not, though he probably did. Only three paintings associated with his name have survived. One, of which there are
Sung versions in the Freer Gallery and the Palace Museum, Peking, illustrates the closing moments in the *fu* of "The Fairy of the
Lo River," by Ts'ao Chih. Both these copies preserve the archaic
style of his time, particularly in the primitive treatment of the
landscape, which provides the setting for the scene where the fairy
bids farewell to the young scholar who had fallen in love with her,
and sails away in her magic boat.

The Lo-shen scroll makes use of the technique of continuous
narration, in which the same characters appear several times,
whenever the story requires. This device seems to have come from
India with the introduction of Buddhism, for there is no evidence
of it in Han art. Probably the Han scrolls most often used the convention employed in the two other surviving works connected
with Ku K'ai-chih, the *Lieh-nü t'u*, illustrating four groups of famous women of antiquity, with their parents,[4] and *The Admonitions of the Instructress to the Court Ladies*, in which the text alternates
with the illustrations. The *Admonitions* scroll, illustrating a poem
by Chang Hua, is not included among recorded works of Ku in
T'ang texts and was first attributed to him in the collection of the
Sung emperor Hui-tsung; there are, indeed, details of the landscape that suggest it may be a copy of the ninth or tenth century.
Yet it clearly derives from a painting by a very early master. The
scene in Fig. 118 shows the emperor gazing doubtfully at a concubine seated in her bed-couch. The couplet (not visible) to the
right runs: "If the words that you utter are good, all men for a
thousand leagues around will make response to you. But if you

117 Hunting scene. Wall painting in the
Tomb of the Wrestlers, T'ung-kou,
Kirin. About fifth century.

118 Attributed to Ku K'ai-chih. The emperor with one of his concubines. Illustration to *The Admonitions of the Instructress*. Detail of a handscroll. Ink and colour on silk. Possibly a T'ang Dynasty copy.

depart from this principle, even your bedfellow will distrust you." The fourth scene, now much faded and damaged, illustrates the virtuous Lady Pan refusing to distract the Han emperor Ch'eng from affairs of state by going out with him in his litter. The same scene, and almost the same composition, appear on a painted wooden screen (Fig. 119) that was discovered in 1965 in the tomb of Ssu-ma Chin-lung, a Chinese official who died at Ta-t'ung in 484, after loyally serving the Northern Wei court, and was buried in the Wei imperial mausoleum. Other scenes on this precious panel illustrate virtuous women of antiquity and, at the top, the emperor Shun meeting his future wives. While it is tempting to think that the treatment of the Lady Pan scene was inspired by a version of the Ku K'ai-chih scroll that had found its way to North China, both may be based on an older traditional rendering of the theme.

When Liang Yüan Ti abdicated in 555, he deliberately consigned to the flames over two hundred thousand books and pictures in his private collection, so it is not surprising that nothing has survived of the works of the other leading masters of the Southern Dynasties who were active in Nanking. The *Li-tai ming-hua chi*, however, records the titles of a number of paintings of this period, from which we know what kinds of subjects were popular. There were the stock Confucian and Buddhist themes, great

119 Filial sons and virtuous women of antiquity. Panel from a wooden screen painted in lacquer. From a tomb dated 484 at Ta-t'ung, Shansi. Northern Wei Dynasty.

子舜

120 The story of the filial Shun. Detail
of an engraved stone slab from a
sarcophagus. Late Northern Wei
Dynasty, about 520–530.

panoramas illustrating the descriptive *fu* and other, shorter
poems; landscapes depicting famous mountains and gardens;
there were scenes of city, village, and tribal life, fantastic Taoist
landscapes and pictures of the figures symbolising the constellations, illustrations of historical events, legends such as the story of
Hsi Wang Mu. Most must have had landscape settings, while several were pure landscapes, and at least three paintings of bamboo
are recorded. The great majority were presumably either standing
screens or long handscrolls.

We can obtain some notion of the style of the time from the
paintings that line the walls of tombs in North Korea, notably the
"Tomb of the Dancing Figures" and the "Tomb of the Wrestling
Scene" (Fig. 117) at T'ung-kou on the Yalu River. Although
painted as late as the sixth century, these lively scenes of feasting
and hunting amid mountains are in the tradition of the Han tomb
paintings at Liao-yang. But to see the most advanced treatment of
landscape in this indigenous style, we must look not at the provincial tomb decorations but at the engraved slabs from North
China, of which the most beautiful examples are the sides of a
stone coffin adorned with incidents in the lives of six famous filial
sons of antiquity. The figures seem hardly more than the excuse
for magnificent landscape panoramas, so richly conceived and so
beautifully drawn that they must surely have been copied from a
handscroll—or, as Sickman suggests, a wall painting—by an ac-

complished artist. Each incident is set off from its neighbours by hills with overlapping tops called *ch'üeh* which have powerful Taoist associations; half-a-dozen kinds of tree are distinguishable, tossed by a great wind that sweeps through their branches, while above the distant hills the clouds streak across the sky. The scene in which the filial Shun escapes from the well into which his jealous stepfather Yao cast him is astonishing in its animation, and only in his failure to lead the eye back through a convincing middle distance to the horizon does the artist reveal the limitations of his time. Though its subject is respectably Confucian, its treatment exudes a joy in the face of living nature that is purely Taoist. It serves also to remind us that in spite of the ever-growing demands of Buddhism for art of an entirely different kind, there already existed at this time a purely native landscape tradition allied to calligraphy and based on the language of the brush.

Buddhist communities were already established in North China before the end of the Han Dynasty. Now, however, political and social chaos, loss of faith in the traditional Confucian order, and the desire to escape from the troubles of the times all contributed to a wave of remarkable religious enthusiasm, and the new doctrine spread to every corner of the empire. Its acceptance, except among the lower strata of society, was not due to blind and innocent faith—for that is not a sentiment to which the educated Chinese are prone—but perhaps to the fact that it was new, that it filled a big gap in men's spiritual lives, and that its speculative philosophy and moral justification of the renunciation of worldly ties appealed to intellectuals, who were now often reluctant to take on the perilous responsibilities of office. The new faith must have proved an effective consolation, if we are to judge by the vast sums spent on the building of monasteries and temples and their adornment during these troubled years.

We must pause in our narrative for a moment to consider the life and teachings of the Buddha, which form the subject matter of Buddhist art. Gautama Śākyamuni, called the Buddha, or the Enlightened One, was born about 567 B.C., the son of a prince of the Śākya clan ruling on the border of Nepal. He grew up surrounded by the luxuries of the palace, married, and had a son Rāhula. His father deliberately shielded him from all contact with the miseries of life beyond the palace gates, but in spite of the care with which his excursions were planned for him, Śākyamuni was finally confronted with the reality of old age, sickness, and death, and he saw a vision of an ascetic, pointing his future path. Deeply disturbed by his experience, he resolved to renounce the world and search for the cause of so much suffering. One night he stole out from the palace, cut off his hair, bade farewell to his horse and groom, and embarked upon his quest. For many years he wandered, seeking, first with one teacher and then with another, the answer to the mystery of existence and a way of release from the intolerable cycle of endless rebirths to which all living things are subject according to *karma*, the inexorable law of cause and effect. Then one day at Bodhgayā, seated under a pippala tree, he entered into a

BUDDHISM

trance. For three days and nights he remained motionless. The demon Māra sent his host to assault him and his three lovely daughters to dance seductively before him, but without moving from where he sat, the Lord rendered the former powerless while the latter he transformed into withered hags. Finally, in the moment of enlightenment, the answer came to him. In his first great sermon in the Deer Park at Benares, he gave his message to the world in the form of the "Four Noble Truths":

All existence is suffering (*dukkha*).
The cause of suffering is craving, lust, desire—even desire for existence itself.
There is an end to suffering, for this craving can be suppressed.
There is a way of suppression, through the Noble Eightfold Path.

The Buddha also taught that there is no such thing as a soul, but that all life is transitory, all in a perpetual state of becoming. By following the Eightfold Path, which involves right conduct, right belief, and right meditation, the devotee can break the cycle of rebirths which binds us eternally to the wheel of existence, and so secure his release and his final merging in eternity like a cup of water poured into the sea. Śākyamuni achieved enlightenment in his lifetime, although he continued to walk the earth, gathering disciples, performing miracles, and spreading his teaching, until his final departure, the *Mahāparinirvāna*, at the age of eighty. His teaching was austere and, moreover, only for the chosen few who were prepared to renounce the world and face the rigours of life as a mendicant or, later, the regimen of the monastery. Its appeal lay partly in its simplicity—a welcome relief from the complexities of Hindu theology and metaphysics—and partly in the hope it offered of release from a destiny from which Hindu doctrine saw no escape.

The new faith grew slowly, and it was not until it was embraced by King Aśoka (272?–232 B.C.) that it became a truly national religion. That monarch devoted himself with such tremendous energy to its propagation that legend has it he erected eighty-four thousand *stūpas* (relic mounds) in a single day, while his monastic and temple foundations were on a scale which many a pious Buddhist ruler has since tried to emulate. His missionary activities brought the faith to Ceylon and to Gandhāra in northwest India, where it came in contact with the religious ideas and artistic forms of the provincial Graeco-Roman world. It was probably in Gandhāra that, under these influences and encouraged by the great conference organised by King Kanishka (second century A.D.) of the Kushans, the first great development in Buddhist doctrine took place. The core of the dogma remained unaltered, but the new schools—who called themselves Mahāyāna ("greater vehicle"), referring derogatively to the more conservative sects as the Hīnayāna ("lesser vehicle")—taught that salvation was open to all men, through faith and works. Now the Buddha ceased to be an earthly teacher, but was conceived of as pure abstraction, as the universal principle, the godhead, from whom truth, in the form of the Buddhist *dharma* ("law"), radiates with a blinding light across the universe. By this elevation to a status parallel to that of the Hindu Brahmā, the Buddha receded far beyond the reach of mortal man. *Bhakti*, the adoration of a personal god, expressed in Hinduism in the love of Krishna, demanded a more approachable deity. So there came into existence the *bodhisattva* ("one destined for enlightenment"), who has postponed his own end that he might bring help and comfort to suffering mankind. Of the *bodhisattvas*, the most popular was Avalokiteśvara ("the Lord who looks down [in mercy]"), who on his translation to China as Kuan-yin became identified both with his female reflex, Tārā, and with the ancient Chinese mother-goddess, and thus imperceptibly acquired female sex—a process that was complete by the end of the tenth century. Almost as important were Manjuśri (Chinese, Wen-shu) the god of wisdom, and Maitreya, the deity who, though now still a *bodhisattva*, will in the next cycle descend to earth as the Buddha; to the Chinese he has become Mi-lo-fu, the pot-bellied "god of wealth" who sits grinning at the entrance of every temple. In time the pantheon grew to extraordinary proportions, the vast array of Buddhas and *bodhisattvas* being attempts to express the infinite aspects and powers of god. These developments were, however, for the theologians and metaphysicians. The common man needed only the comfort of Avalokiteśvara, or the secure knowledge that, merely by speaking once the name of the Buddha Amitābha, he would on quitting this world be reborn in his western paradise beyond the sunset.

121 Śākyamuni Buddha. Gilt bronze. Dated equivalent to 338 A.D. Six Dynasties.

MAP 7 The spread of Buddhism from India into central and eastern Asia.

It was probably in Gandhāra, and under Western influence, that the Buddha was first represented in sculpture. The style of Gandhāra is a curious mixture of the classical realism of Graeco-Roman provincial art with the Indian genius, fostered at the southern Kushan capital of Mathurā, for giving concrete, plastic expression to an abstract, metaphysical concept. From Gandhāra, Buddhism, and with it this new synthetic art, spread northward across the Hindu Kush to central Asia, there to run like a powder trail along the string of oases to the north and south of the Tarim Basin.

122 Types of pagoda. 1–3 derived from the Han timber *lou*: 1. Yünkang (Northern Wei); 2. Sian (T'ang); 3. Canton (Ming). 4 and 5 derived from the Indian *śikhara* tower: 4. Sung-shan (c. 520); 5. Sian (T'ang).

BUDDHIST ART REACHES CHINA

123 Twelve-sided pagoda of Sung-yüeh-ssu on Mount Sung, Honan. Northern Wei Dynasty, about 520.

Buddhist sculpture preceded Buddhist architecture into China, for it was the images—brought in the luggage of missionaries, travellers, and pilgrims, who were no doubt prepared to swear that what they carried was an exact replica of some famous icon in India or central Asia—which were most deeply venerated. The earliest known exactly dated Chinese Buddhist image, cast in 338, is clearly an imitation of a Gandhāran prototype. Such icons were set up in shrines built in the traditional Chinese style, which grew until the monastery or temple became a kind of palace, with courtyards, pavilions, galleries, and gardens. No attempt was made in these timber buildings to imitate the Indian temple. But the *stūpa* presented a different kind of challenge. The monk Sung Yün, returning from Gandhāra early in the sixth century, had described (as doubtless many before him) the gigantic *stūpa* erected by King Kanishka, one of the wonders of the Buddhist world. Built in timber, it was no less than seven hundred feet high, in thirteen storeys, capped by a mast with thirteen golden discs. The Chinese already possessed, in the towers called *lou* and *ch'üeh*, multistoreyed timber buildings which could be adapted to this new purpose (see p. 82). The Chinese examples of this period have all perished, but the pagodas at Hōryūji and Yakushiji near Nara in Japan still stand as monuments to this simple, graceful style. The earliest surviving dateable pagoda on Chinese soil, however, is the twelve-sided stone tower on Mount Sung in Honan, erected in about 520. It has no surviving Chinese antecedents. Its profile echoes the curve of the Indian *śikhara* tower; the arched recesses on the main faces recall the niches on the great *stūpa* at Bodhgayā,

98

and, as Soper has observed, many of the details are Indian, or based on Southeast Asian modifications of the Indian style found in the kingdom of Champa, with which China was now in contact. But gradually the Indian elements were absorbed, and the later stone and brick pagodas imitate, in their surface treatment, the posts, brackets, and projecting roofs of their Chinese timber prototypes.

At Bāmiyān in Afghanistan a high cliff more than a mile in length had been hollowed out into cave shrines decorated with frescoes and bracketed at either end by colossal standing Buddha figures carved out of the rock, plastered and painted. This fashion for decorated cave shrines, which had originated in India, spread to Khotan, Kucha, and other central Asian city-states, where the already syncretic Graeco-Indian tradition of painting and sculpture became mixed with the flat, heraldic, decorative style of Parthia and Sasanian Persia. The routes that skirted the Taklamakan

124 Mai-chi-shan, Kansu. View from the southeast.

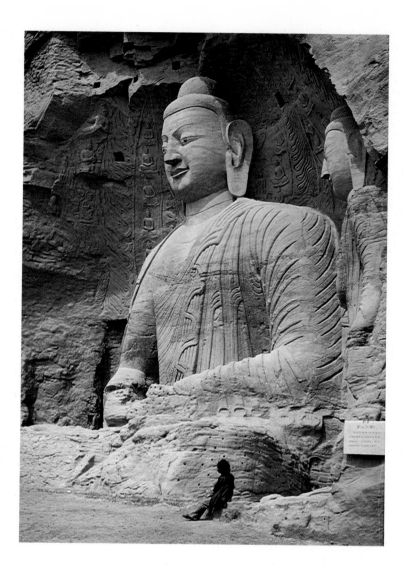

Desert joined at Tunhuang, the gateway to China. There, in A.D.
366, pilgrims had hewn from the soft rock the first of what were
to develop during the next thousand years into a range of nearly
five hundred chambers and niches set about with plaster sculpture
and adorned with frescoes. Further stages on the pilgrim route
into China were marked by cave shrines at Ping-ling-ssu, about
fifty miles southwest of Lanchow, and Mai-chi-shan, twenty-
eight miles southeast of T'ien-shui. The former was only rediscovered in 1951, while restoration of the latter, which had always
been known to the people of the T'ien-shui district, did not begin
till 1953. In their spectacular sites and the quality and richness of
their sculpture these shrines surpass Tunhuang, whose glory lies
chiefly in its paintings.

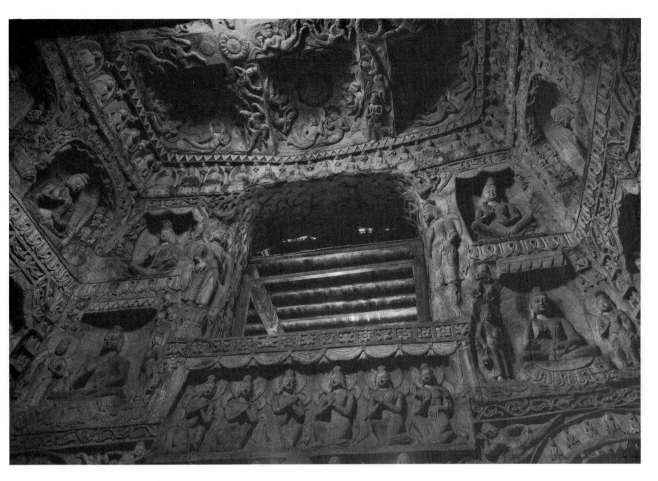

126 Interior of Cave VII, Yünkang. Northern Wei Dynasty, about 470–480.

In 386 the Toba Turks established their ascendancy over North China as the Wei Dynasty, with their capital at Ta-t'ung. Their rulers had embraced Buddhism with enthusiasm, for, like the Kushans in India, they were excluded from the traditional social and religious system of those they had conquered.[5] At the urging of the overseer of monks, T'an-yao, they began, soon after 460, to hew out of the cliffs at Yünkang a series of shrines and colossal figures which were to be a monument not only to Buddhism but also to the splendour of the royal house itself. By the time the capital was moved south to Loyang in 494, twenty large caves and some minor ones had been excavated, while work was resumed under the Sui, and again between 916 and 1125, when Ta-t'ung became the western capital of the Liao Dynasty. The earliest caves—those numbered XVI to XX—were dedicated by the emperor to himself and four earlier Wei rulers, possibly as a penance for the harsh repression of the faith by his Taoist grandfather in 444. These five caves contain huge seated or standing Buddhas cut in the living rock, while the seated Buddha of Cave XX was originally protected by a timber façade of several storeys. This colossus, fifteen

BUDDHIST
SCULPTURE UNDER
THE NORTHERN WEI:
THE FIRST PHASE

metres high, sits in an attitude of meditation; his shoulders and chest are massive and yet finely proportioned, his face is clear-cut with something of the masklike quality often found in Gandhāra, while the drapery is suggested by flat, straplike bands that disappear into points as they pass round the contour of arm or shoulder. Perhaps, as Sickman has suggested, this curious convention is the result of the sculptor's following, and not properly understanding, a line drawing of some Western prototype, for great pains were taken to copy the style of the more venerated images as closely as possible.

By the end of the fifth century a change was beginning to appear in the sculpture at Yünkang, when this solid and somewhat heavy style was modified and refined by the native Chinese predilection for abstract expression in terms of the flowing, rhythmic line. The carvings in Cave VII, one of the most richly decorated of all, bear witness to this transformation. This is one of the "paired" caves dedicated by members of the imperial family about 480 or 490. Every inch of the walls is decorated with reliefs which were once painted in bright colours and testify to the gratitude, to the generosity, and perhaps also to the anxiety about their future destiny of the imperial donors. In long panels, the life of the Buddha is told

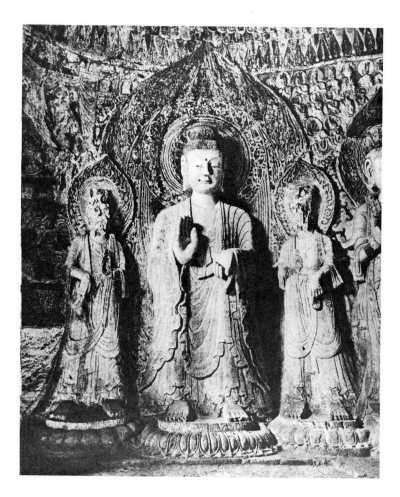

127 Buddha group, south wall of Pin-yang-tung, Lungmen. Limestone. Late Northern Wei Dynasty, probably completed in 523.

in a series of vivid reliefs, while above is the heavenly host—Buddhas, seated or standing, *bodhisattvas*, flying *apsarases*, musicians, and other celestial beings. The decoration of this cave reminds us, in its wealth of detail, its contrast between the realism of the earthly figures and the serenity of the heavenly ones, of the beatific visions of the Italian primitives.

BUDDHIST
SCULPTURE:
THE SECOND PHASE

The Loyang region was closer to the centre of the purely Chinese tradition of pictorial expression in linear, as opposed to plastic, terms; and so it was inevitable that this tendency, already becoming apparent in the later caves at Yünkang, should have found its fulfillment after the move to the south in 494. At Lungmen, only ten miles from the new capital, sculptors found a fine grey limestone which permitted greater refinement of expression and finish than the coarse sandstone of Yünkang. The new style reached its culmination in the cave known as Pin-yang-tung, commissioned by the emperor Hsüan-wu and probably completed in 523. Against each of the interior walls is a large figure of the Buddha, attended by standing *bodhisattvas* or the favourite disciples Ānanda and Kāśyapa. On either side of the entrance, the walls were decorated with godlings in relief, *Jātaka* tales, scenes of the celebrated debate between Vimalakīrti and Manjuśrī, and two magnificent panels showing the emperor and empress coming in procession to the shrine attended by their retinue. (The empress panel, badly damaged in removal many years ago, has been restored and now forms part of the important Chinese collection in Kansas City.) Executed in flat relief, its sweeping linear rhythms and wonderful sense of forward movement suggest the translation into stone of the style of wall painting which must have been current at the Wei court, and is further proof that besides the imported, hieratic forms reserved for the deities themselves there existed another and more purely Chinese style, to which painters and sculptors instinctively turned in representing secular themes.

Because of the great scarcity of Buddhist sculpture from the southern kingdoms, we are apt to think that the stylistic revolution which reached its culmination at Lungmen must have originated in the north and gradually spread southward. But recent discoveries and research suggest that the opposite was the case, and that it was the art of the southern courts centred in Nanking which was the dominating factor in the development of Buddhist sculpture in the Six Dynasties. One of the earliest innovators had been Tai K'uei, a contemporary of Ku K'ai-chih at the Chin court in Nanking. His work, in which he is said to have raised the art of sculpture to a new level, very probably reflected the style of contemporary painting—the flat, slender body, sweeping robes and trailing scarves that we see in copies of the Ku K'ai-chih scrolls. This concept of figure and drapery does not appear in the sculpture of the north until a century later, when we first encounter it in the later stages at Yünkang and the earliest caves at Lungmen, and there is much evidence to show that it was introduced by artists and sculptors from the south.

128 The Wei Empress in procession
with court ladies. Restored stone relief
panel from Pin-yang-tung, Lungmen.
Late Northern Wei Dynasty.

The arrangement of the Pin-yang cave at Lungmen was probably intended to suggest the interior of a temple, whose equipment
would also have included free-standing images in stone, stone votive steles, and gilded bronze images. The steles were carved and
set up in the temple as an act of piety or gratitude by one or more
subscribers, whose names they often bore. They consisted either
of a flat slab shaped like a pippala leaf against which one or, more
often, a group of three figures stands out almost in the round; or
of a rectangular slab decorated, often on all four sides, with Buddhas, *bodhisattvas*, and lesser deities, illustrations to favourite texts
such as the *Lotus Sūtra* (*Saddharmapundarīka Sūtra*) and scenes from
the life of the Buddha carved in relief. Their peculiar interest and
value lie in the fact that they concentrate in little space the essentials of the style and iconography of the period, and that they are
frequently dated.

In Cave 133 at Mai-chi-shan, a group of eighteen of these steles
still stand in their original positions against the walls, where they
were set up by pious devotees. Three of these are splendid examples of the mid-sixth-century style; one a veritable "poor man's
bible." The upper central panel is devoted to the incident in the
Lotus Sūtra in which Śākyamuni by the power of his preaching
causes Prabhūtaratna, a Buddha of the distant past, to appear beside him. In the centre and below are Buddhas flanked by *bodhisattvas*—a simple presentation of the paradise theme. The side panels
show (on the left, going downward) Śākyamuni descending from
the Tuśita heaven where he had preached to his deceased mother;
Śākyamuni as a young prince; the renunciation; and the first

129 Stele illustrating the life of the Buddha and the teachings of the *Lotus Sūtra*. In Cave 133, Mai-chi-shan, Kansu. First half of sixth century.

preaching in the Deer Park. On the right: a *bodhisattva* meditating under a tree; the *Mahāparinirvāna*; Sāmantabhadra on his elephant; the temptations of Māra; and the theological disputation between Manjuśrī and Vimalakīrti (holding the fan).

Very few of the great bronze images of this period have survived. They were nearly all destroyed or melted down in the persecutions which intermittently scarred the history of Buddhism in China. To see the largest, if not the finest, example of an altarpiece in the Wei linear style we must journey to Japan where, in the Kondō ("golden hall") of the monastery of Hōryūji at Nara, is a magnificent Buddha trinity which, though executed by an immigrant from Korea in 623, is a late survival of the style of mid-sixth-century China. Some of the smaller gilded bronze images, made most probably for domestic chapels, escaped destruction. Because of the precision of their modelling and the beauty of their material, these bronzes—ranging from simple seated Buddhas to elaborate altar groups complete with stand, flame *mandorla*, and attendant deities—are among the supreme examples of Chinese

130 Śākyamuni and Prabhūtaratna. Gilt bronze. Northern Wei Dynasty, dated equivalent to 518.

Buddhist art. One of the most perfect examples of the mature Wei style is the exquisite group of Śākyamuni preaching his doctrine to Prabhūtaratna, Buddha of the remote past, dated 518, in the Musée Guimet, Paris. The form is expressively attenuated; the eyes slant, the mouth wears a sweet, withdrawn smile, while the body seems about to disappear altogether under a cascade of drapery that no longer defines the figure beneath but, like the drapery of the Romanesque sculpture of Moissac or Vézelay, in its expression of a state of spiritual ecstasy seems to deny the body's very existence. Here, the influence on sculpture of the sweeping rhythms of the painter's brush is very apparent, while the air of spirituality is certainly enhanced by the extraordinary linear elegance and almost exaggerated refinement of the style of this period as a whole.

131 The development of the Buddha image. 1. Yünkang (c. 460–480); 2. Lungmen (c. 495–530); 3. Ch'i-chou (c. 550–580); 4. Sui (c. 580–620); 5. T'ang (c. 620–750). After Mizuno.

1   2   3   4   5

BUDDHIST
SCULPTURE:
THE THIRD PHASE

After the middle of the sixth century, a further, equally momentous, change came over the style of Chinese Buddhist sculpture. Now the body begins to expand once more, filling the robes, which, instead of fluttering free with a life of their own, begin to mould themselves to the cylindrical form, subtly accentuating its mass. Against these now smooth surfaces, the jewellery of the *bodhisattvas* provides a contrasting ornament; the head becomes rounded and massive, the expression austere rather than spiritual. In the stone sculpture of Northern Ch'i, Chinese craftsmen produced a style in which precision of carving and richness of detail are subordinated to a total effect of grave and majestic dignity. While the change was stimulated by a renewal of Indian influence on Chinese Buddhist art, this time it came not across central Asia, where contact with the West was now broken by fresh barbarian incursions into the Tarim Basin, but up from the Indianised kingdoms of Southeast Asia, with which the court at Nanking had close diplomatic and cultural relations. There are abundant records of Buddhist images being sent to Nanking from Indochina in the sixth century, though none of these has yet been identified. However, in 1953 there was found in the ruins of the Myriad Buddha Temple, Wan-fo-ssu, Ch'iung-lai, near Chengtu, Szechwan, a buried hoard of about two hundred pieces of Buddhist sculpture, some of which clearly show the indirect influence of Gupta art while others have stylistic affinities with the sculpture of the

132 *Bodhisattva*. Stone. Northern Ch'i Dynasty.

133 Minor deities and worshippers. Fragment of a stone relief from Wan-fo-ssu, Ch'iung-lai, Szechwan. Sixth to early seventh century.

Dvāravatī kingdom of Thailand and with figures and reliefs excavated at Dong-duong and other sites in the ancient kingdom of Champa (Vietnam). Nothing comparable to the Ch'iung-lai find has yet been unearthed at Nanking itself, where the destruction of early Buddhist monuments was almost complete; but there is no doubt that the Buddhist art of Szechwan at this time was strongly influenced by artistic developments at the southern capital.

As with sculpture, so did the introduction of Buddhism give birth to a new school of painting of which both the content and the forms were largely foreign. A Sung writer tells of a certain K'ang Seng-hui, a Sogdian, who in A.D. 247 came to the Wu kingdom (Nanking) by way of Indochina "to install icons and practise ritual circumambulation. It so happened that Ts'ao Pu-hsing saw his iconographic cartoons for Buddhas [in the style of] the Western Regions, and copied them; whence it came about that the Ts'ao [style] has been popular through the generations all over the world." (By the end of the sixth century, however, nothing survived of Ts'ao's work "except the head of one dragon in the Privy Pavilion.") The new style culminated in the work of Chang Seng-yu, the greatest of the painters working for the Liang emperors at Nanking. His work was remarkable—according to contemporary accounts—for its realism; he painted dragons on the wall of An-lo-ssu, and when, in spite of his warning, he was persuaded to paint in their eyes, they flew away amid thunder and lightning. He decorated many Buddhist and Taoist temples in Nanking with frescoes; he was a portraitist and also executed long scrolls illustrating such homelier themes as "Han Wu Ti Shooting the Dragon," the "Drunken Monk," and "Children Dancing at a Farmhouse"; but all were lost centuries ago, and none of the later pictures claiming to be copies of his work, such as the "Five Planets and Twenty-four Constellations" in the Abe Collection in Osaka, gives more than a hint of his style. Nevertheless, we may

BUDDHIST PAINTING

134 Buddha preaching the law. Wall painting in Cave 249 (P 101), Tunhuang. Northern Wei Dynasty.

be sure that one feature of this imported manner was the Indian technique of arbitrary shading, found in the wall paintings at Ajantā, which was used to give an effect of roundness and solidity unlike anything that China had seen before.

WALL PAINTINGS
AT TUNHUANG

Fortunately, the wall paintings at Tunhuang, Mai-chi-shan, and Ping-ling-ssu have survived—though for the most part they are but a faint echo of the grand manner of metropolitan China. The first chapel at Tunhuang had been dedicated in 366. Today paintings of the Northern and Western Wei can be seen in thirty-two of the caves, and there were probably many more before dilapidation and later repainting took their toll. Of these, the finest are in Caves 257 (P 110) and 249 (P 101).[6] The vigorous rendering of the preaching Buddha in Cave 249 is a good example of the mixture of styles that we find everywhere at Tunhuang. The stiff heraldic pose of the Buddha shows how the "linear" Chinese manner which we have already seen influencing the sculpture of the period has been frozen into a flat decorative pattern, indicating perhaps the hand of some itinerant painter from central Asia, who has also attempted, not very successfully, to suggest an Indian fullness in the modelling of his attendant *bodhisattvas* and *apsarases*. The subjects of these early frescoes are generally Buddhist trinities, scenes from the life of the Buddha, and endless *Jātaka* tales which, under the guise of recounting incidents in the Buddha's previous incarnations, draw upon a rich storehouse of Indian legend and folklore. It is these delightful scenes, and not the hieratic Buddhas and *bodhisattvas* crudely copying some Western model, that reveal the Chinese journeyman artist at his most spontaneous; indeed, it is not unlikely that while some of the main figures were executed by artists from central Asia and beyond, donors were content to leave these accessory scenes to local talent.

A famous panel in Cave 257 tells the story of the Buddha's incarnation as a golden gazelle. The simple humped hills slant back diagonally in rows like the seated figures in the Han banqueting scenes. Between them, the participants are painted almost in silhouette on a flower-strewn ground. The sense of open space is Chinese, as is the emphasis on linear movement; but the decorative flatness of the figures, the dappled deer and flower-sprinkled ground, have a Near Eastern origin. Most striking are the decorations on the sloping tentlike ceiling of Cave 249 (see below), painted early in the sixth century. While Buddhas dominate the main walls, the ceiling is a riot of celestial beings—Buddhist, Hindu, and Taoist, the latter including Hsi Wang Mu and Tung Wang Kung, with lesser deities. Beneath them runs a frieze of gaily coloured mountains over which mounted huntsmen pursue

135 The Buddha incarnate in a golden gazelle (the *Rūrū Jātaka*). Wall painting in Cave 257 (P 110), Tunhuang. Northern Wei Dynasty.

136 Landscape with fabulous beings, on lower part of ceiling of Cave 249 (P 101), Tunhuang. Northern Wei Dynasty.

137 Chimera. Stone. Third to fourth century.

138 Dragon. Gilt bronze. Northern Wei Dynasty.

their quarry, after the fashion of Han decorative art. These paintings are a vivid illustration of the way in which Chinese Buddhism, at least at the popular level, came to terms with Taoism and native folklore.

FUNERARY SCULPTURE

This was the heyday of Buddhist faith in China. Many people were cremated, denying themselves the elaborate burials that had been characteristic of the Han. But the Confucian rites were not altogether neglected, and some of the imperial burials were as spectacular as ever. The actual tombs of the Liang emperors have never been found among the green hills and rice fields outside Nanking, but much of the monumental sculpture that lined the "spirit way" still survives. The winged beasts of the sixth century are more graceful than those of Han, being animated by a dynamic linear movement which also found expression in miniature in the beautiful gilt-bronze lions, tigers, and dragons of which there are

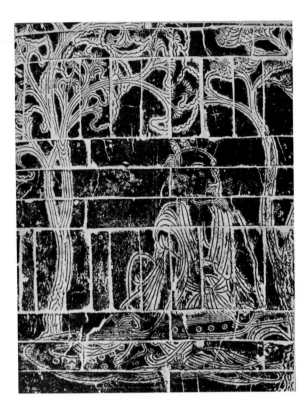

139 Hsi K'ang (223–262), one of "Seven Sages of the Bamboo Grove." Brick tomb relief, Nanking. About fifth century.

many examples in Western museums. Some of the larger tombs in the Nanking region were lined with bricks moulded with lines in thread relief, which, when correctly laid, formed a picture that covered a large area of the wall. These relief pictures, depicting themes such as the "Seven Sages of the Bamboo Grove" which were popular with the southern gentry, may well preserve not only the composition but also the style of early southern masters such as Ku K'ai-chih.

The ceramics industry in North China only gradually recovered from the disasters of the fourth century. The quality and variety of the *ming-ch'i* deteriorated. Much rarer now are the farms and pigsties that give so delightful a picture of Han rural economy. But to compensate, the best of the grave figurines have an almost fairy-like elegance that reminds us of the ladies in the Ku K'ai-chih scrolls, while the horses are no longer the tough, stocky, deep-chested creatures of Han art; they seem, rather, in their heraldic grace of form and the richness of their trappings to evoke a bygone age of chivalry. The Wei figurines are usually dark-bodied and unglazed, but some are painted with colours that have mellowed to soft reds and blues through long burial.

It was not until the sixth century that really fine-quality wares were being made in the north. Some vessels show the same variety and robustness of style that we find in the Buddhist sculpture of the period, borrowing motifs such as the lotus from the repertoire of Buddhist art, and pearl roundels and lion masks in appliqué from Sasanian metalwork. It was a restless and uncertain age in

CERAMICS

III

140 Horse. Painted pottery. Said to be from a tomb near Loyang. Northern Wei Dynasty.

141 Vase. Stoneware slipped and splashed with green under an ivory-white glaze. From a tomb of 575 at Anyang, Honan. Northern Ch'i Dynasty.

Chinese art, although here and there an untroubled mastery was achieved, as in the beautiful porcellaneous vase from the tomb of a Northern Ch'i official buried at Anyang in 575. It is covered with an ivory white, crackled glaze splashed with green—a technique hitherto thought to have been unknown in China before the T'ang Dynasty. This tomb also contained pottery flasks with Sasanian figure subjects in relief under a brown glaze. A similar mixture of Chinese and western Asiatic motifs and techniques can be seen in other crafts in China at this time, notably metalwork and relief sculpture, showing that the cosmopolitanism that we think of as typical of the first half of the T'ang Dynasty was already well established in the sixth century.

So far, very few Six Dynasties kiln sites have been discovered in the north. The position in the lower Yangtse Valley is quite different. Kilns have been located in ten counties in Chekiang alone, while many of their products have been unearthed from dated tombs of the third and fourth centuries in the Nanking region. Of

142 Flask. Stoneware decorated with dancers and musicians in relief under a golden brown glaze. From a tomb of 575 at Anyang, Honan. Northern Ch'i Dynasty.

143 Water container in the form of a lion-dog, Yüeh ware. Stoneware covered with an olive-brown glaze. Chin Dynasty, late third to early fourth century.

these pottery centres, the most important were those in Shang-yü-hsien and around the shores of Shang-lin-hu in Yü-yao-hsien, active into the T'ang and Five dynasties. In addition to celadon, the kilns at Te-ch'ing, north of Hangchow, also produced a ware with a rich black glaze. But in general the early Chekiang celadons show, in the growing strength and purity of their shapes, the final emancipation of the Chinese potter from his earlier bondage to the aesthetic of the metalworker.

Indeed, freedom in the arts seems to be the keynote of this period, not only in technique and design but also in the attitude of the privileged classes toward the arts. For this was the age of the first critics and aestheticians, the age of the first gentlemen painters and calligraphers, the age of the first great private art collections and of the birth of such cultivated pursuits as garden designing and conversation as a fine art. Just as the sixth-century anthologist Hsiao T'ung selected the poems for his *Wen-hsüan* on grounds of literary merit alone, so, it seems, did patrons in the Six Dynasties come for the first time to value their possessions—whether paintings or calligraphy, bronzes, jade, or pottery—simply because they were beautiful.

144 "Chicken ewer," Yüeh ware. Stoneware covered with an olive-brown glaze.

7
The Sui and T'ang Dynasties

The Six Dynasties had been a period when new forms, ideas, and values were first, and often tentatively, tried out—ideas which could not find their fullest expression in those restless centuries but needed an era of stability and prosperity to bring them to fruition. Wen Ti, who founded the Sui Dynasty in 581, was an able general and administrator who not only united China after four hundred years of fragmentation but also carried the prestige of her arms out into central Asia. But his son Yang Ti squandered the resources of the empire on palaces and gardens built on the scale of Versailles, and on vast public works. These included a long section of the Grand Canal, constructed to link his northern and southern capitals, for the building of which over five million men, women, and children were recruited to forced labour. These huge projects, as a Ming historian put it, "shortened the life of his dynasty by a number of years, but benefited posterity unto ten thousand generations." Combined with four disastrous wars against Korea, they were too much for his long-suffering subjects, who rose in revolt. Soon a ducal family of the name of Li joined the insurrection, and the Sui dynasty collapsed. In 617, Li Yüan captured Ch'ang-an, and in the following year mounted the throne as first emperor of the T'ang Dynasty. In 626 he abdicated in favour of his second son, Li Shih-min, who then, at the age of twenty-six, became the Emperor T'ai-tsung, thereby inaugurating an era of peace and prosperity that lasted for well over a century.

T'ang culture was to that of the Six Dynasties as was Han to the Warring States, or, to stretch the parallel a little, Rome to ancient Greece. It was a time of consolidation, of practical achievement, of immense assurance. We do not find in T'ang art the wild and fanciful taste of the fifth century, which saw fairies and immortals on every peak. Nor does it carry us, as does Sung art, into those silent realms where man and nature are one. There is metaphysical speculation, certainly, but it is that of the difficult schools of Mahāyāna idealism which interested a small minority, and is expressed, moreover, in forms and symbols that touch neither the

MAP 8 China in the T'ang Dynasty.

imagination nor the heart. For the rest, T'ang art has incomparable vigour, realism, dignity; it is the art of a people thoroughly at home in a world they knew to be secure. There is an optimism, an energy, a frank acceptance of tangible reality which gives the same character to all T'ang art, whether it be the most splendid fresco from the hand of a master or the humblest tomb figurine made by the village potter.

By the time of his death in 649, T'ai-tsung had established Chinese control over the flourishing central Asian kingdoms of Kucha and Khotan, the conquest of Korea had been begun, Tibet linked to the royal house by marriage, and relations established with Japan and the Southeast Asian kingdoms of Funan and Champa. Ch'ang-an, laid out by the Sui, now became a city of a size and splendour rivalling, if it did not surpass, Byzantium. It was planned on a grid seven miles by six. In the northern sector lay the government buildings and the imperial palace, which was later moved to a cooler, less crowded site outside the northeast corner of the city. In its streets one might have encountered priests from

Han
Dynasty
Ch'ang–an

Imperial Park

Ta–ming–kung

Palace
Administrative
Quarter

Hsing-
ch'ing-
kung

West Market

East Market

Ta–yen Pagoda

Hibiscus
Garden

MAP 9 Ch'ang-an in the T'ang
Dynasty.

India and Southeast Asia, merchants from central Asia and Arabia, Turks, Mongols, and Japanese, many of whom are humorously caricatured in the pottery figurines from T'ang graves. Moreover, they brought with them their own faiths, which flourished in an atmosphere of rare religious tolerance and curiosity. T'ai-tsung himself, though personally inclined toward Taoism, at the same time for reasons of state supported the Confucians and strengthened the administrative system. This astonishing man also treated the Buddhists with respect—notably that great traveller and theologian Hsüan-tsang, who had left China in defiance of an imperial order in 629, and after incredible hardships and delays had reached India, where he acquired a reputation as a scholar and metaphysician. In 645 he returned to Ch'ang-an, bringing with him the texts of the idealistic Vijñānavādin School of the Mahāyāna. The emperor came out to meet him, and his entry into the capital was a public triumph. Never before had Buddhism stood so high in Chinese history; but it was not the only foreign religion on Chinese soil. There were also Zoroastrian temples, Manichaean and Nestorian Christian churches in the capital and, from the mid-eighth century onward, Moslem mosques; and the art of this period is as full of imported motifs as were the streets of Ch'ang-an with foreigners.

That China enjoyed a hundred years of peace and prosperity at home and enormous prestige abroad was due not only to the achievement of Li Shih-min but also to two outstanding personalities who succeeded him. Kao-tsung, who ascended the throne in 649, was a weak and benevolent man, dominated by his concubine, Wu Tse-t'ien, who after his death in 683 had the shocking effrontery to declare herself "emperor." But such was the ability of this cruel and pious woman (her Buddhist patronage is immortalised in some of the finest sculpture at T'ien-lung-shan), that Confucian ministers loyally served her until her forced abdication in 705 at the age of eighty-two brought to an end two decades of stability and peace. Seven years later the throne passed to the man who, as Hsüan-tsung (Ming Huang, 713–756), was to preside over the most brilliant court in Chinese history, a period comparable to the Gupta in the reign of King Harsha or to Florence under Lorenzo de' Medici. Like T'ai-tsung, he cherished and upheld the Confucian order, and in 754 he founded the Imperial Academy of Letters (Han-lin Yüan), which, as Joseph Needham has observed, is older by nearly a thousand years than any existing European academy. All the talent and wealth of the country that was not given to the construction and adornment of Buddhist temples seemed to be concentrated on his court, his palaces, his favourite scholars, poets, and painters, his schools of drama and music, his orchestras (two of which came from central Asia), and, finally, on his mistress, the lovely Yang Kuei-fei. Through her influence, An Lu-shan, a general of Mongol or Tungus origin, had become a favourite with Ming Huang. Suddenly, in 755, he revolted, and the

145 Tumulus and processional way of tomb of Kao-tsung (died 683) and Wu Tse-t'ien (died 705), Ch'ien-hsien, Shensi.

emperor and his court fled in panic from Ch'ang-an. To appease his escort, Ming Huang, now over seventy, was forced to hand his favourite over to the soldiers, who promptly strangled her. A few years later the rebellion was crushed by the efforts of his son Su-tsung; the dynasty staggered to its feet, and there was even something of a revival in the early years of the ninth century; but its power was broken, its glory past, and the long, slow death of the T'ang had already begun.

In 751, Chinese armies in central Asia had been severely defeated by Moslems advancing from the west, with the result that Chinese Turkestan now came permanently under Moslem influence. The Arab conquest of central Asia began the destruction of that chain of prosperous, civilised kingdoms which had provided the overland link between China and the West in the seventh century, a process which was in due course to be completed by the ferocity of the Mongols. Contact with the Western world was now maintained by way of the southern ports. The quays of Canton and other southern ports were thronged with Chinese and foreigners who lived in peaceful prosperity with each other until the peasant rebel Huang Ch'ao massacred the latter in 879. And at Ch'üan-chou in Fukien (Marco Polo's Zayton), recent excavations have revealed that as late as the thirteenth century Hindus, Arabs, Manichaeans, and Jews were settled in that great trading port, whose cosmopolitanism is symbolised by the twin pagodas of the K'ai-yüan temple, built in the twelfth century by Chinese and Indians working side-by-side.

146 The main hall of Fu-kuang-ssu, Wu-t'ai-shan, Shansi. Ninth century.

ARCHITECTURE

As so often happens in history, China became less tolerant as her power declined, and the foreign religions suffered accordingly. The Taoists were jealous of the political power of the Buddhists and succeeded in poisoning the mind of the emperor against them, while the Confucians had come to look upon certain Buddhist practices (particularly celibacy) as un-Chinese. The government also viewed with increasing alarm the vast sums spent on the monasteries and their unproductive inmates, who now numbered several hundred thousand. In 845 all foreign religions were proscribed and all Buddhist temples confiscated by imperial edict. The ban on Buddhism was later relaxed, but in the meantime so thorough had been the destruction and looting that today very little survives of the great Buddhist architecture, sculpture, and painting of the seventh and eighth centuries. Again we must look to Japan, and it is the monasteries at Nara, itself a replica of Ch'ang-an, that preserve some of the finest of T'ang art. Tōdaiji was not an exact copy of a T'ang temple, but in its grandeur of scale and conception it was designed to rival the great Chinese foundations. It was built on a north-south axis with pagodas flanking the main approach. A huge gateway leads into a courtyard dominated by the Buddha Hall (*Daibutsuden*), 290 feet long by 170 feet deep by 156 feet high, housing a gigantic seated Buddha in bronze, consecrated in 752. Much restored and altered, this is today the largest wooden building in the world, though in its time the Chien-yüan-tien at Loyang, long since destroyed, was even larger.

The earliest known T'ang wooden temple building is the small main hall of Nan-ch'an-ssu in Wu-t'ai-hsien, Shansi, built in 782; the largest is the main hall of Fu-kuang-ssu on Wu-t'ai-shan, built in the mid-ninth century. Both of these buildings show a slight curve in the silhouette of the roof that was to become more pronounced with time and to be a dominant feature of Far Eastern architecture. Many theories have been advanced to account for this curve, the most farfetched being that it was intended to imitate the sagging lines of the tents used by the Chinese in some long-forgotten nomadic stage. But we do not need to look so far afield, for the curve is inherent in the Chinese roof truss itself. Unlike the rigid triangular Western truss with its central king post, the Chinese truss consists of a framework of horizontal beams supported on queen posts, surmounted by purlins to which the rafters are fixed. The architect has only to vary the height of the queen posts to arrive at any contour he desires. It is impossible to say just when this curve began to appear. It is perceptible in the sixth century and is used with great delicacy in the Sui, as shown by a beautiful stone sarcophagus of 608 in the Sian Museum. The lift at the corners, as well as adding to the beauty of the roof, helped to accommodate the extra bracketing required to support the enormous overhang of the eaves at that point.

147 The Western rigid truss and the Chinese beam-frame truss compared.

148 The development and decline of the bracket order: 1. T'ang (857); 2. Sung (1100); 3. Yüan (1357); 4. Ming; 5. Ch'ing (1734).

By the T'ang Dynasty, the heavy bracketing system (which, with the column it is poised upon, constitutes the nearest Chinese architecture comes to an "order" in the Western sense), is becoming a little more complex; the brackets extend outward and upward to support two slanting cantilever arms called *ang*, the inner ends of which are anchored to a crossbeam (1). In Sung and Yüan construction, the *ang* ride freely balanced on the bracketing system (2 and 3), creating a dynamic and meaningful play of forces that reminds us of Gothic vaulting. During the Ming and Ch'ing, however, as the details become increasingly fussy and elaborate, the true function of *ang* and bracket is lost, and the whole degenerates into an intricate but structurally meaningless assemblage of carpentry, a mere decorative frieze running along under the eaves (4 and 5).

149 Conjectural reconstruction of the Lin-te-tien of the Ta-ming Kung, Ch'ang-an. T'ang Dynasty.

The sketch on this page shows a conjectural restoration of one of the palaces of the Ta-ming Kung. It is instructive to compare this with the three great halls of the Forbidden City in Peking (see p. 183). While the latter is far larger in scale, the grouping of the buildings is much less interesting. The interlocking of masses on ascending levels buttressed at the sides by wings and towers, which gives such strength to the T'ang complex, was not attempted in Peking. T'ang (and indeed Sung) palaces seem to have been not only more enterprising architecturally but also more natural in scale than the vast, isolated, and coldly ceremonial structures of the Ch'ing Dynasty, and suggest a more human concept of the role of the emperor.

A few T'ang stone and brick pagodas have survived. Some—the pagoda built for Hsüan-tsang's ashes at Ch'ang-an, for example—are straightforward translations of a form of construction derived from the Han timber tower (*lou*). The Chien-fu-ssu at Sian (see Figure 122, No. 5), on the other hand, derives ultimately from the Indian *śikhara* tower of stone, which we have already encountered in its purest form in the pagoda on Mount Sung (see p. 98). Imitation of Indian forms was carried still further in the Treasure Pagoda of the Fu-kuang temple of Wu-t'ai-shan, which originally had a dome, copied perhaps from a sketch or souvenir

150 Pagoda of Hsin-chiao-ssu, Ch'ang-an, Shensi. Brick. Built about 699 to receive the ashes of Hsüan-tsang; rebuilt 882. T'ang Dynasty.

brought back by a returning pilgrim. Under the influence of the mystical Mahāyāna sects, an attempt was even made to incorporate the dome of the *stūpa* into a timber pagoda; none survives in China, but the twelfth-century Tahōtō of Ishiyamadera is a Japanese example of this odd misalliance.

Until the dissolution of the monasteries in 845, their insatiable demands for icons, banners, and wall paintings absorbed the energies of the great majority of painters and sculptors. Some of the sculptors' names are recorded: we read in Chang Yen-yüan's history, for example, of Yang Hui-chih, a painter in the time of Wu Tao-tzu, who "finding that he made no progress, took to sculpture, which he thought was an easier craft." Chang also mentions other pupils and colleagues of Wu who became noted for their work in clay and stone; indeed, as we shall see, T'ang sculpture in its extraordinary linear fluidity seems often to have been formed by the brush rather than the chisel. Very little secular sculpture was carried out, if we except the guardian figures and winged horses and tigers that lined the "spirit way" leading to the tombs. The earliest and most famous example of T'ang funerary sculpture is the set of panels depicting in relief the six favourite chargers of T'ang T'ai-tsung, executed, according to tradition, after designs by the great court painter Yen Li-pen; the style is plain and vigorous, the modelling so flat that the origin of these monumental silhouettes in line drawings seems not at all improbable.

BUDDHIST SCULPTURE: THE FOURTH PHASE

151 Charger and his groom. Stone relief from the tomb of the emperor T'ai-tsung (died 649).

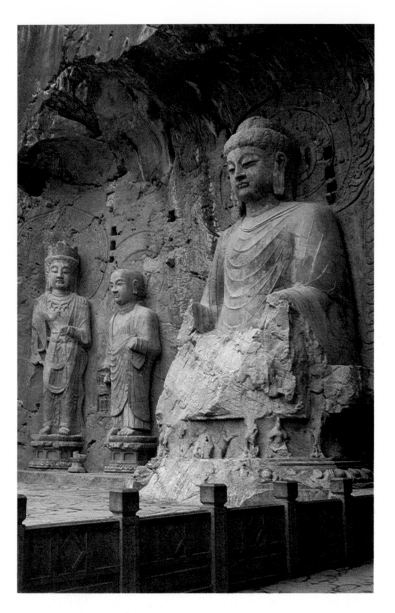

152 Vairoćana Buddha flanked by
Ānanda, Kāśyapa, and attendant
bodhisattvas. Stone. Feng-hsien-ssu,
Lungmen, Honan. T'ang Dynasty,
672–675.

153 Standing Buddha, Udayāna type.
White marble. From Hsiu-te Pagoda
near Ch'ü-yang, Hopei. T'ang Dynasty.

The great Buddhist bronzes of the seventh and eighth centuries
have all disappeared, melted down in the persecution of 845 or lost
through subsequent neglect, and the style can best be seen in the
temples at Nara in Japan. Only in the cave shrines has stone and
clay sculpture survived in any quantity. At Lungmen, in 672, the
emperor Kao-tsung ordered the carving of a colossal figure of the
Buddha Vairoćana flanked by the disciples Ānanda and Kāśyapa,
with attendant *bodhisattvas*. Obviously intended to rival in size and
magnificence the great Buddha of Yünkang, this figure of the
Buddha of Boundless Light far surpasses it in power of modelling, refinement of proportion, and subtlety of feeling. Even
though badly damaged, the Vairoćana well expresses the ideal of
the Mahāyāna, which saw the Buddha not as a great teacher but as
a universal principle radiating out in all directions for all time.

More directly modelled on an Indian prototype—perhaps on a version of the celebrated sandalwood image reputedly made by King Udayāna in the Buddha's lifetime, a copy of which was brought back by Hsüan-tsang in 645—is the thoroughly Gupta torso in marble from Ch'ü-yang-hsien, Hopei, in the Victoria and Albert Museum. This tendency to treat stone as though it were clay reached its climax in the cave shrines carved out at T'ien-lung-shan during the reigns of Wu Tse-t'ien and Ming Huang. Here the figures are carved fully in the round, with the exquisite grace and richly sensuous appeal that we find in Greek sculpture of the fourth century B.C. The modelling has an all-too-Indian suavity and voluptuousness; the drapery seems as though poured over the fleshy body. But, to compensate, there is a new mobility of movement. In these figures, the Indian feeling for solid swelling form and the Chinese genius for expression in terms of linear rhythm are at last successfully reconciled in a great synthesis, producing a style which was to become the basis of all later Buddhist sculpture in China.

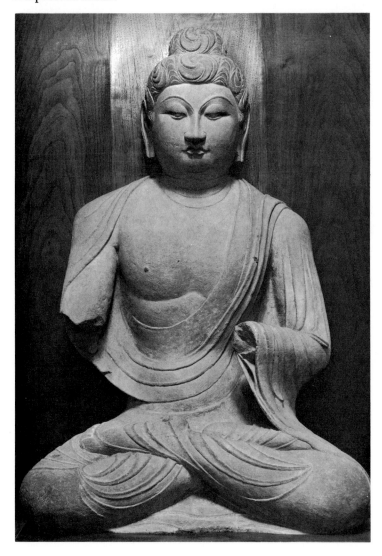

154 Seated Buddha (head restored). Stone. From Cave XXI, north wall, T'ien-lung-shan, Shansi. T'ang Dynasty.

BUDDHIST PAINTING:
FOREIGN INFLUENCES

The Buddhist painting of this period must have contained as rich a mixture of native and foreign elements as did sculpture. During the seventh century, the most popular subjects were those that illustrated the teachings of the T'ien-t'ai sect based on the *Lotus Sūtra*, an encyclopaedic text which in its combination of theology and metaphysics, ethics, magic, and simple human appeal seemed to satisfy all human needs; we already encountered some of its themes on the sculptured steles of the Northern Wei. Even more popular were the teachings of the *Ching-t'u* ("pure land") School, which had cut its way through the growing forest of metaphysical abstractions of the later Mahāyāna with the doctrine that through simple faith one might be reborn in one of the Buddhist paradises and so find release and eternal bliss. By the mid-seventh century, however, new concepts were coming into Buddhism which were eventually to bring about its decline. The later Mahāyāna in India had become deeply coloured by a highly abstract and idealistic metaphysics, on the one hand, and by the practices of the Tantric sects of revived Hinduism, on the other. Tantrism held that by sheer concentration of willpower, aided by magic spells (*mantra*) and diagrams (*mandala*), a deity could be invoked and desirable changes in the order of things thus brought about. This school also believed in the Hindu concept of the *Śakti*, a female emanation, or reflex, of a deity who would be doubly efficacious if presented clasping her in ecstatic union. At its finest, this new art has a formidable power that is overwhelming, but it too easily degenerates into the soulless repetition of magical formulae.[1] It found its true home in the bleak wastes of Tibet, whence it reached out to paralyse the art of Tunhuang during the Tibetan occupation, from about 750 to 848. In course of time, the revolt of the Chinese spirit against the sentimental, the over-intellectual, and the diabolical aspects of these sects found expression in the Ch'an (Zen) School of contemplative mysticism, but as this doctrine did not greatly affect painting until the Sung Dynasty, we will defer discussion of it to Chapter 8.

In 847, the scholar and connoisseur Chang Yen-yüan completed his *Li-tai ming-hua chi* (*Record of Famous Painters of Successive Dynasties*), the earliest known history of painting in the world. This important book, which has, happily, survived, includes a catalogue of the frescoes in the temples of Ch'ang-an and Loyang and is as full of the names of great painters and their works as Baedeker's guide to Florence; but the persecution of 845, coupled with wars and rebellions, fire and sheer neglect, destroyed them all. According to contemporary accounts, the work of the foreign painters aroused much interest and had considerable influence on local artists. During the Northern Ch'i there had been Ts'ao Chung-ta, whose figures, according to Chang Yen-yüan, "were clad in garments which clung to the body; they looked as if they had been drenched in water"—an apt description also of the sculpture at T'ien-lung-shan. The Khotanese painter Yü-ch'ih (or Wei-ch'ih) Po-chih-na had come to Ch'ang-an in the Sui Dynasty; he specialised not only in Buddhist subjects but also in strange objects from foreign lands, and flowers, which he painted with great re-alism. His son (?) I-seng was honoured by T'ai-tsung with a ducal title. "His paintings," says another ninth-century work, the *T'ang-ch'ao ming-hua lu* (*Record of Famous Painters of the T'ang Dynasty*) of Chu Ching-hsüan, "whether votive images, human fig-ures, or flowers and birds, were always foreign-looking and not like Chinese things"; while Chang Yen-yüan said of his brush-work that it was "tight and strong like bending iron or coiling wire." A Yüan critic wrote of him that "he used deep colours which he piled up in raised layers on the silk." His work is of course long since lost, but it seems that his "relief style" of flower painting was not a subtle use of shading to give an effect of solid volume, as is often supposed on the basis of descriptions in early texts, but a much cruder technique wherein the pigment was piled up in a heavy impasto till the flowers actually *did* stand out from the wall. Traces of this technique survive in the much-damaged wall paintings in the caves at Mai-chi-shan.

WU TAO-TZU

While some T'ang painters were no doubt seduced by such devices into thoroughly un-Chinese experiments, Wu Tao-tzu, the great-est of them all, seems from contemporary accounts to have worked in a purely Chinese style, which in its grandeur of concep-tion and fiery energy of execution makes him one with Michelan-gelo. Born about 700, he is said before he died to have painted three hundred frescoes (using the term in the loose sense; they were painted not on wet but on dry plaster) in the temples of Loy-ang and Ch'ang-an. None of his pictures has survived; indeed, by the eleventh century the poet Su Tung-p'o could say that he had seen but two genuine ones, his friend Mi Fu three or four. But we can obtain a vivid idea of the vigour, solidity, and realism of his work from descriptions written by those who had seen it—more vivid, certainly, than is provided by the thirdhand copies, odd rubbings, and sketches on which our estimates are generally based. The twelfth-century writer Tung Yu said of him: "Wu Tao-tzu's figures remind me of sculpture. One can see them sideways and all round. His linework consists of minute curves like rolled copper wire" (another writer says this was more characteristic of his early work: it suggests the influence of Yü-ch'ih I-seng); "however thickly his red or white paint is laid on, the structure of the forms and modelling of the flesh are never obscured." Earlier, Tung Yu had remarked that "when he paints a face, the cheek-bones project, the nose is fleshy, the eyes hollow, the cheeks dim-pled. But these effects are not got by heavy ink-shading. The shape of the features seems to have come spontaneously, yet in-evitably." All spoke of the whirlwind energy of his brush, so re-markable that crowds would gather to watch him as he worked. Perhaps his technique is reflected in the head of the Indian sage Vi-malakīrti painted by an unknown eighth-century artist on the wall of Cave 103 (to right) at Tunhuang. His influence on later figure painting was enormous.

155 The sage Vimalakīrti. Detail of a wall painting in Cave 103 (P 137 M), Tunhuang. T'ang Dynasty, eighth century.

125

THE HŌRYŪJI
KONDŌ CYCLE

No major works survive in China itself to demonstrate that fusion of Indian formal ideals with the traditional Chinese language of the brush which took place in the T'ang Dynasty, and which we have already referred to in sculpture as the "fourth phase." But such a great synthesis did take place, and was in turn passed on to Korea and Japan. About the beginning of the eighth century, the walls of the Kondō of Hōryūji Temple, Nara, were decorated with four large, square panels depicting the paradises of the Buddhas of the four directions, and eight vertical panels with *bodhisattvas*. These paintings, after miraculously surviving for twelve hundred years, were almost totally destroyed by fire in 1949, a disaster to the art world as great as if the frescoes in the Sistine Chapel or those in the cave temples of Ajantā had perished. A part of the most popular paradise—that of Amitābha—is illustrated here. The composition is a simple and serene arrangement of deities, the *bodhisattvas* Mahāsthāmaprāpta and Avalokiteśvara standing on either side of Amitābha, who sits turning the wheel of the law on his lotus throne beneath a bejewelled canopy. The figures are drawn with a sweeping brush-line of extraordinary delicacy and precision which evokes a feeling of the solid form, from which the Indian tactile sensuality has been abstracted. Indeed, except for the iconography and the contours themselves there is little here that is Indian. Arbitrary shading is used with great restraint to amplify the roundness of an arm or chin, but much more is accomplished by the almost imperceptible modulations of the brush-line itself, while the folds of the drapery are emphasised by a kind of shading which—if the *Admonitions* scroll is a faithful copy of the style of

156 The paradise of Amitābha. Detail of a wall painting in the Kondō (Image Hall) of Hōryūji, Nara, Japan. Early eighth century.

Ku K'ai-chih—goes back to the fifth century. Only in the jewellery is there a hint of that rich impasto with which the Yü-ch'ih had astonished Ch'ang-an. Apart from these details, the forms, as Tung Yu said of Wu Tao-tzu, "seem to have come spontaneously, yet inevitably."

Long after the cult of Amitābha had declined in metropolitan China, it lived on in the hearts of the pilgrims and country folk at Tunhuang, who must have gazed with awe and wonder at the huge heavenly visions that filled the walls of the seventh- and eighth-century caves. In a walled-up storeroom at Tunhuang, Sir Aurel Stein found a great hoard of manuscripts and silk banners. Many were craftsman's work, but, taken as a whole, they represent the only considerable group of undoubtedly genuine Chinese silk paintings from the T'ang Dynasty that have survived. The most remarkable is a banner on which are very carefully drawn a series of Buddha figures almost certainly copied from sketches of well-known Indian images made on the spot. One represents the Buddha of the enlightenment at Bodhgāya, two are faithful reproductions of Gandhāran models, another shows the Buddha preaching on the Vulture Peak, while Stein identified yet another

TUNHUANG

as identical in style with two great stucco reliefs which he discovered in the ruins of a monastery in Khotan. The banners also include a number of paradises and single deities (especially the increasingly popular Kuanyin), painted in warm colours, with a wealth of detail and floral ornament. The most appealing and lively parts of these banners are the little panels at the sides, which, like the predella of a quattrocento altarpiece, tell in miniature the story of the Buddha's life on earth, generally in a landscape setting. It seems that until Tibetan esoteric Buddhism laid its cold hand on Tunhuang, the Chinese painters there used a landscape setting wherever they could. Sometimes, indeed, it dominates the theme in a thoroughly un-Indian fashion. In Caves 103 (P 54) and 217 (P 70), for example, the old subdivision into superimposed horizontal scrolls has been replaced by a panoramic landscape of towering peaks that fills the whole wall. There is still a tendency to break it up into smaller connected "space cells," and the transition through the middle distance to the horizon is hardly better managed than on the stone sarcophagus in Kansas City. But other paintings at Tunhuang, notably the landscape vignettes in Cave 323 (P 137M), show that this problem was successfully solved in the eighth century.

COURT PAINTING

158 Pilgrims and travellers in a landscape. Landscape in the boneless style. Detail of wall painting in Cave 217 (P 70), Tunhuang. T'ang Dynasty, eighth century.

We must return from the rustic pleasures of Tunhuang naturalism to the splendour of the T'ang court. A famous scroll in Boston bearing portraits of thirteen emperors from Han to Sui has traditionally been attributed to Yen Li-pen, the son and brother of two famous artists, who had been a court painter in attendance (*taichao*) to T'ai-tsung and rose to the high office of Minister of the Right under his successor. This handscroll—or part of it, for more than half is a copy of the Sung Dynasty—is the very epitome of the Confucian ideal, now restored to its proper place as the pivot of Chinese society. While each group makes a monumental composition by itself, together they form a royal pageant of incomparable dignity. The figures are full, the robes ample, the brush-line fluent and of even thickness. Arbitrary shading is used with restraint to give volume to the faces, more generously in the folds of the robes, as on the Amitābha in the Kondō at Hōryūji.

In recent years our knowledge of T'ang painting has been suddenly enlarged by the opening of a group of richly decorated princely tombs in Ch'ien-hsien to the northwest of Sian. Is it perhaps the hand of a pupil of Yen Li-pen that we see in the lovely paintings that line the tomb of Princess Yung-t'ai? The unfortunate girl was murdered, or forced to commit suicide, at the age of seventeen by the "emperor" Wu Tse-t'ien. When that monstrous woman died, the restored emperor built, in 706, a subterranean tomb for his daughter, of which the walls were adorned with the figures of serving girls. The drawing is free and vivacious, sketchy yet perfectly controlled. These paintings, done solely for the pleasure of the dead princess, bring us closer to an understanding of T'ang courtly wall painting as it approached its climax in the eighth century. Meanwhile, the vast double tomb of Kao-tsung and Wu Tse-t'ien sleeps, unviolated, in the depths of a hill of rock not far away, and until at some future date it is opened, we can only imagine the treasures of art and craft it must contain.

The quality of T'ang court life is further revealed in the paintings attributed to Chou Fang and to Chang Hsüan, a court painter under Ming Huang who was chiefly celebrated for his paintings of "young nobles, saddle horses, and women of rank." So far as is known, none of their works survives in the original, but there exists what is possibly a careful copy of a T'ang painting by one or the other of these masters, *Court Ladies Preparing Silk*, attributed to the Sung emperor Hui-tsung, but more likely a product of his palace studio: it is hard to imagine the emperor having the time to make replicas of this sort, although he often put his name to them. We see a lady, about to pound the silk strands, rolling up her sleeves; another draws out the thread, a third is sewing, on the left a servant fans the charcoal brazier. The colour is rich and glowing, the detail of jewel-like precision. There is neither ground nor background, but the picture has depth, and there is a subtle and uniquely Chinese sense of almost tangible space between the figures.

Court painters such as Chou Fang and Chang Hsüan were kept busy by the emperor, as were the poets, in celebrating the more memorable social and cultural events of court life, and in portrait painting. This included portraits not only of the emperor's favourite concubines and virtuous ministers, but also of strangers from the West whose exaggerated features have been a never-failing source of delight to the Chinese. In more serious vein were portraits of Buddhist priests, such as the series of the patriarchs of

160 Female attendants. Detail of a wall painting in the tomb of Princess Yung-t'ai, Ch'ien-hsien, Shensi. T'ang Dynasty, about 706.

161 Attributed to Sung Hui-tsung (1101–1125). *Court Ladies Preparing Silk.* Detail of a handscroll after a T'ang Dynasty original. Ink and colour on silk. Sung Dynasty.

the *Chen-yen* (Shingon) sect, painted by Li Chen, a contemporary of Chou Fang. Long forgotten in China, the work of this artist has been cherished in Japan for its austere and noble evocation of the spirit of mystical Buddhism.

Court artists were not always treated with the respect they felt was due to them. Chang Yen-yüan tells of the indignity to which the great Yen Li-pen was once subjected, when he was rudely summoned—the courtiers used the term *hua shih*, roughly equivalent to "master craftsman painter" (a term that would never be applied to a scholar, a high official, or a gentleman)—to sketch some ducks that were swimming about on the palace lake in front of T'ai-tsung, after which he advised his sons and pupils never to take up the art. Ming Huang was passionately fond of horses, particularly the tough, stocky ponies from the western regions, and is said to have had over forty thousand in his stables. The striking painting of one of his favourites, Night White, has long been attributed to the noted horse specialist Han Kan. Tethered to a post, the horse rears up with eyes dilated as though the painter had startled him. All but the head, neck, and forequarters are the work of a later restorer, but enough remains to suggest a dynamic energy of movement and solidity of modelling such as we find also in the best of the T'ang pottery figurines.

LANDSCAPE PAINTING

During these prosperous years, when painters were busily occupied with Buddhist frescoes, portrait painting, and other socially useful activities, their hearts, if not their feet, were roaming the hills and valleys far from the glitter of the capital. The tradition of landscape painting which was later to rise to such supreme heights had been born in the Six Dynasties, but it had advanced little—partly because of the ever-increasing demand for Buddhist icons, partly because artists were then still struggling with the most elementary problems of space and depth. But during the T'ang Dynasty these difficulties were mastered.

According to later Chinese critics and historians, two schools of landscape painting came into being in the T'ang Dynasty. One, practised by the court painter Li Ssu-hsün and his son Li Chao-tao, painted in the precise line technique, derived from earlier artists such as Ku K'ai-chih and Chan Tzu-ch'ien, adding decorative mineral colours; the other, founded by the poet-painter Wang Wei, developed monochrome landscape painting in the *p'o-mo* ("broken ink") manner. The first, later called the Northern School, becomes in course of time the special province of court painters and professionals, while the second, the so-called Southern School, was the natural mode of expression for scholars and amateurs. As we shall see when we come to a discussion of Ming painting, this doctrine of the Northern and Southern schools, and of the founding role of Wang Wei, was invented by a group of late Ming scholar-critics to bolster up their belief in the superiority of their own kind of painting over that of the professionals and court painters of the day. But I mention it here because it has dominated Chinese thinking about landscape painting for nearly four hundred years. In fact, the line between the two kinds of painting was not so sharply drawn in the T'ang Dynasty. Wang Wei's elevation to this pinnacle in the history of Chinese painting was an expression of the belief, shared by all scholar-painters from the Sung Dynasty onward, that a man's painting, like his handwriting, should be the witness, not to his skill with the brush, but to

162 Attributed to Han Kan (active 740–760). *Night White*, a favourite horse of T'ang Ming Huang. Handscroll. Ink on paper. T'ang Dynasty(?).

163 Style of Wang Wei (?). *Riverside under Snow*. Part of a handscroll(?). Ink and colour on silk. About tenth century.

his quality as a man. Because Wang Wei was the ideal type of man, it was argued, he must also have been the ideal type of painter.

A gifted musician, scholar, and poet, Wang Wei (699–761?) joined the brilliant group of painters and intellectuals around Ming Huang's brother Prince Ch'i. He got into political difficulties at the time of the An Lu-shan rebellion, but was extricated by his brother and restored to imperial favour. When his wife died in 730 he became a devout Buddhist, though whether this influenced his painting is not known. He was famous in his lifetime for his snow landscapes, but the work for which he is best remembered by later painters is a long panoramic handscroll depicting his country estate, Wang-ch'uan, outside Ch'ang-an. This picture disappeared long ago, and although the general composition has been preserved in many later copies, one of which was engraved on stone in the Ming Dynasty, these give little idea of the style, still less of the technique, of the original. Perhaps the nearest we shall ever get to his intensely poetic relationship with nature is the beautiful little *Riverside Under Snow*, formerly in the Manchu Household Collection and now believed to be lost. To judge from reproductions, it might be a late T'ang or tenth-century painting in his manner. The landscape conventions are archaic, the technique simple, yet no early Chinese landscape painting evokes more movingly the atmosphere of a river bank in the depths of winter, when the snow covers the ground, the roofs, and the bare branches, and men hurry home to their cottages at dusk.

It is difficult to write with any certainty about the style of T'ang landscape painting when almost all we have to go on are the frescoes and banners from Tunhuang and the recently discovered paintings in the T'ang tombs. But enough has been revealed to suggest that by the eighth century three styles had come into being, which might be called the *linear*, the *boneless*, and the *painterly*. In the linear style, which traces its origin back to Ku K'ai-chih and beyond, the forms are drawn in fine, clear lines of more-or-less even thickness and filled with washes of colour, as in the landscape from the tomb of I-te of which a detail is illustrated here. In the boneless style, exemplified in the detail from Cave 217 at Tunhuang (figure 158), colour is broadly applied in opaque washes with little or no outline, a technique which seems to have been reserved for wall painting. In the third style, the painterly, an articulated, calligraphic line is combined with broken interior ink washes to produce a richly integrated texture. This style, in the development of which Wang Wei's contemporary Chang Tsao rather than Wang Wei himself was a key figure,[2] seems to have become fully expressive in the eighth century, and can be illustrated, in rather crude form, by the detail from one of the Tunhuang banners shown on p. 127. The painterly style was to develop into the mainstream of ink landscape painting in the hands of major painters of later dynasties, while the linear style sank for the most part to the level of the professional craftsman painters, and the boneless style, at least in China, sank out of sight altogether.

In the last century of T'ang, the focus of cultural activity shifted away from Ch'ang-an and Loyang to the southeast, which was

164 Landscape in the linear style. Copy
of wall painting in the tomb of I-te,
Ch'ien-hsien, Shensi. T'ang Dynasty,
706.

rapidly becoming more populous and more prosperous. It was in
the region of Nanking and Hangchow that landscape painters
now made their most daring experiments in "breaking the ink,"
while the breakdown of traditional restraints on artistic, as on social, behaviour encouraged the eccentrics to indulge in techniques
of ink-flinging and -splashing quite as wild as those of the New
York School of the 1950s. The work of these expressionists, alas,
is lost, but their styles were taken up by some of the Zen painters
of the tenth century and again in the late Southern Sung.

The objects, apart from paintings and sculpture, with which our
Western collections illustrate the achievements of T'ang culture
are, for the most part, grave goods. These, though they have an
appealing vigour and simplicity, bear little relation to the finest of
T'ang decorative arts. But masterpieces of T'ang crafts were
placed in the tomb as well, and sometimes buried for other reasons. In 1970, two pottery jars were unearthed at Ho-chia-ts'un,
crammed with gold and silver vessels and other treasures, believed
to have been buried when their owner fled from the rebel An Lu-
shan in 756. Among the finest pieces was the covered jar illustrated
here, decorated with parrots and peonies in gilt repoussé.

DECORATIVE ARTS

165 Covered jar with swing handle, decorated with parrots amid peonies. Beaten silver with traced decoration in gilt. Excavated at Ho-chia-ts'un, Sian. T'ang Dynasty, eighth century.

166 Octagonal wine cup. Beaten silver with traced and relief decoration in gilt. Excavated at Ho-chia-ts'un, Sian. T'ang Dynasty, eighth century.

But if all of it were put together it would not give the over-whelming impression of the splendour and refinement of T'ang decorative art that we get from one single collection in Japan. In 756 the empress Kōken dedicated to the great Buddha of Tōdaiji at Nara the treasures her deceased husband Shōmu had collected in his lifetime. These and other objects were put in a treasury, called the Shōsōin, in which they have survived virtually intact until this day. This remarkable collection contains furniture, musical instruments, and gaming boards painted, lacquered, or inlaid with floral and animal designs in mother-of-pearl, tortoise-shell, gold, and silver; there are glass vessels from the Arab world, silver platters, jugs and ewers, mirrors, silk brocades, weapons, pottery, maps, paintings, and calligraphy. What is astonishing about this collection is the triumphant confidence with which the Chinese craftsman—assuming most of these pieces to be of Chinese origin, or copies of Chinese work—has mastered foreign forms and techniques. This is particularly true of the art of the goldsmith and silversmith, which came into its own in the T'ang Dynasty. Hitherto, silverwork had been largely dominated by bronze design, but under Near Eastern influence it was emancipated. Some silver vessels, such as the two huge bowls in the Shōsōin, were cast, but precious metals were scarce, and a massive appearance was often gained with little material by soldering thin sheets together to form the outer and inner surface, which also made it possible to trace designs in the metal, both outside and inside. Many of the shapes such as the stem cup, foliated bowl, and flat platter with animal designs in repoussé, and the octagonal cup illustrated here, are of Persian origin; the decoration, applied with a typically T'ang combination of lavishness and delicacy, includes animals

167 "Lion-and-grape" mirror. Bronze. T'ang Dynasty.

and figures, hunting scenes, flowers, birds, and floral scrolls, generally chased or engraved, and set off against a background of rows of tiny punched circles, a technique borrowed from Sasanian metalwork.

The extravagant taste of the T'ang Dynasty also demanded that mirror backs be gilded or silvered. The old abstract and magical designs have now been replaced by a profusion of ornament whose significance is auspicious in a more general way. Symbols of conjugal felicity, entwined dragons, phoenixes, birds, and flowers in relief or inlaid in silver or mother-of-pearl account for most of the designs. Two beautiful mirrors in the Shōsōin retain something of the ancient symbolism of the TLV design by bearing landscapes of foam-washed peaks ringed with clouds and set about with fairies, immortals, and other fabulous creatures; while the influence of Manichaean symbolism may be seen, as Cammann has suggested, in the "lion-and-grape" design which was extremely popular for a short time; its sudden disappearance may have coincided with the suppression of foreign religions in 843/45.

CERAMICS

T'ang ceramics, too, made much use of foreign shapes and motifs. The metal ewer was copied in stoneware, often with appliqué designs in relief under a mottled green and brown glaze; the rhyton was reproduced from an old Persian shape; the circular pilgrim bottle, which appears in the blue-glazed pottery of Parthian Persia and Syria, reappears in China, decorated rather roughly in relief with vintaging boys, dancers, musicians, and hunting scenes. The Hellenistic amphora in Chinese stoneware loses its static symmetry; the playful dragon handles, the lift and buoyancy of its silhouette, the almost casual way in which the glaze is splashed on, all bespeak the touch of the Chinese craftsman, who brings the clay to life under his hands.

The T'ang Dynasty is notable in the history of Chinese ceramics for the dynamic beauty of its shapes, for the development of coloured glazes, and for the perfecting of porcelain. Now, no longer are potters limited to the simple green- and brown-tinted glazes of the Han. A white ware with blue-green splashes was already being made in North China under the Northern Ch'i Dynasty (550–577). The fine white earthenware of the T'ang Dynasty is often clothed in a polychrome glaze, made by mixing copper, iron, or cobalt with a colourless lead silicate to produce a rich range of colours, from blue and green to yellow and brown; this glaze is applied more thinly than before, often over a white slip, is generally very finely crackled, and stops short of the base in an uneven line. Dishes are stamped with foliate or lotus patterns and decorated with coloured glazes, which are confined by the incised lines of the central design, whereas elsewhere the colours tend to run together. The T'ang love of rich effects is seen also in the marbled wares, made by mixing a white and a brown clay together and covering the vessel with a transparent glaze. The more robust T'ang wares were exported to the Near East, where they were imitated in the poor-quality clays of Persia and Mesopotamia.

168 Ewer with dancer and dragons in relief under a polychrome glaze. Earthenware. T'ang Dynasty.

There were two main centres for the production of these coloured wares in North China. The Sian region made vessels and figurines with a light buff earthenware body, while kilns in Honan, using clay with a much higher kaolin content, made wares with a fine white body akin to porcelain—although a good deal softer. After the An Lu-shan rebellion of 755 the production of these coloured wares declined in Shensi and Honan, but it continued in Szechwan, in the newly prosperous city of Yangchow where the Grand Canal meets the Yangtse River, and in the far north under the Liao Dynasty.

In the meantime, however, as the north declined the southeast grew in prosperity. Before the end of the dynasty, Yüeh ware had reached a high pitch of perfection at the Shang-lin-hu kilns near Hangchow. The body is porcellaneous; bowls and vases (the most common shapes) are sometimes decorated with moulded or incised flowers and plants under an olive-green glaze. The soft-bodied North China wares have a flat or slightly concave base, but the Yüeh wares have a fairly high, and often slightly splayed, foot.

169 Jar decorated with splashed polychrome glaze. Earthenware. T'ang Dynasty.

It was probably in the Sui Dynasty that the Chinese potters perfected true porcelain, by which is meant a hard, translucent ware fused at high temperature with the aid of a high proportion of felspar, causing it to ring when struck. In 851 a work entitled *The Story of China and India* by an unknown author appeared at Basra; it contained information about the Cantonese supplied by a merchant named Sulaiman, who writes of them: "They have pottery of excellent quality, of which bowls are made as fine as glass drinking cups; the sparkle of water can be seen through it, although it is pottery."[3] Indeed, this white ware was already in demand far beyond China's shores, for fragments of both green Yüeh ware and white porcelain were found in the ruins of the Abbasid city of Samarra, which was the summer residence of the caliphs from 836 to 883. Although the site was occupied after that date, the greater part of the huge quantity of shards belongs to the

170 Lobed bowl, Yüeh ware. Stoneware covered with greyish-olive glaze. T'ang Dynasty.

171 Vase, possibly Hsing ware. Porcelain covered with a creamy white glaze. T'ang Dynasty.

years of its heyday and bears witness to a flourishing export trade in Chinese ceramics.

What was this mysterious white ware? An almost pure white porcelain was being produced in Kung-hsien, Honan, very early in the seventh century, but there was another T'ang ware that was whiter and finer still. An *Essay on Tea* (the *Ch'a-ching*), written, it is believed, by the poet Lu Yü in the latter half of the eighth century, says that for drinking tea one should use Yüeh bowls, which gave it the colouring of ice or jade, or the ware of Hsing-chou, which was as white as snow or silver. In spite of intensive searches in recent years in the Hsing-chou area, now called Nei-ch'iu-hsien, no kilns producing a pure white ware were found there. But in 1980 and 1981, investigators discovered in four kilns in Lin-ch'eng-hsien, a little to the north, remains of porcelain that exactly fits Lu Yü's description of "Hsing ware." These scholars point out that early writers—and Lu Yü was, after all, a poet—were not always precise in designating the source of ceramic wares, citing the example of T'ang Ting ware, which was actually made not in Ting-hsien but in neighbouring Ch'ü-yang-hsien.

The white porcelain soon became popular and was widely imitated, notably in the white-slipped stonewares of Hunan and Szechwan. At the same time, the number of kilns making the finer wares began to multiply. In the latter half of the dynasty, white porcellaneous wares were made—if a single reference in a poem of Tu Fu is acceptable evidence—at Ta-yi in Szechwan; while pale bluish-white ware, the predecessor of the lovely Sung *ch'ing-pai* (*ying-ch'ing*), was already being produced in the Shih-hu-wan kilns near Ching-te-chen, and at Chi-chou, both in Kiangsi. Yüeh-type celadons were being manufactured near Changsha in Hunan, and in Hsiang-yin-hsien north of the city, where some of the earliest experiments in underglaze and enamel painting in China were undertaken. A hard grey stoneware, ancestor of the famous splashed Chün wares of the Sung Dynasty, was made in kilns at Huang-tao in Chia-hsien, not far from Chün-chou. The full, massive shapes covered with a rich brown or black felspathic glaze are often made even more striking by bluish-white phosphatic splashes.

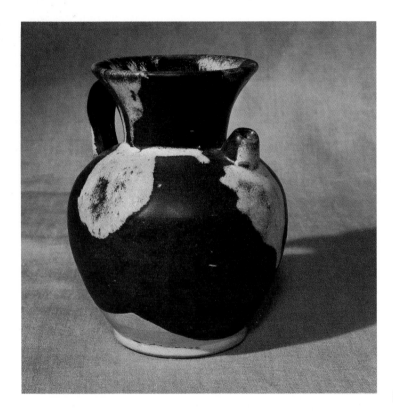

172 Jar, Huang-tao ware. Stoneware covered with a brownish-black glaze with phosphatic splashes. T'ang Dynasty.

173 Camel carrying a band of musicians. Earthenware painted and polychrome-glazed. From a tomb at Sian, Shensi. T'ang Dynasty.

The fact that most of the T'ang wares we enjoy today were made, not for the collector's pleasure, not even for domestic use, but simply as cheap grave goods probably accounts for their unsophisticated charm and vigour. These qualities are most apparent in the great numbers of figurines placed in the tombs, which give a vivid picture of daily life in T'ang times. They vary in size from animals and toys a few inches high to gigantic horses, Bactrian camels, armed men, and fantastic squatting guardian creatures popularly called *ch'i-t'ou* or *pi-hsieh*. They include a fascinating array of officials, servants, dancing girls, and musicians; indeed, among them women predominate. Women rode horseback with the men and even played polo. A passage in the "Treatise on Carriages and Dress" in the *Chiu T'ang-shu* (*Old T'ang History*) records that "at the beginning of the K'ai-yüan period [713–742] the palace ladies who rode behind the carriages all wore central Asian

174 Seated woman. Earthenware painted and polychrome-glazed. From a tomb at Loyang, Honan. T'ang Dynasty.

175 Tomb guardian trampling on a demon. Earthenware painted and polychrome-glazed. T'ang Dynasty.

hats, exposing the face, without a veil. Suddenly, their hair also was exposed when they broke into a gallop. Some were wearing men's dress and boots."[5]

Something of the gaiety of this courtly life is recaptured in these pottery figurines. The fairylike slenderness of the Six Dynasties women gives way in the fashion of the eighth century to an almost Victorian rotundity—Yang Kuei-fei herself was said to have been plump. But these women make up in character what they lack in elegance, while Chinese potters derived much amusement from caricaturing the extraordinary clothes, the beards and great jutting noses of the foreigners from central and western Asia. The human figurines were almost always made in moulds, the front and back being cast separately, while the larger figures and animals were made in several pieces, generally with the base, or underside of the belly, left open. Though sometimes left in the slip and painted, they were most often lavishly decorated with three-colour glazes, which in time acquired a minute crackle very difficult for the forger to imitate.

The most spectacular of the T'ang figurines are the fierce armed men who are often represented standing on demons. They may represent actual historical figures. Once, when the emperor T'ai-tsung was ill, ghosts started screeching outside his room and throwing bricks and tiles about. A general Chin Shu-pao, who claimed that he had "chopped up men like melons, and piled up corpses like ant-hills," offered, with a fellow officer, to stand guard outside the imperial sickroom, with the result that the screeching and brick-throwing abruptly ceased. The emperor was so pleased that he had the generals' portraits painted to hang on either side of his palace gate. "This tradition," the T'ang book tells us, "was carried down to later years, and so these men became door-gods."[6]

8

The Five Dynasties and the Sung Dynasty

T'ang China never fully recovered from the An Lu-shan rebellion, and gradually what had been a great empire shrank, in both body and spirit. The loss of central Asia to Islam, the Tibetan invasion, rebellions by warlords and peasants and the consequent break-down in the irrigation system on which prosperity and good order depended, all made the downfall of the dynasty inevitable. In 907, China finally disintegrated into the state of political chaos dignified by the name of the Five Dynasties. The title is an arbitrary one, chosen to cover those royal houses which had their capitals in the north; set up mostly by military adventurers, they had such grandiose names as Later T'ang, Later Han, and Later Chou. Between 907 and 923, Later Liang had four rulers belonging to three different families. Although the south and west were divided among the Ten (Lesser) Kingdoms, in fact those regions were far more peaceful and prosperous. Szechwan, as before when the country was disunited, was, until the destruction of Former Shu by Later T'ang in 925, a flourishing kingdom, distinguished for its scholars, poets, and artists who had come as refugees from the T'ang court, bringing with them something of the imperial splendours of Ch'ang-an and Loyang. The style of late T'ang decorative art is reflected in the jades, wall painting, silverwork, and relief sculpture in the tomb of the Former Shu ruler Wang Chien, who died at Chengtu in 918.

Meanwhile, as before, the northern barbarians watched with patient interest the disintegration of their old enemy. In 936, the first ruler of Later Chin made the fatal gesture of ceding to the Khitan the area between Peking and the sea south of the Great Wall, with the result that once again the nomads had a footing on the edge of the North China Plain. Ten years later they established the kingdom of Liao over a wide area of North China, which was not to be finally restored to Chinese hands for over four hundred years.

In 959, the last emperor of the Later Chou died and in the following year the regent, General Chao K'uang-yin, was persuaded to ascend the throne as the first emperor of a new dynasty. At first

176 Warrior supporting funerary platform in tomb of Wang Chien, Chengtu, Szechwan. Stone. Five Dynasties, 918 A.D.

141

it seemed that the Sung would be just one more in a succession of short-lived houses. But Chao was an able man; in sixteen years of vigorous campaigning he had practically united China, though, as Goodrich observed, the Sung armies never succeeded in breaking the iron ring that had been forged around the imperial boundaries by the Khitan (until 1125), the Jurchen Tungus (until 1234), and the Mongols in the north; by the Tangut, a Tibetan people (c. 990–1227), and the Mongols in the northwest; and by Annam and Nan-chao in the southwest. In 1125, the dynasty suffered a disaster from which it barely recovered when the Jurchen raided the capital at Kaifeng and captured the whole court, including the emperor Hui-tsung, famous throughout history as a painter, collector, and connoisseur. In 1127, a young prince and the remaining officials fled south beyond the barrier of the Yangtse, where the court wandered from place to place for several years before they set up what they hoped was to be their temporary capital at Hangchow. The Jurchen, who named their dynasty Chin, were now in control of all China north of the Yangtse–Yellow River watershed. Like the Liao, they were only prevented from further incursions into Sung territory by the enormous tribute China paid every year, chiefly in coin and rolls of silk, until Genghis Khan with his savage hordes descended from the north, obliterating friend and foe alike.

MAP 10 China in the Sung Dynasty.

Hemmed about by hostile powers, the Sung looked inward upon herself. Han China had lived in a fabulous world whose boundaries were mythical K'un-lun and P'eng-lai far beyond the horizon; T'ang China flung out her arms to embrace central Asia and welcome all that the West had to offer. Sung China, at peace with itself and buying peace with its neighbours, proceeded to examine the world with a new curiosity, a deeper reverence. She rediscovered the world of feeling and imagination which had been revealed to her in the Six Dynasties but had been lost again under the strong light of T'ang positivism. It was this depth of philosophical insight, combined with a perfect balance of creative energy and technical refinement, that made the tenth and eleventh centuries one of the great epochs in the history of Chinese art.

During this time, China was ruled by a succession of emperors more truly cultivated than any before or since. Under them, the intellectuals who ran the government were an honoured élite, permitted to remain seated in the imperial presence and to debate rival policies with complete freedom. Their prestige was perhaps partly due to the rapid spread of printing, for which Chengtu, the capital of Shu, was already the chief centre in the ninth century. There, the first paper money had been printed, between 932 and 953 the first edition of the *Classics* was issued in 130 volumes, and before the end of the tenth century the Buddhist *Tripitaka* in over 5,000 volumes, and the Taoist canon. With the aid of this new craft it became possible to synthesise knowledge as never before, and there began the unending compilation of dictionaries, encyclopaedias, and anthologies which was to become ever more characteristic of Chinese intellectual activity until the revolution. It was this desire for intellectual synthesis which led to the founding by Chou Tun-i and Chu Hsi of the doctrine of Neo-Confucianism, in which the Confucian moral principle (*li*) became identified with the Taoist first cause (*t'ai-chi*) seen as both a metaphysical and a moral force, and at the same time was enriched by a theory of knowledge and a way of self-cultivation derived partly from Buddhism. To the Neo-Confucianist, *li* became the governing principle which gives to each form its inherent nature. By "investigating things"—that is, by a process of study, part scientific, part intuitive, and leading outward from the near and familiar—the cultivated man could deepen his knowledge of the world and of the workings of *li*. The intense realism of Northern Sung painting, whether revealed in the painter's knowledge of the texture of rocks, the true form of flowers and birds, or the construction of a river boat, bears witness to the profound and subtle examination of the visible world which found philosophical expression in Neo-Confucianism.

An important by-product of the Confucian revival, or parallel manifestation of the same backward-looking impulses perhaps, was the new interest taken in ancient arts and crafts, creating a demand for reproductions of archaic ritual vessels and implements, in bronze and jade, which was to grow with the centuries. While there is little secure evidence for dating these reproductions, the general opinion is that those of the Sung Dynasty are on the whole

177 Winged lion in the style of the Warring States period. Bronze inlaid with gold and silver. Attributed to the Sung Dynasty.

more accurate and archaic in feeling than those of Ming and Ch'ing. Illustrated catalogues of the bronzes and jades in the collection of the emperor Hui-tsung were published in the twelfth century and subsequently reprinted in more unreliable editions that served as the source for many of the fanciful reproductions of later centuries.

殿堂等七鋪作
鋪作副階五
雙槽草架側樣第十二

殿側樣十架椽身內雙槽殿身
外轉七鋪作重栱出雙抄兩下
昂裹轉六鋪作重栱出雙抄單
階外轉五鋪作重栱出單抄單
昂裹轉五鋪作出雙抄
並各計心
以上

178 Seven-tiered bracket for a palace hall. Illustration from the Sung Dynasty architectural manual, *Ying-tsao fa-shih* (1925 edition). Woodcut.

ARCHITECTURE

179 Twelve-sided pagoda of Fu-kung-ssu, Ying-hsien, Shansi. Sung Dynasty, 1058.

It is in character with the synthesising trend of the period that the first great manual of architectural practice, the *Ying-tsao fa-shih*, presented to the emperor in 1100, should have been written in the Sung Dynasty. The author, Li Chieh, a practising architect in the Board of Works, combines historical scholarship with a considerable amount of straightforward technical information on materials and construction, which in his time was becoming increasingly complex and refined—if not so grand in scale as in the T'ang Dynasty. The *ang*, for example, is now no longer a simple cantilevered arm jutting out to hold up the eaves; it is cut loose from supports at either end and poised on the top of an intricate bracketing system, held in balance by a complex play of stresses and strains. In time, this intricacy for its own sake will lead to degeneration, but in Sung timber construction it combines structural boldness with refinement of detail. Sung taste also preferred the delicate to the robust, the tall and slender to the gigantic and solid, and Kaifeng was a city of spires. Temples had roofs of yellow tiles and were floored with yellow and green. Timber and stone pagodas now acquired little projecting roofs at each storey, curving up at the point where two faces met.

144

As the Toba Wei had fostered Buddhism because they themselves were aliens on Chinese soil, so did the Liao and Chin, and
under their patronage there was a revival of the faith in North
China, as well as in the Sung domain itself. The twelve-sided pagoda of Fu-kung-ssu at Ying-hsien in Shansi (1058) is one of the
few surviving examples of a major Sung pagoda, rich in detail,
dynamic in bracketing, noble in proportion. In the city of Ta-
t'ung in northern Shansi, a secondary capital under both Liao and
Chin, two important temples stand side-by-side: Lower Hua-
yen-ssu (Fig. 181), completed in 1038 under the Liao, and still virtually intact, and Upper Hua-yen-ssu, rebuilt after a fire in 1140,
although the five great Buddhas were remade in the Ming Dynasty and the frescoes repainted late in the nineteenth century. At
Lower Hua-yen-ssu, not only is the sculpture original but the
walls retain the original *sūtra* cases fashioned like scaled-down pavilions, their intricate carpentry providing a rare example of the
style of the period. In this sumptuous shrine, architect and sculptor have combined their arts in the service of theology to create a
fabulous Buddha world by which the worshipper, on entering the
hall, is surrounded and enveloped. Buddhas, *bodhisattvas*, guardi-
ans, and *arhats* take their apportioned place in a gigantic three-
dimensional *mandala*, the total effect of which is to saturate the eye,
and the mind of the believer, with the manifold and all-embracing
powers of God.

One of the most impressive—and deceptive—examples of Liao-
Chin sculpture is the set of pottery figures of *lohan* (*arhats*) which
were found some years ago in a cave at I-chou near Peking. One is
in the British Museum, five others in Western collections. The
vigorous modelling, the dignity and realism, and above all the
three-colour glaze, all suggested a T'ang date at a time when the
possibility of art of any quality being produced under the Liao and
Chin was not seriously considered. But it is now known that
North China at this time was the centre of a flourishing culture in
which the traditions of T'ang art were preserved, with subtle differences, not only in sculpture but also in ceramics, and there is no
disgrace in assigning them to the Liao or Chin. These figures, and
others executed in dry lacquer, are not so much portraits of individual monks as expressions of a variety of spiritual states. In the
face of the young *arhat* in the Nelson Gallery is portrayed all the inward struggle, the intensity of concentration, of the meditative
sects of which Ch'an was the chief. When we turn to the figure in
the Metropolitan Museum, we see, in the bony skull, lined features, and deep-set eyes of an old man, the outcome of that struggle; it has taken its toll of the flesh, but the spirit has emerged serene and triumphant.

But not all sculpture of this period was an archaistic revival or a
prolongation of the T'ang tradition. The figures in wood and
plaster represent an evolution beyond the T'ang style. The Buddhas and *bodhisattvas* are still fully modelled—even to the extent of
a fleshiness that can be displeasing—but what they have lost in dynamic energy they gain in a new splendour of effect. They stand

SCULPTURE

180 Lohan. Pottery covered with green
and brownish-yellow glaze. From I-
chou, Hopei. Liao Dynasty, tenth to
eleventh century.

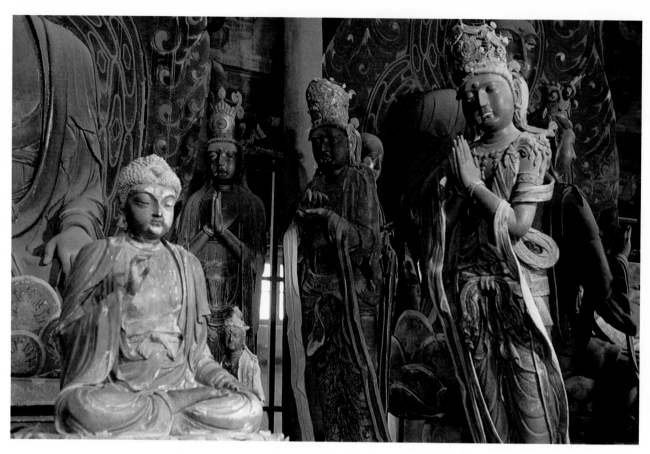

181 Interior of Lower Hua-yen-ssu, Ta-t'ung, Shansi. Liao Dynasty, 1038.

against walls covered with huge frescoes painted in the same ample and spectacular manner. In fact, so closely does the style of the one echo that of the other that Sickman's vivid description of the sculpture could apply equally to the painting:

> An almost uncanny impression of movement, as though the gods were stepping forward with an easy, stately pace, or had just taken their seats on the lotus throne, is produced by the great agitation and restless movement of the garments and encircling scarves. These latter accessories are especially important in creating an almost spiral movement in three dimensions as the long, broad ribbons trail over the arms, loop across the body and curve around the back. In the actual carving the folds are deep, with sharp edges, so that the maximum contrast is obtained between highlight and shadow. Frequently the ends of garments and scarves are caught up in whorls and spirals obviously derived from the calligraphic flourishes of painting.[1]

This suave and restless splendour was clearly designed, like that of the high Baroque art with which it has so much in common, to capture the attention of the worshipper through its emotional appeal. It is no accident that it finds its most splendid expression in the figures of Kuanyin, the comforter, the giver of children, the preserver from peril of all those who call upon her name. She looks down upon suffering humanity with calm detachment; yet she is not indifferent, and her regard is full of sweetness without

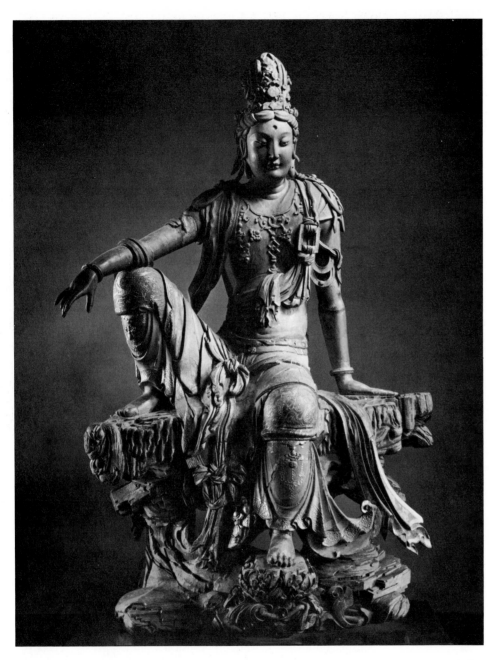

182 Kuanyin. Sculpture in wood and gesso, painted and gilded. Late Sung or Yüan Dynasty.

being sentimental. In this beautiful figure, a potential extravagance of effect is held delicately in check by the refinement of Sung taste.

At another level, Sung sculpture could be anything but refined. Although, after the mid-T'ang, institutional Buddhism appealed less and less to the intelligentsia, its doctrines of rewards and punishments continued to exert their hold on the common people. Some very down-to-earth Sung religious art was produced for the edification of the masses. Among the most astonishing examples of Sung sculptural realism is the figure of a soul suffering the torments of hell, one of hundreds of reliefs carved by unknown

183 Soul suffering the torments of hell. Stone relief sculpture on a cliff at Ta-tsu, Szechwan. Sung Dynasty.

craftsmen on the cliff at Ta-tsu in Szechwan. These vivid carvings belong to a tradition of popular didactic sculpture that survived till recent times in Buddhist and Taoist temples and has been vigorously revived in the People's Republic, a striking example being the *Rent Collection Courtyard* of 1965, illustrated on page 260.

CH'AN PAINTING IN THE FIVE DYNASTIES

Buddhism as a popular religion, however, never fully recovered from the suppression of 845. During the later T'ang the speculative and Tantric sects decayed, partly because they had no roots on Chinese soil. But for the Ch'an sect (known in Japan as Zen) the position was different. Like Taoism, it emphasised quietism, self-cultivation, the freeing of the mind from all intellectual and material dross so as to leave it open and receptive to those flashes of blinding illumination when suddenly, for a moment, the truth is revealed. To create the right atmosphere for meditation, the Ch'an monks built their temples in beautiful secluded places, where the only sound might be the wind in the trees and the rain falling on the stones of the temple courtyard. Their aims, and the very techniques by which they were to be realised, had much in common with those of the Taoists, although they were a good deal more strenuous. So it was chiefly in Ch'an that Buddhism, after being on Chinese soil for nearly a thousand years, finally came to terms with Chinese ideals.

In seeking a technique with which to express the intensity and immediacy of his intuition, the Ch'an painter turned to the brush and monochrome ink, and with the fierce concentration of the calligrapher proceeded to record his own moments of truth in the outward forms of Buddhas and *arhats* or, indeed, of any subject that he chose to paint. Already in the last century of the T'ang Dynasty there were artists practising techniques as wildly eccentric as those of any modern Western action painter. None of their work survives, but contemporary descriptions of it suggest that these individualists were either Ch'an adepts or were fired by the same impulse toward irrationality and spontaneity as that which inspired the Ch'an painters. Only slightly later was Kuan-hsiu who, after a lifetime of painting Buddhist subjects in the lower Yangtse region, came, full of years and honour, to the court of Wang Chien at Chengtu, where he died in 912. His *arhats* were drawn with that exaggeration bordering on perversity which is typically Ch'an; with their bony skulls, huge eyebrows, and pronounced Indian features, they have the ugliness of caricature, as if only by deliberate distortion can the sudden, electrifying experience of the Ch'an mystic be suggested. For the experience itself is incommunicable; all the artist can do is to give the viewer a shock which may jolt him into awareness. But even to suggest that these paintings have a purpose may be suggesting too much, and we should see them simply as pictorial metaphors for an event, or "happening," in the mind that cannot be described. "Illumination," they seem to say, "is like this."

The few surviving copies of Kuan-hsiu's work are treasured in Japan, where Zen long outlasted its popularity in China. When Kuan-hsiu died, his mantle fell upon Shih K'o, a wild and eccentric individual who, according to an eleventh-century historian, "liked to shock and insult people and compose satirical rhymes about them." By this time, writers were fond of classifying painters into three grades: *neng* (capable), *miao* (wonderful), and *shen* (divine, superhuman); but for Shih K'o and his like even *shen* was not enough, for it still implied obedience to the rules. For them they coined the term *i*, meaning "completely unrestrained by

184 In the manner of Shih K'o (active mid-tenth century). *Two Minds in Harmony.* Part of a handscroll. Ink on paper. Sung Dynasty.

rules." "Painting in the *i* style," said another author, "is most difficult; those who follow it . . . despise refinement and rich colouring and draw the forms quite sketchily, but grasp the natural (*tzu-jan*) spontaneously." The notion of *i* was to crop up again and again in the history of Chinese painting to describe painters who, so far as the orthodox canons were concerned, were *hors concours*.

185 Attributed to Ku Hung-chung (tenth century). *A Night Entertainment of Han Hsi-tsai*. Detail of a handscroll. Ink and colour on silk. Possibly a Sung Dynasty copy.

In the meantime, quite another tradition was flourishing at Nanking, whose painters might have raised their hands in horror at the antics of the fauves up in Chengtu. There, Li Hou-chu, the "emperor" of Southern T'ang, had recreated in miniature the luxury and refinement of the T'ang court under Ming Huang. One recent writer describes the art produced under his patronage as the twilight of the T'ang, another as "premature Sung"; all we can say is that it provides an important link between the two great epochs. Under his patronage, the spirit of Chou Fang and Chang Hsüan was reborn in Chou Wen-chü and Ku Hung-chung. The painting of which a detail is reproduced here is probably a very close copy, dating from about the twelfth century, of a scroll by Ku Hung-chung depicting the nocturnal revels of the vice-president Han Hsi-tsai, rumours of whose thoroughly un-Confucian behaviour with singing and dancing girls, of whom he had at least a hundred, had reached the ears of the emperor. Li Hou-chu sent a painter in attendance (*tai-chao*) to observe and record what was going on, and then confronted Han Hsi-tsai with the evidence of his dissipation. The scene looks respectable enough, but the casual attitudes of Han, his friends, and his singing girls, the meaningful glances, the figures half-hidden behind bed-curtains, are all highly suggestive; indeed, not the least intriguing thing about this picture is the way in which licentiousness is suggested in a formal language of such exquisite refinement and dignity. The painting, which the fourteenth-century writer T'ang Hou considered "not a pure and fitting object for a high-class collection," is also extremely revealing as a document on tenth-century costume, furniture, and porcelain, and shows how lavishly paintings, including monochrome landscapes, were used in interior decoration, forming panels on the beds as well as tall free-standing screens. It would seem that the hanging scroll has not yet become fashionable.

The last great exponent of the T'ang figure-painting tradition was Li Kung-lin (1046–1106), better known as Li Lung-mien from the name of his country estate of which he, in emulation of Wang Wei, painted a long, panoramic handscroll. Several versions of it exist. Li Lung-mien moved in an intellectual circle at court that included the poet Su Tung-p'o and the historian Ou-yang Hsiu, while it is recorded that even the great statesman Wang An-shih, who was "careful in choosing his friends," condescended to visit him. In early life he was a famous painter of horses—until, so the story goes, a Taoist told him that if he continued much longer in this vein he would become like a horse himself, whereupon he switched to other themes. He was thoroughly eclectic, spending years in copying the old masters, and though his own technique was restricted largely to ink-line (*pai-miao*), his subject matter included everything from horses and genre scenes to Taoist fairy landscapes, Buddhist figures, and paintings of Kuanyin amid rocks, of which he created an ideal conventional type. His sweeping brush-line, characterised by a typically Sung refining of the manner of Wu Tao-tzu, also provided a model for figure painters that endured down to Ming times.

186 Attributed to Li Lung-mien (c. 1040–1106). *Horse and Groom*. One of five tribute horses. Detail of a handscroll. Ink and colour on paper.

The reverence for the past revealed in Li Lung-mien's sedulous copying of the old masters is from now on to loom large in Chinese connoisseurship and to present the most formidable problems to the expert. In the case of a master we may assume that

CONNOISSEURSHIP

his motives were the honourable ones of training his hand and of transmitting the ancient models in the spirit of the sixth principle of Hsieh Ho. To paint in the manner of Wu Tao-tzu, therefore, was no less original than for a pianist to play the works of Bach and Beethoven; for what the artist sought was not originality but a sense of identity, both with nature and with the tradition itself. The Western artist particularises; and his painting is generally the result of a direct examination of what is before his eyes. The Chinese painter generalises, and his work, ideally, reveals not the particular but the quintessential forms of nature, animated by his élan and by his mastery of the brush. To achieve this he must, like the pianist, have the language of expression at his fingertips so that no technical impediment, no struggle with form or brushwork, should come between the vision and its realisation. An important part of his training is the study of the old masters. He might perhaps make an exact reproduction by tracing (*mu*), he might copy the picture with the original before him (*lin*), or he might freely interpret the manner of the master (*fang*). Paintings in either of the first two categories which passed into the hands of unscrupulous collectors or dealers would often acquire false signatures, seals, and colophons, and the new attribution would then be attested by further colophons. In many cases, such are the vicissitudes through which the painting has passed that the authenticity of an ancient masterpiece can never be proved, and the most that can be said is that a given work is in the style of a certain master or period and *looks* old enough, and good enough, to be genuine. Sometimes a painting is exposed as a copy by the subsequent appearance of a still finer version. In this most difficult branch of connoisseurship there is not an expert who has not been deceived, and the recent tendency in the West has been perhaps toward an excessive caution not shared by the majority of Chinese and Japanese connoisseurs.

LANDSCAPE
PAINTING:
THE CLASSICAL IDEAL
IN NORTH CHINA

This uncertainty applies particularly to the few great landscape paintings of the Five Dynasties and early Sung which are generally attributed to such masters as Ching Hao, Li Ch'eng, Tung Yüan, and Chü-jan, all of whom were working in the tenth century, and Fan K'uan, Hsü Tao-ning, and Yen Wen-kuei, who were active into the eleventh. In the hundred years between 950 and 1050 a galaxy of great names succeed each other in what must be looked upon as the supreme moment in classical Chinese landscape painting. Ching Hao, who was active from about 900 to 960, spent much of his life in retirement amid the mountains of eastern Shansi. An essay attributed to him, the *Pi-fa chi* (*Record of Brush Methods*) or *Hua shan-shui lu* (*Essay on Landscape Painting*), puts his thoughts on the art into the mouth of an old man whom he pretends he met when wandering in the mountains, and who gave him a lecture on principles and technique. The old man tells him of the six essentials in painting: the first is spirit, the second rhythm, the third thought, the fourth scenery, the fifth brush, and the sixth ink; a more logical system than that of Hsieh Ho, for it

187 Attributed to Li Ch'eng (919–967).
Buddhist Temple in the Hills after Rain.
Hanging scroll. Ink and colour on silk.
Northern Sung Dynasty.

proceeds from the concept to its expression, and thence to the
composition, truth to nature (scenery), and finally technique. The
sage further distinguishes between resemblance, which repro-
duces the outward, formal aspect of objects, and truth, which involves the inner reality, the synthesis of the two producing a
perfect integration of form and content. He seeks a just corre-

樹纔老葉溪
澗凍擁関仙
居家上属不
莊物柁間遊
似丟山早見
氣如蒸
己卯春月
尚題

188 Kuo Hsi (eleventh century), *Early
Spring*. Hanging scroll dated equivalent
to 1072. Ink and colour on silk.
Northern Sung Dynasty.

spondence of the type of brush-stroke with the object depicted. He insists that flowers and trees should be those appropriate to the season, and that men be not larger than trees—not simply for the sake of objective realism, but because only by faithfully reproducing the visible forms of nature can the artist hope to express, through them, their deeper significance. To default in this, therefore, is a sign that the artist has not fully understood how nature operates.

This doctrine of a realism raised to the level of idealism is elaborated in a well-known essay by the eleventh-century master Kuo Hsi, who combined in his spectacular landscapes the strong drawing and jagged silhouette which we associate with Li Ch'eng, with a modelling of relief in ink-wash which was probably derived from the late T'ang individualists. Kuo Hsi was to Sung landscape what Wu Tao-tzu had been to T'ang Buddhist art—a painter of enormous energy and output, who loved to cover large walls and standing screens with monumental compositions. In his *Advice on Landscape Painting* (*Shan-shui hsün*), he insists again and again on the necessity, amounting to an ethical obligation, for the artist to study nature in every aspect, to mark the procession of the seasons, the way the same scene may look at morning and evening; to note and express the particular, unique character of every changing moment; to select with care; to impart movement to water and cloud, for, as he says, "watercourses are the arteries of a mountain; grass and trees its hair; mist and haze its complexion." Indeed, as the painter knows the very mountains to be alive, so must he transmit that life (*ch'i*) into the mountains that he paints.

How was it then, one might ask, that the Chinese painter, who insisted on truth to natural appearance, should have been so ignorant of even the elementary laws of perspective as the West understands it? The answer is that he deliberately avoided it, for the same reason that he avoided the use of shadows. Scientific perspective involves a view from a determined position and includes only what can be seen from that single point. While this satisfies the logical Western mind, it is not enough for the Chinese painter. Why, he asks, should we so restrict ourselves? Why, if we have the means to depict what we know to be there, paint only what we can see from one viewpoint? The Sung Dynasty critic Shen Kua took Li Ch'eng to task for "painting the eaves from below" and thereby putting an arbitrary restriction on his power to "view the part from the angle of totality." "When Li Ch'eng paints mountains, pavilions, and buildings," he writes in his *Meng-ch'i pi-t'an*,

PERSPECTIVE

> he paints the eaves from below. He believes that looking up one perceives the eaves of a pagoda as a person on the level ground and is able to see the beams and rafters of its structure. This is absurd. All landscapes have to be viewed from "the angle of totality to behold the part," much in the manner in which we look at an artificial rockery in our gardens. If we apply Li's method to the painting of real mountains, we are unable to see more than one layer of the mountain at a time.

155

Could that be called art? Li Ch'eng surely does not understand the principle of viewing the part from the angle of totality. His measurement of height and distance certainly is a fine thing. But should one attach paramount importance to the angles and corners of buildings?[2]

THE AIMS OF THE LANDSCAPE PAINTER

The composition of a Chinese painting is not defined by the four walls of its mount as is a European painting within its frame. Indeed, the Chinese artist hardly thinks of it as a "composition" at all. Those formal considerations to which the Western painter devotes so much attention, he takes very largely for granted. Rather is his picture, as Shen Kua suggests, a fragment—chosen as it were at random, yet profoundly significant—of eternity. What the Chinese artist records is not a single visual confrontation but an accumulation of experience touched off perhaps by one moment's exaltation before the beauty of nature. The experience is transmitted in forms that are not merely generalised but also richly symbolic. This kind of generalisation is quite different from that of Claude Lorrain and Poussin, whose idyllic landscapes deliberately evoke a long-forgotten golden age. The Chinese artist may paint a view of Mount Lu, but the actual shape of Mount Lu is of little interest to him in itself; the mountain is significant only if, in contemplating it, wandering through it, painting it, he is made aware of those things that for him make Mount Lu, for the moment, the very embodiment of mountainness. Likewise, the bird on a branch painted by some Sung academician is not a thing in itself, defined by its frame, but seems poised in limitless space, a symbol chosen by the artist to express what we might call the bird-on-bough aspect of eternity. We are often told that the Chinese painter leaves large areas of the picture space empty so that we may "complete it in our imagination." But that is not so. The very concept of completion is utterly alien to the Chinese way of thinking. The Chinese painter deliberately avoids a complete statement because he knows that we can never know everything, that what we can describe, or "complete," cannot be true except in a very limited sense. All he can do is to liberate the imagination and set it wandering over the limitless space of the universe. His landscape is not a final statement, but a starting point; not an end, but the opening of a door. For this reason, Rembrandt's drawings, and the work of the modern abstract expressionists, are much closer to the spirit of Chinese art than are the idealised, classical compositions of European landscape painters of the seventeenth century.

In the passage I have quoted above, Shen Kua clearly explains the attitude behind the "shifting perspective" of Chinese painting, which invites us to explore nature, to wander through the mountains and valleys discovering fresh beauty at every step. We cannot take in so great a panorama at a glance; indeed, the artist intends that we should not. We would need perhaps days or weeks to walk the length of the stretch of countryside he presents in his scroll; but by revealing it to us little by little as we proceed, he combines the element of time with that of space in a four-dimensional synthesis such as Western art has not achieved until modern

189 Fan K'uan (active late tenth to early eleventh century), *Travelling amid Mountains and Gorges*. Hanging scroll. Ink and colour on silk. Northern Sung Dynasty.

times. The nearest parallel is to be found not in European art but in music, in which the theme unfolds and develops in time. As we unroll as much of the great panorama as we can comfortably pass from right hand to left (never opening it out fully as is done in museums), we find ourselves drawn unwittingly into the scene spread out before us. The artist invites us to follow him down the winding paths, to wait at the river bank for the ferryboat, to walk through the village—disappearing from view for a few moments, perhaps, as we pass behind a hill—to re-emerge and find ourselves standing on the bridge, gazing at a waterfall; and then perhaps to saunter up the valley to where a monastery roof can just be seen above the treetops, there to rest, fan ourselves after our exertions, and drink a bowl of tea with the monks.

Only by a shifting perspective, which opens out a fresh view at every turn of the path, is such a journey possible. Indeed, we can only truly appreciate a great Chinese landscape painting if it does have this power to send our spirits wandering. At the end of the scroll, the artist will leave us standing at the lake shore, gazing out across the water to where distant peaks rise through the haze, while an infinity of space stretches above them, carrying us with it beyond the horizon. Or he may close the scroll with a rocky tree-clad spur in the foreground, and thus bring us back to earth once more.

This power in a great Chinese landscape painting to take us out of ourselves was widely recognised as a source of spiritual solace and refreshment. Kuo Hsi opens his essay by declaring that it is the virtuous man above all who delights in landscapes. Why the virtuous man particularly? Because, being virtuous (in other words, a good Confucian), he accepts his responsibilities to society and the state, which tie him down to the urban life of an official. He cannot "seclude himself and shun the world," he cannot wander for years among the mountains, but he *can* nourish his spirit by taking imaginary journeys through a landscape painting into which the artist has compressed the beauty, the grandeur, and the silence of nature, and return to his desk refreshed.

FAN K'UAN The great masters of the tenth and eleventh centuries are sometimes called classical because they establish an ideal in monumental landscape painting to which later painters returned again and again for inspiration. In every case, the attributions to such masters as Ching Hao, Li Ch'eng, Kuan T'ung, and Kuo Chung-shu are merely traditional. But by a miracle there has survived one masterpiece bearing the hidden signature of the great early Sung painter Fan K'uan which is almost certainly an original from his hand. Born about the middle of the tenth century, and still living in 1026, Fan K'uan was a shy, austere man who shunned the world. At first, like his contemporary Hsü Tao-ning, he modelled himself on Li Ch'eng, but then it came to him that nature herself was the only true teacher, and he spent the rest of his life as a recluse in the rugged Ch'ien-t'ang Mountains of Shansi, often spending a whole day gazing at the configuration of rocks or going out on a winter night to study with great concentration the effect of moonlight upon the snow. If we were to select one single painting to illustrate the achievement of the Northern Sung landscape painters, we could not do better than to choose his *Travelling amid Mountains and Gorges*, in which we see a train of pack horses

190 Chang Tse-tuan (late eleventh to early twelfth century), *Life along the River on the Eve of the Ch'ing-ming Festival*. Detail of a handscroll. Ink and slight colour on silk. Northern Sung Dynasty.

emerging from a wood at the base of a huge precipice. The composition is still in some respects archaic; the dominating central massif goes back to the T'ang Dynasty, the foliage retains several early conventions while the texture strokes (*ts'un*) are still almost mechanically repeated and narrow in range; their full expressive possibilities are not to be realised for another two hundred years. Yet this painting is overwhelming in its grandeur of conception, its dramatic contrasts of light and dark in the mist, rocks, and trees, and above all in a concentrated energy in the brushwork so intense that the very mountains seem to be alive, and the roar of the waterfall fills the air around you as you gaze upon it. It perfectly fulfills the ideal of the Northern Sung that a landscape painting should be of such compelling realism that the viewer will feel that he has been actually transported to the place depicted.

The high point of Sung realism was reached in a remarkable handscroll depicting life on the outskirts of the capital just before the Ch'ing-ming festival in spring. The artist reveals an encyclopaedic knowledge of the look of houses, shops, restaurants, and boats, and of the variety of people of high and low degree who throng the streets. His vision is almost photographic, while he displays complete mastery of shadowing (in the hulls of the boats) and foreshortening. It is worth noting that the painter, Chang Tse-tuan, otherwise almost unknown, was a member of the scholar-gentry and that he did not consider it beneath him to concern himself with so mundane a subject. But the Ch'ing-ming scroll, painted perhaps around 1120, is both the climax and the swan song of pictorial realism as an ideal for painters of his class: from now on, the literati will leave this kind of painting to the academicians and professionals.

TUNG YÜAN AND CHÜ-JAN

These painters were all men of North China, nurtured in a hard, bleak countryside whose mood is well conveyed in the austerity of their style. The painters of the south lived in a kinder environment. The hills of the lower Yangtse Valley are softer in outline, the sunlight is diffused by mist, and winter's grip is less hard. In the works of Tung Yüan and Chü-jan, both active in Nanking in the middle decades of the tenth century, there is a roundness of contour and a looseness and freedom in the brushwork that are in marked contrast to the angular rocks and crabbed branches of Li Ch'eng and Fan K'uan. Shen Kua said that Tung Yüan "was skilled in painting the mists of autumn and far open views" and that "his pictures were meant to be seen at a distance, because their brushwork was very rough." Tung also, rather surprisingly, worked in a coloured style like that of Li Ssu-hsün. The revolutionary impressionism which Tung Yüan and his pupil Chü-jan achieved by means of broken ink-washes and the elimination of the outline is well illustrated by Tung Yüan's scroll depicting scenery along the Hsiao and Hsiang rivers in Hunan, sections of which are now in the museums in Peking and Shanghai. In this evocation of the atmosphere of a summer evening, the contours of the hills are soft and rounded and the mist is beginning to form among the trees, while here and there the diminutive figures of fishermen and travellers go about their business. Over the scene hangs a peace so profound that we can almost hear their voices as they call to each other across the water. Here for the first time an element of pure lyricism appears in Chinese landscape painting.

191 Attributed to Tung Yüan (tenth century). *Scenery along the Hsiao and Hsiang Rivers.* Detail of a handscroll. Ink and colour on silk. Early Sung Dynasty(?).

THE PAINTING OF THE LITERATI

Vestiges of Northern Sung realism lingered on in the Southern Sung Academy, and in professional painting even through the Ming and Ch'ing dynasties—as, for example, in the landscape by Yüan Chiang illustrated on page 229—but this apparent realism was a mere convention: the artist was no longer looking at nature with fresh eyes, he was simply concocting pictures out of his head. But even while a realism based on genuine observation was reaching its climax in the Northern Sung period, the seeds of a very different notion of the purposes of painting were taking root in the minds of a small circle of intellectuals of whom the leaders were the great poet Su Tung-p'o (1036–1101), his teacher in bamboo painting Wen T'ung (died 1079), Mi Fu (or Mi Fei, 1051–1105), and the scholar and calligrapher Huang T'ing-chien (1045–1107). Su Tung-p'o put forward the revolutionary idea that the purpose of painting was not representation but expression. To them, the aim of a landscape painter was not to evoke in the viewer the same kind of feelings as he would have if he were actually wandering in the mountains himself, but to reveal to his friends something of his own mind and feelings. They spoke of merely "borrowing" the forms of rocks, trees, or bamboo in which, for the moment, to find "lodging" for their thoughts and feelings. Of a panorama of the Hsiao and Hsiang rivers such as that attributed to Tung Yüan they might say, not "From this you can tell what the scenery of Hsiao and Hsiang is like," but "From this, you can tell what kind of a man Tung Yüan was." Their brushwork was as personal and as revealing of character as was their handwriting.

So it was that in their painting, the passion of a Fan K'uan for the hills and streams gave way to a more urbane, detached attitude; for they avoided becoming too deeply involved either in nature or in material things. Above all, they were gentlemen, poets, and scholars first, and painters only second; and, lest they be taken for professionals, they often claimed that they were only playing with ink and that a certain roughness or awkwardness was a mark of unaffected sincerity. By choice, they painted in ink on paper, deliberately avoiding the seduction of colour and silk. It is not surprising that of all the streams of Chinese pictorial art, the painting of the high officials (*shih-ta-fu hua*) and of the literati (*wen-jen hua*) is hardest to appreciate. The lines that the Sung scholar Ou-yang Hsiu wrote of the poetry of his friend Mei Yao-ch'en would apply equally well to the paintings of Su Tung-p'o, Wen T'ung, or Mi Fu:

192 Attributed to Su Tung-p'o (1036–1101). *Bare Tree, Bamboo and Rocks.* Handscroll. Ink on paper.

193 Mi Yu-jen (1086–1165), *Misty Landscape*. Hanging scroll. Ink on paper. Southern Sung Dynasty.

His recent poems are dry and hard;
Try chewing on some—a bitter mouthful!
The first reading is like eating olives,
But the longer you suck on them, the better the taste.[3]

Just what brought about this momentous change in the educated man's view of the purposes of art is not quite clear. The germs of it might be found in the life and work of the T'ang poet-painter Wang Wei, regarded by the later literati as the founding father of this tradition of landscape painting; but its emergence as a philosophy of art belongs to the Sung, and seems to go hand-in-hand with the tendency, which found its subtlest and most complex expression in the philosophy of the second generation of Neo-Confucianists, to unite all phenomena, natural forces, qualities of mind, in a universal system of relationships that can only be grasped through intuition. The very existence of such a synthetic philosophy—the ancient *pa-kua* had been a primitive attempt in the same direction—encouraged thinkers to leap from the object of experience straight to the general, all-embracing principle without investigating it for itself. As this approach to knowledge took stronger hold on intellectuals, more and more did it discourage both scientific investigation and realism in art, while the gulf that began increasingly to separate the intellectual élite from the rest of society ensured that henceforth scholars would no longer concern themselves (except in their capacity as administrators) with worldly affairs. It would have been utterly impossible, for instance, for a gentleman in the Yüan, Ming, or Ch'ing Dynasty to have painted a scroll like Chang Tse-tuan's panorama illustrated on page 159.

Whatever the causes of this momentous shift in emphasis—and there are many—it is well illustrated in the handful of surviving paintings that have been attributed to members of this small group of Northern Sung scholar-painters. The short handscroll illustrated here was first attributed to Su Tung-p'o in the thirteenth century, and its actual author is unknown. But it is typical of the taste and technique of the eleventh-century scholar-painters in its choice of medium, its dry, sensitive brushwork, its avoidance of obvious visual appeal, and in the sense that this is a spontaneous statement as revealing of the man himself as of what he depicts.

The work of these early scholar-painters was always original, not because they strove for originality for itself but because their art was the sincere and spontaneous expression of an original personality. One of the most remarkable of these men was Mi Fu, critic, connoisseur, and eccentric, who would spend long evenings with his friend Su Tung-p'o, whom he first met, probably in Hangchow, in 1081, surrounded by piles of paper and jugs of wine, writing away at top speed till the paper and wine gave out and the small boys grinding the ink were ready to drop with fatigue. In painting landscapes, Mi Fu, it is said, abandoned the drawn line altogether, forming his mountains of rows of blobs of wet ink laid on the paper with the flat of the brush—a technique probably derived from Tung Yüan's impressionism and highly evocative of the misty southern landscape that Mi Fu knew so well. This striking Mi-dot technique, as it came to be called, had its dangers, however; in the hands of the master or of his son Mi Yu-jen (1086–1165), who seems to have modified it somewhat, it achieved marvels of breadth and luminosity with the simplest of means, but it was fatally easy to imitate.

So radical was this technique of Mi Fu's that the emperor Hui-tsung would have none of his work in the imperial collection, nor would he permit the style to be practised at court. It is not known whether an official painting academy ever existed before the Southern Sung. Painters at the T'ang court had been given a wide variety of civil and military ranks, most of which were sinecures. Wang Chien, ruler of Former Shu, seems to have been the first to give his painters appointments in his own Hanlin Academy of Letters, and this practice was followed by the Southern T'ang emperor Li Hou-chu at Nanking, and by the first emperors of the Sung. Contemporary writers often speak of distinguished painters as being in attendance (*tai-chao*) in the Yü-hua-yüan (Imperial

SUNG HUI-TSUNG AND THE ACADEMY

194 Sung Hui-tsung (reigned 1101–
1125), *The Five-Colour Parakeet.*
Hanging scroll. Ink and colour on silk.
Northern Sung Dynasty.

Academy of Painting); yet no such institution is ever mentioned in the Northern Sung history, and if such a body did in fact exist, it was presumably a subdivision of the Hanlin Academy.

The tradition of direct imperial patronage culminated in Hui-tsung (1101–1125), the last emperor of Northern Sung, whose passion for pictures and antiquities blinded him to the perils into which his country was drifting. In 1104 he set up an official School of Painting (*Hua-hsüeh*) in the palace, but in 1110 this was abolished and painting was once more put under the Hanlin Academy. Hui-tsung kept tight control over the painters at court. He handed out the subjects to be painted and set examinations as though the painters were candidates for administrative posts. The theme was generally a line from a poem, and distinction went to the most ingenious and allusive answer. When, for example, he chose the theme "A Tavern in a Bamboo Grove by a Bridge," the winner did not put in the tavern at all but simply suggested it by a signboard set among the bamboos. Thus, what Hui-tsung required of these artists was not mere academic realism so much as the kind of intellectual agility, the avoidance of the obvious, the play upon ideas that was expected also of literary scholars. But the emperor, himself a painter of great ability, tolerated no indiscipline in the ranks. He imposed a dictatorship of form and taste upon his academicians as rigid as that of Le Brun over the artists working for Louis

XIV, who were in much the same position. The penalty for independence was dismissal. For all his talent and enthusiasm, his influence cannot have been beneficial. The imposition of a rigid orthodoxy laid the foundation for a decorative, painstaking "palace style" which was to govern court taste until modern times, while his insatiable and somewhat unscrupulous demands as a collector—demands which no owner could refuse—helped to ensure the destruction, in the disastrous events of 1125/27, of most of the still-surviving masterpieces of ancient art.

Whenever Hui-tsung produced a masterpiece, the painters in the academy vied with each other in copying it and if they were lucky succeeded in having their versions inscribed with the emperor's own cypher. So closely indeed did they model their work on his that it is now almost impossible to disentangle the one from the other, though some attempts have been made to do so. It would even be wrong to assume that the better the painting the more likely it is to be from the imperial hand. The pictures associated with his name are for the most part quiet, careful studies of birds on branches—*A Dove on a Peach Tree*, *Sparrows on Bamboo*, and so on—painted with exquisite precision, delicate colour, and faultless placing. Often their beauty is enhanced by the emperor's highly elegant calligraphy which, we may be sure, was not infrequently applied also as a mark of approval to paintings executed by members of the academy. A typical product of this sophisticated circle is the famous *Five-Colour Parakeet*, which bears a poem and signature penned by the imperial brush. This exquisitely balanced picture reveals a certain stiffness (much clearer in the original than in the photograph), an anxiety to be correct at all costs—just the qualities we might expect to find in Hui-tsung himself.

The art of flower painting which Hui-tsung and his academicians practised was not, in origin, wholly Chinese. Buddhist banner paintings brought from India and central Asia were richly set about with flowers, painted in a technique which influenced the late-sixth-century master Chang Seng-yu. Speaking of some of Chang's paintings in a temple at Nanking, a T'ang author had written: "All over the gate of the temple 'flowers-in-relief' are painted. . . . Such flowers are done in a technique brought here from India. They are painted in vermilion, malachite greens, and azurite blues. Looking at them from a distance, one has the illusion that they are [carved] in relief, but close at hand they are seen to be flat."[4] T'ang Buddhist art is rich in this decorative style of flower painting, but by the tenth century it had become an art in its own right. Later painters loved to animate their flower studies with birds, and thus "birds and flowers" (*hua-niao*) became recognised as an independent category in the repertoire.

The tenth-century master Huang Ch'üan is said to have invented a revolutionary technique of flower painting at the court of Wang Chien in Chengtu. He worked almost entirely in delicate, transparent washes of colour, sometimes laid one over the other, a

BIRD AND
FLOWER PAINTING

style, requiring great skill in handling the medium, that is related to the boneless technique we have already encountered in landscape painting.

The technique of his contemporary and great rival at Nanking, Hsü Hsi, was apparently quite different, for he drew his flowers and leaves swiftly in ink and ink-wash, adding only a little colour. Huang Ch'üan's style was considered the more skillful and decorative, and eventually became more popular with professionals and court painters, while Hsü Hsi's, because it was based on the free use of brush and ink, found favour among the literati. Huang's son Huang Chü-ts'ai, among others, successfully combined elements of both styles. No original from the hand of Huang Ch'üan or Hsü Hsi has survived, but their techniques are still popular with flower painters today.

A comment by the critic Shen Kua on the work of Huang and his son, on the one hand, and Hsü, on the other, throws an interesting light on the standards by which this kind of painting was judged in the Sung Dynasty.

The two Huangs' flower paintings are marvellous [*miao*] in their handling of colours. Their brushwork is extremely fresh and finely detailed. The ink lines are almost invisible, and are supplemented only by washes of light colours. Their sort of painting you might call sketching from life. Hsü Hsi would use his ink and brush to draw in a very broad way, add a summary colouring, and that would be all. With him the spiritual quality is pre-eminent, and one has a special sense of animation. Ch'üan disliked his technique, called his work coarse and ugly, and rejected it as being without style.[5]

This was the true professional speaking.

195 Attributed to Huang Chü-ts'ai (933–993). *Pheasant and Sparrows amid Rocks and Shrubs*. Hanging scroll. Ink and colour on silk. Northern Sung Dynasty.

196 Attributed to Li T'ang (c. 1050–1130). *A Myriad Trees on Strange Peaks*. Fan. Ink and colour on silk. Sung Dynasty.

When, after the disaster of 1125, the Sung shored up the ruins of their house amid the delights of their "temporary" capital at Hangchow, they set out to recapture the dignity and splendour of the old life at Kaifeng. At Wu-lin outside the city, a formal Academy of Painting, *Hua-yüan*, was set up, for the first and only time in Chinese history. Venerable masters from the north were assembled there to reestablish the tradition of court painting, and no national catastrophe, it seemed—provided that it was ignored—could disturb the even tenor of their life and art. The classic northern tradition was transformed and transmitted to the Southern Sung by Li T'ang, *doyen* of Hui-tsung's academy. History credits Li T'ang with a monumental style based on the *fu-p'i ts'un* ("axe-cut texture stroke"), a graphic description of his method of as it were hacking out the angular facets of his rocks with the side of the brush. A powerful landscape in this technique in the Palace Museum, Taipei, signed and dated equivalent to 1124, may be a later copy, and it is likely that no original from his hand survives today. Perhaps the little fan painting, *A Myriad Trees on Strange Peaks*, brings us as close to his style as we shall ever get. He was an old man when Kaifeng fell, and most of his work must have perished with the imperial collection. But copies, attributed paintings, and literary sources suggest that his style and influence were dominant in the twelfth century, making him a vital link between

LI T'ANG

197 Attributed to Chao Po-chü (1120–1182). *Rocky Mountains along a River in Autumn*. Detail of a handscroll. Ink and mineral colour on silk. Southern Sung Dynasty.

the remote grandeur of Northern Sung and the brilliant romanticism of Southern Sung painters such as Ma Yüan and Hsia Kuei.

The first great Southern Sung landscape painter of whom we have any knowledge was Chao Po-chü, a member of the Sung imperial family who as a youth had been in Hui-tsung's academy—and lived on to become a favourite of Kao-tsung (1127–1162) and a high office-holder in Chekiang. He is said to have excelled in landscapes with figures in the green-and-blue style that had originated with Li Ssu-hsün. His handscroll, *Rocky Mountains along a River in Autumn*, of which a detail is illustrated here, combines restrained echoes of the precise, decorative T'ang manner with a monumental *intimisme* that is typical of Sung landscape painting at its best.

198 Ma Yüan (active 1190–1225), *On a Mountain Path in Spring*, with a poem by Yang Mei-tzu, consort of Ning-tsung. Album-leaf. Ink and colour on silk. Southern Sung Dynasty.

MA YÜAN AND HSIA KUEI

Perhaps because of its obvious visual and emotional appeal, the work of the Ma-Hsia School, as it is called, has come in Western eyes to represent the very quintessence of Chinese landscape painting, and not only in the West, for this style was to have a profound influence too on the development of landscape painting in Japan. Its language of expression was not altogether new. We have found an anticipation of its spectacular tonal contrasts in Fan K'uan and Kuo Hsi, its clawlike trees and roots in Li Ch'eng, its axe strokes in Li T'ang. But in the art of Ma Yüan and Hsia Kuei these elements all appear together, united by a consummate mastery of the brush which would border on mannerism if it were not so deeply infused with poetry. Without this depth of feeling, the style is in itself decorative and easily imitated in its outward aspects—qualities which were to be seized upon by the painters of the Kanō School in Japan. What is new is the sense of space, achieved by pushing the landscape to one side, opening up a vista of limitless distance. There are many night scenes, and the atmosphere is often redolent of a poetic sadness that hints at the underlying mood of Hangchow in this age of deepening anxiety.

Ma Yüan became a *tai-chao* at the end of the twelfth century, Hsia Kuei early in the thirteenth. It is not always easy to disentangle the style of the one from the other. If we say, looking at the

199 Hsia Kuei (active 1200–1230), *Pure and Remote View of Hills and Streams*. Detail of a handscroll. Ink on paper. Southern Sung Dynasty.

Four Old Recluses in Cincinnati attributed to Ma Yüan, that his brushwork is bold and fiery, we will find the same quality even more brilliantly displayed in Hsia Kuei's *Pure and Remote View of Hills and Streams*, in the Palace Museum collection, Taipei. It is hard to believe that this almost violently expressionistic work was painted by a senior member of the Imperial Academy. Both he and Ma Yüan used Li T'ang's axe stroke *ts'un* with telling effect, both exploited brilliantly the contrast of black ink against a luminous expanse of mist; all we can say is that of the two Ma Yüan generally seems the calmer, the more disciplined and precise, Hsia Kuei the expressionist, who may in a fit of excitement seem to stab and hack the silk with his brush. The brilliant virtuosity of his style appealed strongly to the Ming painters of the Che School (see p. 206), and there is little doubt that the great majority of paintings generally attributed to Hsia Kuei are in fact pastiches by Tai Chin and his followers. For there is in the real Hsia Kuei a noble austerity of conception, a terseness of statement, a brilliant counterpoint of wet and dry brush, a sparing and telling use of *ts'un*, which his imitators failed altogether to capture.

The art of Hsia Kuei is not far removed, in the explosive energy of its brushwork, from that of the Ch'an Buddhist masters, who at this time were living not far from the capital in point of distance—their monasteries lay in the hills across the West Lake from Hangchow—but who were in their lives and art far removed from the court and all it stood for. Of these, the chief were Liang K'ai,

CH'AN PAINTING

200 Mu-ch'i (active mid-thirteenth
century), *Evening Glow on a Fishing
Village*, one of "Eight Views of the
Hsiao and Hsiang Rivers." Detail of a
handscroll. Ink on paper. Southern Sung
Dynasty.

who after rising to be *tai-chao* under Ning-tsung (1195–1224), retired to a temple, taking with him the brilliant brush style of Hsia
Kuei, and Mu-ch'i, who from his monastery, the Liu-t'ung-ssu,
dominated the Ch'an painting of the Hangchow region throughout the thirteenth century. There was hardly a subject that Much'i did not touch. Landscapes, birds, tigers, monkeys, *bodhisattvas*—all were the same to him. In all he sought to express an essential nature that was not a matter of form, for his forms may break
up or dissolve in mists—but of inner life, which he found because
it was in the painter himself. His famous *Six Persimmons* is the supreme example of his genius for investing the simplest thing with
profound significance. Less often recognised is his power of monumental design, shown above all in the central panel of his great
triptych in Daitokuji, Kyōto, depicting the white-robed Kuanyin
seated in meditation amid the rocks, flanked by paintings of a
crane in a bamboo grove, and gibbons in the branches of a pine
tree. Whether or not these scrolls were painted to hang together is
immaterial, for, in Ch'an Buddhism, all living things partake of
the divine essence. What is most striking about these scrolls, and
common to all the best Ch'an painting, is the way in which the artist rivets the viewer's attention by the careful painting of certain
key details, while all that is not essential blurs into obscurity, as in
the very act of meditation itself. Such an effect of concentration
and control was only possible to artists schooled in the disciplined
techniques of the Ma-Hsia School; the brush style of the literati,
for all its spontaneity, was too relaxed and personal to meet such a
challenge.

DRAGONS   The influence of the academic attitude toward art in the Sung Dynasty is revealed in a growing tendency to categorise. The catalogue of the emperor Hui-tsung's collection, *Hsüan-ho hua-p'u*,
for instance, was arranged under ten headings: Taoist and Buddhist themes (which, though less popular than before, still preserved a prestige conferred by tradition); figure painting (including portraits and genre); palaces and buildings (particularly those
in the ruled *chieh-hua* style); foreign tribes; dragons and fish; landscapes; domestic animals and wild beasts (there was a whole

201 Mu-ch'i, *The White-Robed Kuanyin*, flanked by crane and gibbons. Central portions of three hanging scrolls. Ink on silk. Southern Sung Dynasty.

school of painters specialising in water buffaloes); flowers and birds; ink bamboo; and vegetables and fruit. The last category requires no special mention; and bamboo we will leave to Chapter 9. But before leaving the subject of Sung painting we must say a word on the subject of dragons. To the man-in-the-street the dragon was a benevolent and generally auspicious creature, bringer of rain and emblem of the emperor. To the Ch'an Buddhists he was far more than that. When Mu-ch'i painted a dragon suddenly appearing from the clouds, he was depicting a cosmic manifestation and at the same time symbolising the momentary, elusive vision of truth which comes to the Ch'an adept. To the Taoists, the dragon was the *Tao* itself, an all-pervading force which momentarily reveals itself to us only to vanish again and leave us wondering if we had actually seen it at all. "Hidden in the caverns of inaccessible mountains," wrote Okakura Kakuzō,

> or coiled in the unfathomed depths of the sea, he awaits the time when he slowly rouses himself to activity. He unfolds himself in the storm clouds; he washes his mane in the blackness of the seething whirlpools. His claws are in the forks of the lightning, his scales begin to glisten in the bark of rain-swept pine trees. His voice is heard in the hurricane which, scattering the withered leaves of the forest, quickens the new spring. The dragon reveals himself only to vanish.[6]

Ts'ao Pu-hsing in the third century had been the first prominent painter to specialise in dragons, but the greatest of all was Ch'en Jung, who combined a successful career as an administrator during the first half of the thirteenth century with a somewhat unorthodox technique as a dragon painter. His contemporary, T'ang Hou, tells us that when he was drunk he would give a great shout, seize his cap, soak it with ink and smear on the design with it, afterwards finishing the details with a brush. His celebrated *Nine*

202 Ch'en Jung (active 1235–1260), *The Nine Dragons*. Detail of a handscroll. Ink on paper. Southern Sung Dynasty.

Dragons, painted in 1244, could well have been executed thus, the dragons with his brush, the clouds with his cap; indeed, on the original the imprint of some textile in the clouds can be seen quite clearly.

CERAMICS: NORTHERN WARES

203 Vase, *mei-p'ing*. Stoneware covered with black glaze. From Ho-pi-chi, Honan (?). Northern Sung Dynasty.

The art of the Sung Dynasty which we admire today was produced by, and for, a social and intellectual élite more cultivated than at any other period in Chinese history. The pottery and porcelain made for their use is a natural reflection of their taste. Some T'ang wares may be more robust, Ch'ing wares more perfectly finished, but the Sung have a classical purity of form and glaze that holds a perfect balance between the vigour of the earlier wares and the refinement of the later. Although some of the porcelain for the Northern Sung court came from kilns as far away as Chekiang and Kiangsi, the most famous of the Northern Sung *kuan* ("official") wares was manufactured in the kilns at Chien-tz'u-ts'un, near Ting-chou in Hopei, where a white porcelain was already being made in the T'ang Dynasty. The classic Ting ware is a finely potted, high-fired white porcelain, with a creamy white glaze that has a brownish tinge where it runs into the "tear-marks" described in early texts. The floral decoration of earlier pieces such as the masterly tomb pillow illustrated here was freely carved in the "leather-hard" paste before firing; later, more elaborate patterns were impressed in the paste from pottery moulds. As the vessels were fired upside down, the rims of bowls were left unglazed and often had to be bound with bronze or silver. Chinese connoisseurs recognise, in addition to the true *pai* ("white") Ting, a fine-grained *fen* ("flour") Ting, a *tzu* ("purple"—actually soy-sauce

204 Funerary pillow, Ting ware. Porcelain covered with creamy white glaze. Northern Sung Dynasty.

205 Bottle with copper-bound rim, Ju ware. Stoneware covered with dove's-egg-blue glaze. Northern Sung Dynasty.

206 Pitcher, northern celadon. Stoneware with carved decoration under an olive-green glaze. Northern Sung Dynasty.

brown) Ting, and a coarse yellowish *t'u* ("earth") Ting. Varieties of Ting and near-Ting, however, are not always easy to distinguish.

The extensive surveys and excavations of recent decades have made it apparent that not only was one type of ware often made in a number of different kilns, with the inevitable local variations in character and quality, but also that one kiln centre might turn out a wide range of products. To take two examples, Koyama Fujio and, more recently, Chinese investigators discovered in the ruins of the Ting kilns white, black, and persimmon-red glazed porcelain, unglazed, painted porcelain, pottery with white slip, with patterns in iron oxide, with carved designs, with black, and with buckwheat brown glaze. The Sung kilns at Ho-pi-chi, T'ang-yin-hsien, Honan, first investigated in 1955, while turning out chiefly plain white wares also produced coloured wares, white wares with coloured decoration, cups glazed black outside and white inside, a high-quality Chün-type stoneware, and black glazed vases with vertical yellowish ribs in relief, such as the lovely vessel illustrated here. The value and beauty of the Ting wares lies not merely in their glaze and decoration but also in the exquisite purity of their shapes, many of which were copied not only in other Sung kilns but also in the Korean wares of the Koryŏ period. After the fall of Kaifeng in 1127, wares of Ting type were made at Chi-chou in central Kiangsi, very probably by refugee potters who had fled to the south.

Since the Sung Dynasty, Chinese connoisseurs have classed Ting-yao as a "classic" ware of Northern Sung, together with Ju-yao, Chün-yao, and the now legendary Ch'ai-yao, which had a glaze "blue like the sky after rain." When the too-fastidious emperor Hui-tsung decided that, presumably because of its "tear-

207 Jar, Chün ware. Stoneware covered with lavender-blue glaze splashed with purple. Sung Dynasty.

208 Jar, Tz'u-chou ware. Stoneware slipped and painted in black under a transparent glaze. Sung Dynasty.

209 Vase, *mei-p'ing*, Tz'u-chou ware. Stoneware with designs carved through black to white slip under a transparent glaze. From Hsiu-wu, Honan. Sung Dynasty.

drops" and metal rim, Ting-yao was no longer good enough for palace use, kilns were set up to make a new *kuan* ware, both at Ju-chou and within the confines of the capital itself. The latter kilns have long since been buried or swept away in the floods that periodically inundate the Yellow River Valley, and it is not known for certain what kind of porcelain they produced, although the Palace Museum authorities in Taiwan have recently published a number of fine pieces, close both to Ju-yao and to Hangchow *kuan-yao*, as products of the Kaifeng imperial kilns. Ju-yao, one of the rarest of all Sung porcelains, has been more positively identified. It has a buff or pinkish-yellow body, covered with a bluish-grey glaze with a lavender tint, netted over with a fine crackle-like mica. The shapes, chiefly bowls, brush washers, and bottles, are of an exquisite simplicity matching the quality of the glaze. Ju-chou was also one of several centres in addition to the large factory in T'ung-ch'uan-hsien, north of Sian, that produced "northern celadon"—an apt name for a stoneware often richly decorated with carved or moulded floral designs under a dull green glaze. A kind of celadon had been made at Yao-yao in T'ung-ch'uan-hsien as early as the Six Dynasties, but when the Sung expanded to absorb Chekiang, production and quality in the Yao-yao kilns seem to have been influenced by the Yüeh potters, some of whom may have been sent to North China.

Much more closely related to Ju, however, is the well-known Chün ware, made not only at Chün-chou and Ju-chou but also at other centres in the neighbourhood of Ho-pi, Anyang, and Tz'u-chou. The finest Chün was of palace quality, and so is sometimes called *kuan* Chün by Chinese collectors. The potting is much heavier than that of Ju-yao, however, and myriads of tiny bubbles, which burst on the surface of the thick lavender-blue glaze, give it a seductive softness and warmth. It was the Chün potters who discovered that spots of copper oxidised in the glaze during firing produced crimson and purple splashes, a technique which they used with exquisite restraint. On later varieties of Chün ware, however, such as the numbered sets of flower pots and bulb bowls made in the Ming Dynasty at Te-hua and Canton, these flambé effects were often used with tasteless extravagance.

The Tz'u-chou wares represent perhaps the most striking example of the extent to which the discoveries of the last fifteen years have altered the ceramic picture. Tz'u-chou is a convenient name for a large family of North China stonewares decorated chiefly by painting under the glaze or by carving or incising through a coloured slip. The technique of underglaze painting had been tentatively tried out in Hunan during the T'ang Dynasty, but the Tz'u-chou potters of the Sung used it with easy mastery. The unaffected grace and confidence of the brush drawing give the Tz'u-chou wares an immediate appeal, although until very recently they have been considered too close to a peasant art to command the respect of educated people in China itself.

The kilns at Tz'u-chou are well known, and still active today, but recent Chinese excavation and research have revealed that the "North China decorated stoneware," as perhaps it ought to be called, was made across the breadth of the country, from Shantung to Szechwan. Of the known kilns, the most important so far excavated, in addition to Tz'u-chou itself, are Ho-pi (already mentioned), the stratified kilnsite at Kuan-t'ai on the Honan-Hopei border, among whose products was a white ware with designs incised or stamped through the glaze to a darker body, and the kilns at Hsiu-wu (or Chiao-tso) on the Shansi-Honan border, which turned out striking vases with floral designs reserved on black or boldly carved through a black glaze.

Before the end of the Sung Dynasty, North China potters, not only at Tz'u-chou but at kilns in Honan, Shansi, and Shantung, had developed the revolutionary technique of overglaze painting. Their delightful bowls and dishes decorated with birds and flowers swiftly sketched in tomato-red, green, and yellow over a creamy glaze are the earliest examples of the enamelling technique that was to become so popular in the Ming Dynasty.

At the fall of the T'ang, the northeast was lost to a Khitan tribe who called their dynasty Liao (907–1124). We have already noted how a "T'ang revival" school of Buddhist art was flourishing at Yünkang and elsewhere under their patronage, and have assigned the famous ceramic Lohans to this period. Liao sites in Manchuria have yielded fragments of Chun-, Ting-, and Tz'u-chou-type wares, but Japanese scholars and collectors and, more recently, Chinese archaeologists have also recovered large quantities of a distinct local ware that combines something of the sgraffiato floral decoration of Tz'u-chou with the three-colour glazes and the robust—though now provincial and often ungainly—shapes of the T'ang Dynasty, such as the chicken ewer, pilgrim flask, and trumpet-mouthed vase. The finest Liao wares are the equal of Sung porcelains in elegance, and even the rough grave wares such as the imitation of a leather water-flask carried at the saddle have the same spontaneous, unsophisticated charm that we admire in mediaeval European pottery.

The ceramics illustrated in this chapter offer a vivid comparison of the difference in taste between North and South China. The north had an ancient ceramic tradition and vast numbers of kilns; the northerners made bold technical experiments and liked vigorous carved designs, splashed glazes, and strong colours. The wares of the south, until the Yüan Dynasty at least, are quieter, more conservative, more apt to echo antique shapes, seldom venturing beyond celadon and monochrome black or white.

Among the most striking of the northern wares are those with a black glaze, which used to be called Honan *temmoku*. This name forms a link with South China, for it was in the south that tea-drinking had first become popular during the T'ang Dynasty and it was discovered that a black glaze effectively set off the pea-green colour of the tea. *Temmoku* is the Japanese equivalent of T'ien-mu, a mountain near Hangchow, whence certain of these southern wares were shipped to Japan. The true *temmoku*, made at Chien-an in Fukien as early as the tenth century, consisted almost exclu-

210 Bowl, Tz'u-chou ware. Stoneware decorated with coloured enamels over a creamy white glaze. Late Sung or Yüan Dynasty.

211 Traveller's flask. Stoneware with cockscomb relief ornament in green enamel over white glaze. North China. Liao Dynasty.

SOUTHERN WARES

212 Tea bowl, Fukien *temmoku* ware. Stoneware with black "hare's fur" glaze. Southern Sung Dynasty.

sively of the type of tea bowls which proved so popular in Japan. They have a dark stoneware body decorated with a thick, oily iron glaze running to big drops at the foot. The colour is basically a very dark brown verging on black, often streaked with blue or steel grey, producing marks known as "hare's fur," or bluish "oil spots" caused by the coagulation of grey crystals. These were imitated in a rather coarse, lustreless ware made at Chi-chou in Kiangsi—often confusingly called *Kian ware* in older books—and at other kilns in Fukien such as Kuang-che, Fu-ch'ing, and Ch'uan-chou.

When, after a few years at Hangchow, the Southern Sung court began to realise that this was to be more than a temporary halting place, steps were taken to enlarge the palace and government offices and to set up factories to manufacture utensils for court use which would duplicate as closely as possible those of the old northern capital. The supervisor of parks, Shao Ch'eng-chang, who was in charge of this work, established a kiln near his own office (*Hsiu-nei Ssu*) on Phoenix Hill just to the west of the palace, which lay at the southern end of the city. There, according to a Sung text, Shao's potters made "a celadon which was called *Nei-yao* [palace ware]. Its pure body of exceptional fineness and delicacy, its clear and lustrous glaze, have been prized ever since." The Phoenix Hill area has been repeatedly built over, and the kilns have not been discovered, nor is it known how long they were in operation. But before long another imperial factory was set up to the southwest below the suburban Altar of Heaven (*Chiao-t'an*). This has become a place of pilgrimage to ceramics enthusiasts, who over the years have picked up quantities of shards of the beautiful "southern *kuan*" which graces many Western collections. Its dark body is often thinner than the glaze, which is layered, opaque, vitrified, and sometimes irregularly crackled, ranging in colour from a pale bluish-green through blue to dove grey. The ware has an air of courtly elegance combined with quietness and restraint that made it a fitting adornment for the Southern Sung court.

We should not try to draw too sharp a line between Hangchow *kuan* ware and the best of the celadons made at Lung-ch'üan in

MAP 11 Kiln sites in the Hangchow area.

176

213 Tripod incense burner, southern *kuan* ware. Stoneware with crackled bluish-green celadon glaze. Southern Sung Dynasty.

southern Chekiang. The imperial kilns at Hangchow made a light-bodied ware in addition to the dark, while Lung-ch'üan turned out a small quantity of dark-bodied ware as well as the characteristic light grey. It seems certain that the finest Lung-ch'üan celadons were supplied on official order and could hence be classed as *kuan*.

Probably of all Sung stonewares the celadons are the most widely appreciated—outside China, at least. The name is believed to have been taken from that of Céladon, a shepherd dressed in green who appeared in a pastoral play, *L'Astrée*, first produced in Paris in 1610. These beautiful wares, known to the Chinese as *ch'ing tz'u* ("blue-green porcelain"), were made in a number of kilns, but those of Lung-ch'üan were the finest, as well as the most abundant, and were, indirectly, the heirs of the Yüeh wares. The light-grey body of Lung-ch'üan ware burns yellowish on exposure in the kiln, and wears an unctuous iron glaze ranging in colour from leaf-green to a cold bluish-green, which is sometimes, though by no means always, crackled. Crackle, originally an accidental result of the glaze shrinking more than the body when the vessel cooled after firing, was often exploited for its decorative effect, as in the *ko*-type celadons, in which a closer, secondary crackle was also developed. To the finest Lung-ch'üan celadons, which

214 Vase, Lung-ch'üan (*kinuta*) ware. Stoneware with grey-green celadon glaze. Southern Sung Dynasty.

215 Vase, *ch'ing-pai* or *ying-ch'ing* ware. White porcelain. Southern Sung Dynasty.

have a lovely, cloudy blue-green colour, the Jananese gave the name *kinuta* ("mallet"), perhaps after the shape of a particularly famous vase. Almost every shape appears in the Lung-ch'üan repertoire: many are purely ceramic, but we also encounter adaptations of archaic bronze forms, notably incense burners in the form of the three- and four-legged *ting*—a mark of that antiquarianism which was now begining to develop in Chinese court art and was to have an ever-increasing influence on cultivated taste.

We can trace the development of the Chekiang celadons through dated pieces well into the Ming Dynasty, when the potting becomes heavier, the glaze greener and more glassy, and the scale more ambitious.

Celadon, including coarser varieties made in South China, bulked large in China's export trade from the Southern Sung onward. Of the over six thousand pieces recovered from a ship destined for Japan that went down off Sinan, South Korea, shortly after 1331, most were celadons. The ware has turned up in sites from New Guinea and the Philippines to East Africa and Egypt, while, as every amateur knows, it was much in demand among Arab potentates, partly perhaps because it was believed to crack or change colour if poison touched it.

Also exported in large quantities (although it was originally a purely domestic ware) was a beautiful translucent porcelain with a granular, sugary body and pale bluish glaze. Some doubt as to its respectability in Chinese ceramic history was long caused by the fact that the name for it used in the West is *ying-ch'ing*, a recent term which was invented by Chinese dealers to describe its shadowy blue tint, and for which scholars had searched in vain in Chinese works. In fact, its original name, *ch'ing-pai* ("bluish-white"), occurs frequently in texts going back to the Sung Dynasty—although Chinese writers are very inconsistent, and the term may on occasion, in later periods at least, have meant blue and white. Because of its high felspar content, the hard clay could be potted in shapes of wonderful thinness and delicacy. The tradition, which began humbly in the T'ang kilns at Shih-hu-wan some miles to the west of Ching-te-chen, achieved a perfect balance between living form and refinement of decoration in the Sung wares, whose shapes included teapots, vases, stem cups, and bowls, often with foliate rim and dragons, flowers, and birds moulded or incised with incredible lightness of touch in the thin paste under the glaze. Already in the Sung Dynasty *ch'ing-pai* wares were being imitated in many kilns in South China, and a good proportion of their output was exported to Southeast Asia and the Indonesian Archipelago, where the presence of *ch'ing-pai*, celadon or the white wares of Te-hua in Fukien in an archaeological site often provides the most reliable means of dating it.

9
The Yüan Dynasty

During the twelfth century, China had come to uneasy terms with her northern neighbours and, after her custom, civilised them. But beyond them across the deserts of central Asia there roamed a horde which Fitzgerald called "the most savage and pitiless race known to history"—the Mongols. In 1210 their leader, the great Genghis Khan, attacked the buffer state of Chin, and in 1215 destroyed the capital at Peking. In 1227 he destroyed the Hsi-hsia, leaving only one-hundredth of the population alive, a disaster by which the Northwest was permanently laid waste. Three years later Genghis died, but still the Mongol hordes advanced, and in 1235 they turned southward into China. For forty years the Chinese armies resisted them, almost unsupported by their own government. But the outcome was inevitable, and even before the last Sung ruler perished in 1279, the Mongols had proclaimed their dynastic title, calling themselves the Yüan. China was spared the worst of the atrocities which had been visited upon all other victims, for, as a Khitan advisor had pointed out, the Chinese were more useful alive, and taxable, than dead. But the wars and breakup of the administration left the Mongols masters of a weak and impoverished empire, whose taxpayers had been reduced from a hundred million under the Sung to fewer than sixty million. Although Kublai Khan (1260–1294) was an able ruler and a deep admirer of Chinese culture, the Mongol administration was ruthless and corrupt. Seven emperors succeeded one another in the forty years following the death of Kublai.

In 1348, Chinese discontent against the harsh rule of the last Khan broke into open rebellion. For twenty years rival bandits and warlords fought over the prostrate country, which the Mongols had long since ceased to control effectively. Finally, in 1368, the Khan fled northward from Peking, the power of the Mongols was broken forever, and the short, inglorious rule of the Yüan was at an end. In conquering China they had realised the age-long dream of all the nomad tribes, but in less than a century the Chinese drained them of the savage vitality which had made that conquest possible and threw them back into the desert, an empty husk.

Politically the Yüan Dynasty may have been brief and inglorious, but it is a period of special interest and importance in the history of Chinese art—a period when men, uncertain of the present, looked both backward and forward. Their backward-looking is shown in the tendency, in painting as much as in the decorative arts, to revive ancient styles, particularly those of the T'ang Dynasty, which had been preserved in a semi-fossilised state in North China under the alien Liao and Chin dynasties. At the same time, the Yüan Dynasty was in several respects revolutionary, for not only were those revived traditions given a new interpretation but the divorce between the court and the intellectuals brought about by the Mongol occupation instilled in the scholar class a conviction of belonging to a self-contained élite that was not undermined until the twentieth century and was to have an enormous influence on painting.

In the arts and crafts, the Yüan Dynasty saw many innovations, a reaction against Sung refinement and a new boldness, even garishness, in decoration. Some of these changes reflect the taste of the Mongol conquerors themselves and of the *Se-mu*, the non-Chinese peoples such as Uighurs, Tanguts, and Turks whom the Mongols had swept up in their *Drang nach Osten* and established as fief-holders and landlords in occupied China—a new and partly Sinicised aristocracy which the dispossessed Chinese gentry, particularly in the south, looked on with a mixture of envy and contempt.

216 Incense burner, *liu-li* ware. Pottery covered with polychrome lead glaze. Excavated in the remains of the Yüan capital Ta-tu (Peking). Yüan Dynasty.

The Mongols dragooned artisans and craftsmen of all the conquered races into their service, organising them in quasi-military units. Although there were central Asians, Persians, and even Europeans among them, the dominating influence on the arts was of course Chinese. Yet, Marco Polo's description of Kublai's palace at Khanbalik, or Cambaluc as he called it,[1] and Friar Odoric's account of the Mongol summer palace at Shang-tu (Coleridge's Xanadu), show that while the buildings were mostly Chinese in style, the Mongols displayed their new wealth in the lavish use of gold and brilliant colours, the very antithesis of Sung taste, while they betrayed their nomad origins in the thick mats, furs, and carpets that covered the floors, and the skins that draped the walls, of the imperial apartments, giving them the air of some unbelievably sumptuous yurt. The brightly glazed incense-burner shown here, which was excavated from a Yüan mansion in Peking in 1964, vividly illustrates the demand of the invaders, and of the Chinese traders who profited by the occupation, for objects that were traditionally Chinese in form but showy, even barbaric, in flavour.

ARCHITECTURE

Very little is left above ground of Kublai's Khanbalik, and the city that we see today is essentially the creation of the Ming emperor Yung-lo, who moved the capital back from Nanking to Peking in 1421, and of his Ming and Ch'ing successors. The Ming capital, which came to be called the Tartar City after its occupation by the

FORBIDDEN
CITY

OUTER CITY
(CH'ING PERIOD)

TEMPLE &
ALTAR OF
HEAVEN

217 Sketch map of the Yüan Dynasty
Ta-tu (broken line) compared with
Peking of Ming and Ch'ing (unbroken
line).

Manchus in 1644, is actually smaller than that laid out by the Mongols, though the total area was greatly increased again when the Manchus created to the south the Chinese City for the native inhabitants. Peking consists of a city within a city within a city. Surrounded by a wall fifteen miles long, the Tartar City comfortably holds the Imperial City with a perimeter of six-and-a-half miles, in the heart of which lies the Purple Forbidden City—the Imperial Palace itself. At the extreme southern end of a north-south axis that stretches for seven-and-a-half miles lie the three-tiered marble Altar of Heaven and the circular Ch'i-nien-tien (Hall of Annual Prayers)—the Temple of Heaven whose blue-tiled roofs are familiar to every visitor to Peking.

Ancient Chou ritual, to which the Ming and Ch'ing rulers rigidly conformed, had prescribed that the Son of Heaven should rule from "three courts." Accordingly, the heart of the Forbidden City is dominated by three great halls of state, the San Ta Tien, set one behind the other at the climax of the great axis. The first from the south, and the largest, is the T'ai-ho-tien (Hall of Supreme Harmony) used by the emperor for his grander audiences, raised on a huge platform and approached by marble staircases. Behind it lies the waiting hall, Chung-ho-tien (Hall of Middle Harmony), while beyond is the Pao-ho-tien (Hall of Protecting Harmony), used for state banquets. The private apartments, offices of state, palace workshops and gardens occupy the northern half of this vast enclosure. Not many of the palace buildings we see today are the original structures, however. The T'ai-miao (Grand Ancestral

218 Aerial view of the heart of Peking. Down the centre runs the lake of the New Summer Palace, Wan-shou-shan; to the right is the moated rectangle of the Purple Forbidden City, with the three halls of state, San Ta Tien, clearly visible on the north-south axis. Prospect Hill lies in the rectangle to the north, while to the south is the main gate of the Forbidden City, T'ien-an-men. Since this photograph was taken, in about 1945, the city walls have been torn down, the area to the south of T'ien-an-men has been cleared to make a huge square, with the Great Hall of the People on the west side, and new streets and apartment blocks have taken the place of many of the narrow lanes and courtyard houses of the old Peking.

Shrine) is indeed Ming, having been rebuilt in 1464 after a fire; but the history of the T'ai-ho-tien is more typical. First built by Yung-lo in 1427, it was largely rebuilt on the same plan in 1645, while a further reconstruction was started in 1669 and not finished till thirty years later. It was again rebuilt in 1765, since when it has been frequently restored and repainted, though so conservative were the Ch'ing architects that it is unlikely that they departed much from the Ming original—which was itself a cautious repetition of the style of the fourteenth century.

Indeed, from Yüan times onward, Chinese architecture became less and less adventurous. Gone are the daring experiments in quadripartite gables, spiral canopies, and dynamic bracketing that give such interest and vitality to Sung architecture. Now each

219 The Three Great Halls, San Ta
Tien, of the Forbidden City, looking
south.

building is a plain rectangle. The eaves have become so heavily
loaded with unnecessary carpentry that the architect has to place
an extra colonnade under their outer edge to support the weight,
thus making superfluous the elaborate cantilevered system of
brackets and *ang*, which now shrinks away to a decorative and
meaningless frieze or is masked behind a band of scrollwork sus-
pended from the eaves. The splendour of the Forbidden City lies
not in its details but, rather, in its rich colour, now wonderfully
mellowed by age, the magnificently simple sweep of its roofs, and
the stupendous scale of its layout. These buildings were all of timber. A few barrel-vaulted stone or brick temple halls were built in
the sixteenth century but, as before, the use of the vault and dome
was largely confined to tombs, a typical example being the tomb
of the Wan-li emperor in the Western Hills, the excavation of
which, completed in 1958, occupied a team of Chinese archaeologists for two full years.

Like other invaders before them, the Mongols supported the
Buddhists as a matter of policy. They were particularly attracted
to the esoteric and magical practices of the Tibetan Lamaists, who
were encouraged to set up their temples in Peking. The Buddhist
architecture and sculpture produced by Chinese craftsmen under
their patronage represents no real advance upon that of the Sung,
except perhaps in sheer scale and magnificence. The effect of the
Mongol invasion on painting was far more profound. There were
still Ch'an masters, such as Yen Hui and Yin-t'o-lo, for example,
and professional painters who satisfied the conservative trend in
courtly taste with works in the manner of Ma Yüan or who car-

ART UNDER
THE MONGOLS

220 Ch'ien Hsüan (c. 1235–after 1301), *Wang Hsi-chih Watching Geese*. Detail of a handscroll. Ink and colour on paper.

ried on the tradition of monumental landscape painting that had survived in the north under the patronage of enlightened Chin rulers; but such professional painters are barely mentioned in the literature of Chinese painting, which was written by the scholars themselves, and we know very little about them. The southern gentry, viewed with deep suspicion by the Mongols, deprived of the right to rise in public service, kept themselves alive by teaching, practising medicine, or fortunetelling, while some of the better-off devoted their enforced leisure to the writing of a new kind of fiction and drama which has permanently enriched Chinese literature. With few exceptions, the great scholar-painters also put themselves beyond the conqueror's reach.

Ch'ien Hsüan (c. 1235–after 1301), already middle-aged when the Sung Dynasty fell, lived out his life in retirement, loyal to the last. Two small album-paintings, of a squirrel and a sparrow (if indeed they are his) show him as a sensitive exponent of Sung *intimisme*, but in his gentle way he was a revolutionary too. His choice of the archaic T'ang style for his charming handscroll of the calligrapher Wang Hsi-chih watching geese, and indeed of the subject itself, may be seen both as a rejection of the Sung culture that had betrayed itself and as the beginning of the restoration of the art of a more glorious past that was henceforward to be a preoccupation of the scholar-painters.

It would be strange indeed if so splendid a court as that of Kublai Khan had attracted no painters of talent, and in Ch'ien

Hsüan's pupil Chao Meng-fu (1234–1322), the emperor found a man ideally suited to bridge the gulf that lay between his régime and the Chinese educated class. Chao was a descendant of the first Sung emperor and had already served the old dynasty in a minor post for several years when Kublai appointed him. His first job was the writing of memorials and proclamations, but he soon rose to the rank of cabinet minister, confidential advisor to the emperor, and secretary to the Hanlin Academy. Though he often regretted his decision to collaborate (made the more reprehensible by his close family relationship to the Sung royal house), it was men of his kind who civilised the Mongols and thus indirectly encompassed their eventual downfall. Chao Meng-fu was also a great calligrapher, versed in all the styles from the archaic "big seal" script, through the clerical (*li*) style and the standard (*k'ai*) style, to the running draft character.

I have said little in this book about the eloquent and exacting art of calligraphy, an art whose finer points can only be appreciated with long study and training. "Affection for the written word," wrote Chiang Yee, "is instilled from childhood in the Chinese heart." From the merchant who hoists up his newly written shop sign with ceremony and incense to the poet whose soul takes flight in the brilliant sword dance of the brush, calligraphy is revered above all other arts. Not only is a man's writing a clue to his temperament, his moral worth, and his learning, but the uniquely ideographic nature of the Chinese script has charged each individual character with a richness of content and association the full range of which even the most scholarly can scarcely fathom.

Our illustrations show the main stages in the development of the Chinese script from the earliest known writing, the crude pictographs and ideographs scratched on the oracle bones (*chia-ku-wen*) and sunk in the ritual bronzes (*chin-wen*) of the late Shang

CALLIGRAPHY

221 Oracle bone script, *chia-ku-wen*. From Anyang. Shang Dynasty.

222 Seal script, *chuan-shu*. Rubbing from one of the Stone Drums. Chou Dynasty.

224 Draft script, *ts'ao-shu*. Ch'en Shun (1483–1544), part of the inscription on his *Studies from Life*, 1538. Handscroll. Ink on paper. Ming Dynasty.

223 Clerical script, *li-shu*. Rubbing from a stone slab. Han style. After Driscoll and Toda.

225 Regular script, *k'ai-shu*. Emperor Hui-tsung (reigned 1101–1125), part of his *Poem on the Peony*, written in the "thin gold" (*shou-chin*) style. Handscroll. Ink on paper. Sung Dynasty.

Dynasty. After the fall of the Shang, this script, which got its forms most probably from writing on clay with a stylus, evolved into the monumental "big seal" (*ta-chuan*) script seen on the long bronze inscriptions of the middle Chou period.

As China expanded and fragmented during the Warring States period, regional variants of the *ta-chuan* script developed. By the third century B.C. the *ta-chuan* had evolved into the more refined *hsiao-chuan* ("small seal"), which became the official script of the Ch'in Dynasty. The "small seal" script went out of fashion in the Han Dynasty, but it still survives in modern times for seal-carving and the occasional formal inscription, to which it lends an antique flavour. At the same time a new style was evolving, the *li-shu* ("clerical script"), based not on the even line of the stylus but on the free, pliant movement of the brush, in which the strokes vary in thickness and weight, and angles are accentuated by the turn of the brush. Examples of *li-shu* freely written on bamboo slips of

186

震大明湖時來泉上
蒸華不注波瀾聲
熱東海枯雲霧潤
久恐元氣洩歲旱不
地湧出白玉壺谷靈
濼水發源天下無
趵突泉

226 Running script, *hsing-shu*. Chao
Meng-fu (1254–1322), part of his *Pao-t'u
Spring Poem*. Handscroll. Ink on paper.
Yüan Dynasty.

the pre-Ch'in period have been found, but the style is more familiar on rubbings taken from stone inscriptions of the Han Dynasty
which display its potential for monumental form at its best.

Some Chinese characters have as many as twenty or more
strokes. According to tradition, it was the need for a script that
could be written quickly in the heat of battle that gave birth to the
highly cursive "draft script" (*ts'ao-shu*). In fact, some such abbre-
viated script must have been in existence for some time for practical and commercial uses, but in the Han it developed into an art
form in its own right. Indeed, in the turbulent post-Han period it
became, in company with the intellectual Taoism fashionable at
the time, something of a cult among the literati. Meantime, the
rather formal and angular Han *li-shu* was evolving naturally into
the more flowing and harmonious "regular script" (*k'ai-shu*, or
cheng-shu), which has, with its variants, remained the standard
form, learned by every child, up to the present day.

Every later style of script has its own *hsing* ("running") variety.
The southern calligrapher Wang Hsi-chih (303–379) and his sons
developed a supple *k'ai-shu* and a *hsing-shu*, of which an example is
illustrated here. The somewhat "feminine" elegance of the southern style is often contrasted with the more "masculine" scripts of
the north, which continued to preserve some of the angular
strength of the old Han *li-shu*. Through the Six Dynasties the two
traditions, southern and northern, developed side-by-side. When
China was reunited under the Sui and T'ang some great calligraphers, notably Yen Chen-ch'ing, succeeded in reconciling the archaic power of the northern style with the elegant fluidity of the
southern.

By this time the main traditional schools were well established.
Beyond them lay the calligraphy of the individualists, Zen adepts,

227 Crazy draft script, *k'uang-ts'ao-shu*.
Hsü Wei (1521–1593), poem.
Handscroll. Ink on paper.

Taoist eccentrics and drunkards, each of whom created his own style of *k'uang* ("crazy") *ts'ao-shu*, in which energy, oddity, and illegibility competed for the honours. A gentleman in Chao Meng-fu's position might admire writing of this kind, but he would be very unlikely to practise it himself.

CHAO MENG-FU

Chao Meng-fu's popular fame rests not only on his calligraphy, however, but also on his almost legendary skill in the art of painting horses, so much so that almost any good example with a respectable claim to antiquity used to be attributed to him. As court painter to the Mongols it would be surprising if his oeuvre had *not* contained a number of pictures of the animal so dear to their hearts. But it is chiefly as a landscape painter that Chao Meng-fu must be remembered. He might, indeed, have said of himself, with Cézanne, "I am the primitive of the way I have discovered."

228 Chao Meng-fu (1254–1322), *The Autumn Colours on the Ch'iao and Hua Mountains*. Detail of a handscroll dated equivalent to 1295. Ink and colour on paper. Yüan Dynasty.

He occupies a pivotal position in the history of Chinese landscape painting, for, living at a time when the Sung tradition had exhausted itself, or exploded into Zen gestures with the brush, he united a direct, spontaneous expression of feeling with a deep reverence for the antique. Looking back beyond the orthodox Sung styles, he rediscovered the poetry and the brushwork of the long-neglected southern manner of Tung Yüan and Chü-jan. In doing so, he opened the way not only for the next generation of Yüan amateur painters—notably the Four Masters discussed below—but for almost all subsequent scholarly landscape painting up to the present day. In his most famous surviving landscape, painted to evoke for a friend the ancestral homeland he had never seen, Chao Meng-fu with dry scholarly wit combines references to the quaintly archaic landscape style of the T'ang Dynasty and to the broad, calm vision of Tung Yüan.

The movement of which Chao Meng-fu was the initiator found its fulfillment half a century later in the Four Great Masters of the Yüan Dynasty: Huang Kung-wang, Ni Tsan, Wu Chen, and Wang Meng. The oldest was Huang Kung-wang (1269–1354), a detail of whose greatest surviving work, *Living in the Fu-ch'un Mountains*, is reproduced here. Little is known about his career except that for a time he held a minor official post and that he retired to a life of scholarship, teaching, painting, and poetry in his native Chekiang. His masterwork was painted slowly, as the mood took him, over a period of three years, being finished in 1350. The treatment is magnificently broad, relaxed, and unaffected, with not the least hint of the decorative silhouette, the "one-corner composition," and other mannerisms of the Hangchow Academy. We feel that this is the painter himself speaking from the depths of his heart. Colophons by the Ming painters Shen Chou and Tung Ch'i-ch'ang both mention Tung Yüan and Chü-jan as having inspired Huang Kung-wang, but the spontaneity of his

THE FOUR GREAT MASTERS OF LANDSCAPE PAINTING

229 Huang Kung-wang (1269–1354), *Living in the Fu-ch'un Mountains*. Detail of a handscroll dated equivalent to 1350. Ink on paper. Yüan Dynasty.

屋角春風多杏花小齊容膝
庚年華金梭曜水池魚戲彩鳳
栖林澗竹斜暈 清瓌霸玉屑
蕭 白髮岸烏紗而今不二韓
廉瀆市上懸壺來之酵甲寅三
月目樣斯 前復攜此畫來索
靜臞此圖為仁仲醫師且錫山
仁仲醫師則仁仲燕
歸故鄉登斯齋
暖吾志也雲林子識

壬子歲七月五日雲林生寫

230 Ni Tsan (1301–1374), *The Jung-hsi
Studio*. Hanging scroll. Ink on paper.
Yüan Dynasty.

touch shows clearly that he caught the spirit of antiquity without
becoming its slave.

This noble simplicity of utterance was carried even further by
Ni Tsan (1301–1374), a wealthy country gentleman who, to escape
ruinous taxation, spent his later years drifting in a houseboat
through the lakes and hills of southeastern Kiangsu, putting up at
monasteries and staying with friends. The establishment of the
Ming Dynasty in 1368 enabled him to return to his old home and

231 Wang Meng (1308–1385), *Thatched Halls on Mount T'ai*. Hanging scroll. Ink and colour on paper. Yüan Dynasty.

die in peace. To the Ming *wen-jen* he was the ideal type of untram-melled scholar-painter. If Huang Kung-wang was austere, then what word can we use to describe Ni Tsan? A few bare trees on a rock, a few hills across the water, an empty pavilion; that is all. The forms are spare and simple. The ink is dry and of an even greyness, touched here and there by sparsely applied *ts'un*, set down, very black, with the side of the brush; it was said of Ni Tsan that "he was as economical of ink as if it were gold." No conces-

232 T'ang Ti, (1296–1340), *Fishermen Returning through a Wintry Forest.* Hanging scroll. Ink and colour on silk. Yüan Dynasty.

sions are made to the viewer; no figures, no boats or clouds enliven the scene, and nothing moves. The silence that pervades the picture is that which falls between friends who understand each other perfectly. The innumerable imitations of his style produced by later artists show clearly how much strength is hidden in his apparent weakness, how much skill in his fumbling with the brush, what richness of content in his emptiness.

A very different type of artist was Wang Meng. He had held office under the Mongols, served as a magistrate after the Ming restoration, and died in prison in 1385. He was a master of a close-knit texture made up of tortuous, writhing lines and a rich variety of *ts'un*; but though he seems to leave nothing out, his touch is sensitive and his composition clear-cut. He is one of the few Chinese painters—Shih-ch'i is perhaps another—who, though using a brush technique of restless intensity, can achieve a final effect of repose.

Now for the first time it became natural for the artist, following the example of Ch'ien Hsüan and Chao Meng-fu, to find his inspiration not in nature so much as in art itself—a new and indeed revolutionary attitude to painting that was to have a profound influence on later generations. Up till the Yüan, one painter had built upon the achievement of his predecessors in enriching his pictorial vocabulary and drawing closer to nature, as Kuo Hsi had built upon Li Ch'eng, Li T'ang on Fan K'uan. Now the succession was broken, as artists began to range back over the whole tradition, reviving, playing variations upon, painting "in the manner of" the great masters, particularly those of the tenth and eleventh centuries. T'ang Ti, for instance, revived and transformed the styles of Li Ch'eng and Kuo Hsi, Wu Chen and Huang Kung-wang paid tribute to Tung Yüan, while others transformed the tradition of Ma Yüan and Hsia Kuei into styles that the professionals could practise. If henceforth this "art-historical art," as it has been called, was to be nurtured and enriched by the great tradition, it was also imprisoned within it, and it took a very strong artistic personality to break free. A second and almost as far-reaching consequence of the Mongol occupation was that the scholar-painters became so alienated from the court and its culture that a gulf opened between court painting and that of the literati that survived up to the end of the Ch'ing Dynasty.

With the Yüan scholar-painters the literary and poetic associations of painting acquired a new value and importance. It became customary for the painter himself to write a poem or inscription on the painting, which might be joined by others written by friends and later admirers, till the picture was almost obliterated under inscriptions and seals which, far from ruining it in Chinese eyes, might greatly enhance its value. From then on also, scholar-painters preferred, like the calligraphers, to work on paper, which, besides being a great deal cheaper than silk, was more responsive to the touch of the brush.[2]

BAMBOO PAINTING

It is not surprising that the difficult art of bamboo painting should have found special favour in the Yüan Dynasty, for it was a natural subject for the proud and independent *wen-jen*, who lived out their secluded lives far from the Mongol court. To them, indeed, the bamboo was itself a symbol of the true gentleman, pliant yet strong, who maintains his integrity unsullied no matter how low the adverse winds of circumstance may bend him. The lithe grace of its stalk and the dashing sword-point of its leaves offered the perfect subject to his brush; but, above all, the painting of bamboo in monochrome ink brought the painter closest to that most difficult of arts, calligraphy. In painting bamboo, the form and place of every leaf and stalk must be clearly adumbrated; the awkward juncture cannot be hidden in mist as in landscape painting; the gradations from black ink in the near leaves to pale in the distance must be precisely judged, the balance of stalks to leaves, of leaves to empty space, exactly struck. Having achieved this the painter

233 Li K'an (active 1260–1310), *Ink Bamboo*. Detail of a handscroll. Ink on paper. Yüan Dynasty.

234 Wu Chen (1280–1354), *Bamboo*. Album-leaf dated equivalent to 1350. Ink on paper. Yüan Dynasty.

must still know how the bamboo grows, and give to his own the springing movement of the living plant. A great bamboo painting is a virtuoso performance of a very high order.

The art had first become fashionable in the Six Dynasties,[3] when it was the custom, except when painting on a very small scale, to outline the stem and leaves in ink and fill them with body colour. This painstaking technique was chiefly handed down by the academicians, though the Sung artist Ts'ui Po and the fourteenth-century master Wang Yüan also used it occasionally. Bamboo painting seems to have gone somewhat out of fashion during the T'ang Dynasty (Hui-tsung had no T'ang specimens in his collection), but had become widely popular by Northern Sung, when its greatest exponents were Wen T'ung and the poet and calligrapher Su Tung-p'o. In the Yüan Dynasty several of the great literati, notably Ni Tsan and Chao Meng-fu, were accomplished painters of bamboo in monochrome ink; in this most exacting art Chao Meng-fu had a rival in his wife Kuan Tao-sheng, one of China's greatest women painters. Li K'an (c. 1260–1310), who took as his master Wen T'ung, devoted his life to bamboo, which he studied both as an amateur botanist and as a painter. His illustrated manual on the bamboo, *Chu-p'u hsiang-lu*, became an essential tool in the hands of every practitioner, as well as providing the starting point for all later writers on the subject. A more natural and spontaneous rendering of the subject than Li K'an ever achieved is the little album-leaf by Wu Chen illustrated here, remarkable for its economy of statement and subtle union of the twin arts of painting and calligraphy.

235 Dish. Porcelain, covered with celadon glaze, leaving the dragon and clouds in biscuit relief. Yüan Dynasty.

CERAMICS

It used to be thought that the decorative arts in China declined, if they did not actually come to a standstill, in the Yüan Dynasty, but now it is realised that this was, on the contrary, a period of innovation and technical experiment. In ceramics, for example, new techniques such as painting in underglaze red or blue were discovered or imported, and old techniques, such as modelling in relief under the glaze, were revived. The northern kilns, except for those at Tz'u-chou and Chün-chou, barely survived the Liao, Chin, and Mongol invasions, and now the focus of the ceramic industry shifted permanently to the centre and south. The kilns at Lung-ch'üan and Li-shui in Chekiang continued to produce celadons on a large scale—indeed, production must have increased to keep pace with the demand for exports to the Near East which the *Pax Tartarica* had stimulated. A baluster vase dated 1327 in the Percival David Foundation in London is typical of the more baroque preferences of the period, being elaborately and somewhat tastelessly decorated with floral scrolls moulded in relief under the glaze. More daring was the technique of leaving the central decorative motif on a dish, such as a dragon, unglazed in relief. Sometimes these reliefs were modelled by hand, but the presence in the Percival David Foundation of a celadon dish and a flask bearing identical dragons (the former unglazed and the latter glazed) indicates that moulds were also used. It is possible that spotted celadon (*tobi-seiji*) may also have been a Yüan innovation. There are signs,

236 Vase and stand. *Ch'ing-pai* porcelain with relief and pearl-bead decoration under bluish-white glaze. Yüan Dynasty.

237 Kuanyin. *Ch'ing-pai* porcelain. Excavated in the remains of the Yüan capital, Ta-tu (Peking). Yüan Dynasty.

however, that by the mid-fourteenth century the quality of Lung-ch'üan wares was beginning to fall off, the probable reason being the competition from the factories at Ching-te-chen in Kiangsi.

During the Sung Dynasty, the finest products of the Ching-te-chen kilns had been white porcelains, chiefly *ch'ing-pai* ware and an imitation of the northern Ting-yao. But by the beginning of the fourteenth century new techniques were already being explored. The *Annals of Fou-liang*, written before 1322, notes that at Ching-te-chen "they have experts at moulding, painting, and engraving." Painting we will consider in a moment. Moulding and engraving can be seen in the so-called *shu-fu* ("privy council") wares. It seems likely that the *shu-fu* was the first ware to be made at Ching-te-chen on imperial order. It comprises chiefly bowls and dishes with incised, moulded, or slip decoration—generally consisting of flower sprays, lotus leaves, or phoenixes amid clouds—under a bluish-white (*ch'ing-pai*) glaze. Sometimes the characters "*shu-fu*" are included, or other auspicious words such as *fu* ("happiness"), *shou* ("long life"), or *lu* ("emolument"). Closely related to these are the stem cups, ewers, bottles, and jars whose decoration consists of applied reliefs, often in zones separated by pearl beading, and the figurines, chiefly the *bodhisattvas*, which were used in domestic shrines. Several exquisite examples, including the Kuanyin illustrated here, have been excavated from Yüan-period sites in Peking.

UNDERGLAZE RED AND BLUE

Another of the innovations at Ching-te-chen which may have occurred before the middle of the fourteenth century was painting in copper red under the glaze, a technique that may have originated in Korea. Some of the most attractive early Chinese examples are the bottles with graceful pear-shaped body and flaring lip decorated with sketchily drawn flower-sprays or clouds. During the Ming Dynasty the designs become more elaborate, but the copper red had a dull colour and a tendency to run, and was consequently abandoned in the fifteenth century in favour of the more manageable underglaze cobalt blue. For a while, attempts were made to combine not only underglaze copper red and cobalt blue but also beading, carving, and openwork. The wine jar illustrated here, excavated at Pao-ting in Shensi, is a splendid example of the extravagant blending of techniques that is so typical of Yüan taste.

In the whole history of ceramics, probably no single ware has been so much admired as Chinese blue and white. It has been imitated in Japan, Indochina, and Persia, and it was the inspiration of the pottery of Delft and other European factories; its devotees have ranged from the headhunters of Borneo to Whistler and Oscar Wilde, and its enchantment is still at work. There is much debate as to when blue and white was first made in China. Underglaze painting had been practised in Hunan and Szechwan as early as the T'ang Dynasty, more successfully in the Tz'u-chou wares of the Sung. There are reports of blue-and-white shards being found in the dedicatory deposit of a Sung pagoda in Chekiang, but the earliest securely dated piece yet discovered was found in a tomb of 1319 at Chiu-chiang in Kiangsi, while the most famous is the pair

239 Pair of vases dedicated to a temple in Kiangsi in 1351. Porcelain decorated in underglaze blue. Yüan Dynasty.

238 Wine jar. White porcelain decorated with openwork panels and painting in underglaze red and blue. Excavated at Pao-ting, Hopei. Yüan Dynasty.

of vases in the Percival David Foundation in London, dedicated to a temple in Kiangsi in 1351, which show a mature handling of this difficult technique. The earliest textual reference—if indeed the term *ch'ing-hua* ("blue-green flower") means blue and white, and not some other ware—occurs in the *Ko-ku yao-lun* of 1387–1388, which dismisses it, along with five-colour wares, as "very vulgar." The general opinion is that the technique was developed at Ching-te-chen at the beginning of the fourteenth century. It may have been influenced by a technique brought from Persia to the early Mongol capital at Karakoram in the thirteenth century and thence transmitted to China.

The pieces that can with confidence be dated in the Yüan period include large, boldly decorated dishes, pear-shaped vases, ewers and flasks in Near Eastern shapes, bowls, and stem cups. Decoration includes Near Eastern ogival panels and Chinese dragons, lotus and chrysanthemum scrolls, and narrower bands of petals some of which had already appeared in the Ch'i-chou wares of the Southern Sung. By the time the David vases were made, the potters and painters at Ching-te-chen had fully mastered their art, and the vases and dishes of the next hundred years are unequalled for their splendour of shape and beauty of decoration. The drawing is free and bold, yet delicate, the blue varying from almost pure ultramarine to a dull, greyish colour with a tendency to clot and turn black where it runs thickest—a fault that was eradicated by the sixteenth century and cleverly imitated in the eighteenth.

10
The Ming Dynasty

The ferment into which central China had sunk as the Mongols lost control of the country was finally resolved when in 1368 Chu Yüan-chang, in turn shepherd, monk, bandit, warlord, and emperor, sent his armies north to occupy Peking, from which the last Yüan ruler had fled. He proclaimed himself emperor of the Ming Dynasty, set up his capital in Nanking, and within four years had not only recovered all the territories held by the T'ang at the height of their power but had extended his control over the Trans-Baikal region and Manchuria as well. He built at Nanking a capital with a city wall twenty miles in circumference, the longest in the world, and under him and his successor central and southern China enjoyed a new importance and prosperity. But in 1421 the third emperor, the usurper Yung-lo,[1] moved his capital back to Peking whence he had received his chief support in his struggle for power, and it was he who rebuilt it on the scale we see today. But Peking, on two counts, was a bad site. It was situated too far to the north of China's new economic centre of gravity, the Yangtse Valley, and it was also highly vulnerable: China's northern enemies—now the Manchus—had only to cross the Great Wall to be at the gates of the city. The troubles that beset the Ming Dynasty throughout its subsequent history were largely due on the one hand to the remoteness of the capital from the parts of China that mattered most—the centre and south—and on the other hand to the constant tension along the Great Wall, which lay only forty miles from Peking. Yung-lo was aggressive and secured the frontier, but his successors were weak and corrupt, the victims of eunuchs at court and rebellions in the provinces, and before long the northern defences were left unguarded.

We have already drawn a parallel between the Warring States and classical Greece on the one hand and Han China and ancient Rome on the other. It is said that history never repeats itself, but the similar relationship of Ming China to Sung is too close to be passed over. For the mixture of power and corruption, grandeur and lack of imagination that characterised the Roman Empire is equally marked in the Ming Dynasty, which took as its model not

240 The Great Wall at Pa-ta-ling.
Chiefly Ming period.

the weak and dreamy Sung, whom they despised, but the splendour, the vigour—and, be it said, the occasional vulgarity—of T'ang. In the early fifteenth century Ming China was immensely powerful. Her navies roamed the southern seas under the remarkable admiral Cheng Ho, a eunuch in high favour with the emperor. But he was not bent on conquest: the Chinese have never been interested in stretching their empire beyond the seas. The admiral's five expeditions between 1405 and 1433 were carried out for the purpose of showing the flag, making alliances, and opening up trade routes, and incidentally collecting curiosities for the entertainment of the court. China had no other interest in the outside world. Before the end of the century, however, Vasco da Gama had rounded the Cape of Good Hope; by 1509 the Portuguese were in Malacca, by 1516 in Canton, and China was finally forced to take account of the existence of the Western barbarians by reason of their aggressive conduct around her own shores.

The splendour of the Ming court concealed a creeping paralysis. Officials, selected by civil service examinations which centred round the stultifying complexities of the "eight-legged essay," became increasingly conservative and conventional in outlook. The energies of savants at court were devoted less to original scholarship than to the preparation of such vast works as the *Yunglo ta-tien*, an encyclopaedia in 11,095 volumes compiled between 1403 and 1407. The Sung emperors had been men of taste and education, able to inspire the best in their scholars and painters; the Ming emperors were for the most part ruffians, usurpers, or weak victims of court intrigue. As a result, the palace tradition in painting petered out in a frozen academicism, and for significant devlopments we must look not to the court but to the scholars, collectors, and amateurs, many of them men of private means, who carried on the tradition that had been established by the indepen-

241 The Liu-yüan Garden. Soochow, Kiangsu.

dent literati of the Yüan Dynasty. If the history of later Chinese painting is to be told in the lives and work of the scholar-gentry—and there are many in China today who would dispute this—then we must focus our attention from now on almost exclusively on the corner of southeastern China that embraces southern Kiangsu and northern Chekiang, a region rich in agriculture, silk, and thriving cities where most of the material and cultural wealth was now created and enjoyed. Here, chiefly in Soochow, the landed gentry of the fifteenth century cultivated their estates, digging pools and heaping up artificial hills to create those famous gardens in which scholars, poets, and painters could enjoy the fruits of the good life. Several of these gardens in Soochow and Wuhsi, with their pavilions and winding paths, their fancy rocks dredged out of the bed of Lake T'ai (and often "improved" by rock specialists), have been restored for the pleasure of the modern visitor, among them the Garden to Linger In (Liu Yüan) and the Garden of the Clumsy Politician (Cho-cheng Yüan). One of the court-

MAP 12 Artistic centres of southeastern China.

yards of the Garden of the Master of the Fishing Nets (Wang-shih Yüan), copied with scrupulous care in the Metropolitan Museum of Art, New York, is further enriched with the exquisite group of rocks illustrated here, which was rescued from an abandoned garden in Soochow.

In and around Soochow also were concentrated the great private collections, those, for example, of Hsiang Mo-lin (1525–1590) and Liang Ch'ing-piao (1620–1691) whose seal on a painting, if accepted as genuine, was often all the collector required to attest to its authenticity. It was these and other private collectors in the southeast, rather than the Ming emperors, who preserved the remaining masterpieces of Sung and Yüan, some of which were to find their way back into the imperial collection in the eighteenth century.

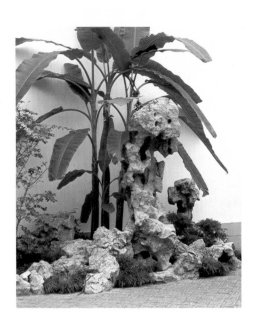

242 Arrangement of rocks from a Soochow garden.

The good life meant leisure, not only for the practice of the arts but also for the pleasures of philosophy. There were many schools active in the Ming, most of which were Neo-Confucian with a colouring of Buddhist and Taoist ideas. The Northern Sung Neo-Confucianists had stressed the importance, in self-cultivation, of the "investigation of things," which included not only the mind, and the underlying principles of things, but phenomena and objects in themselves. By the Ming, however, study of the external world had largely given way to study of such questions as the relationship between mind and principle and between knowledge and action. For a rigorous analysis of things, Ming thinkers such as Wang Yang-ming substituted a tendency to generalise about them. The painting of the Ming scholars, like their thinking, tended to be more intuitive and generalised, as if their predecessors had learned all they needed from the study of the natural world, and now they had only to "borrow," as Su Tung-p'o had put it, mountains and water, rocks and trees, as vehicles for the expression of thought and feeling.

Ming painting consequently does both less and more than that of the Sung: less in that it tells us so little about nature as we see it—compare, for example, the landscapes of Shen Chou and Wen Cheng-ming in this chapter with those of Fan K'uan and Chang Tse-tuan—and more in the sense that the painting is now made to carry a much richer freight of poetic and philosophical content; or, to put it another way, the painter is saying things which cannot be fully expressed in terms of the conventional language of landscape. It was to help carry that freight, to extend, as the Chinese put it, the idea beyond the pictorial image itself, that the painter's inscription became longer and more richly poetic or philosophical in tone. Thus did the art of painting at its upper levels become more and more interwoven with the ideals and attitudes of the élite, and more and more remote from the experience of the rest of society.

This was a great age of art scholarship. Not only the connoisseurs and collectors but the painters themselves were students of the tradition, often deriving inspiration less from nature than from the great works of the old masters which they studied and copied as an essential part of their artistic activity.

The encyclopaedic knowledge of the styles of the old masters which amateur painters begin to display at about this time was aided by the development of colour printing. The earliest colour printing known in China—indeed, in the world—is a two-colour frontispiece to a Buddhist *sūtra* scroll, dated 1346. Under the Ming, erotic books were illustrated in line blocks using up to five colours. One of the first books to include full-colour printing was the *Ch'eng-shih mo-yüan* (*Mr. Ch'eng's Miscellany*), published in 1606, for which a few of the monochrome illustrations were copied from prints given to the author by the great Jesuit missionary Matteo Ricci. The art of colour printing reached its peak in the rare group of anonymous seventeenth-century prints known as the Kaempfer Series, after an early collector of them, and in the

COLOUR PRINTING

243 *Pomegranates*. Colour woodblock print from the Kaempfer Series. Seventeenth century.

244 *Lotus Leaves and Root*. Colour woodblock print from the *Treatise on the Paintings and Writings of the Ten Bamboo Studio*. Ming Dynasty, early seventeenth century.

Shih-chu-chai shu-hua p'u (*Treatise on the Paintings and Writings of the Ten Bamboo Studio*), published in 1633. Thereafter, handbooks on the art of painting as a pastime were to proliferate, the most famous being the *Chieh-tzu-yüan hua-chüan* (*Painting Manual of the Mustard Seed Garden*), first published in five parts in 1679, later expanded, and still used as a technical primer by Chinese students and amateurs today.

In the late seventeenth century, Chinese colour prints reached Japan, stimulating the growth of the art, although full-colour printing was not perfected in Japan till the middle of the eighteenth century. But, while in Japan the colour print developed as a vital art form in its own right, of which the masters recognised and exploited the very limitations of the medium, in China it was, like so much else, the servant of painting, and was always at its best when it most nearly gave the effect of ink and watercolour. After a sad decline in the nineteenth century, the art was revived in the 1920s, and the Jung-pao-chai studio in Peking has become famous both for its decorated letter papers and for its faithful replicas of paintings printed with up to two hundred individual blocks.

MING COURTLY AND PROFESSIONAL PAINTING

At the Ming court there was no personality of the stature of Chao Meng-fu to mediate between the academicians and the literati, who kept their distance and made no attempt to influence court art for the better. The Ming emperors, following the T'ang model, made the Bureau of Painting a subdivision of the Hanlin Academy, but it was no longer the centre of culture and art that it had been in former times. It was set up in the Jen-chih Palace within the Imperial City, and a special office under the Directorate of Palace Eunuchs was established to control it. Painters were honoured with high military titles (to distinguish them from civil officials!) and treated with great favour. This favour, however, depended upon absolute obedience to a rigid code of rules and regulations. They lived, moreover, in terror of their lives. Under Hung-wu, four court painters, including Chou Wei and Chao Yüan, were executed for having incurred that savage monarch's displeasure, and it is astonishing that any good work was produced at all. By the time of the Hsüan-te emperor (Hsüan-tsung, 1426–1435), who was a painter himself, the lot of the senior court artists had much improved, and they were now given the time-honoured rank of *tai-chao*, yet Tai Chin could be dismissed from the emperor's service because he had allegedly painted the garment of a fisherman red, the colour reserved for officials at imperial audiences.

245 Lü Chi (late fifteenth to early sixteenth century), *Pair of Wild Geese on a Snowy Bank*. Hanging scroll. Ink and colour on silk. Ming Dynasty.

Among the most talented of the court painters was Pien Wen-chin (c. 1400–1440), who specialised in painting birds and flowers in the careful, decorative, outline-filled-with-colour style of the Five Dynasties master Huang Ch'üan. In his day he was considered one of the three greatest artists living; and, indeed, his works have a delicacy and perfection of drawing and colour which link him rather to Hui-tsung than to any of the host of decorators who turned out paintings by the hundred to adorn the innumerable

246 Shih-jui (mid-fifteenth century),
Strolling among Flowers. Detail of a
handscroll. Ink and colour on silk. Ming
Dynasty.

rooms of the palace. Dominant among these was the late-fifteenth-century painter Lü Chi, whose magnificently decorative compositions, rich in colour, definite and precise in form, conservative in style, were exactly suited to the taste of his imperial patrons. In landscape, the models for the professionals were Ma Yüan and Hsia Kuei, partly because they too had been academicians, partly because the basis of their work, like that of the flower painters, was not self-expression but technique, and technique could be learned. Ni Tuan, for example, modelled himself on Ma Yüan, Chou Wen-ching on both Ma Yüan and Hsia Kuei, Li Tsai—who is said to have impressed the great Japanese landscape painter Sesshū—on Ma Yüan and Kuo Hsi, while Shih-jui, in a beautiful handscroll reproduced here, skillfully combined the monumental manner of the Northern Sung with the rich mineral-blue-and-green colouring of a still older tradition. In most of their works, however, the element of mystery in the Sung romantics has hardened into a brilliant eclecticism, its poetry into prose.

Tai Chin (1388–1452), a highly skilled landscapist at the Ming court, was a native of Hangchow in Chekiang, where the styles of

247 Tai Chin (1388–1452), *Fishermen*. Detail of a handscroll. Ink and colour on paper. Ming Dynasty.

the Southern Sung academy still lingered on in the fifteenth century. After his dismissal and return to Hangchow, his influence in the area became so wide as to give the name of his province to a very loosely connected group of professional landscape painters. The Che School, as it was called, embodied the forms and conventions of the Ma–Hsia tradition but treated them with a quite unacademic looseness and freedom, as is shown for instance in the detail from Tai Chin's handscroll, *Fishermen*, in the Freer Gallery. Other outstanding artists of the Che School were Wu Wei and Chang Lu, both of whom specialised in figures in a landscape setting. At the very end of the dynasty, the Che School enjoyed a brief final flowering in the elegant and eclectic art of Lan Ying (1578–1660).

PAINTING OF
THE LITERATI:
THE WU SCHOOL

During the prosperous middle years of the Ming Dynasty, the Wu district was the artistic capital of China and Shen Chou (1427–1509) its greatest ornament, and so regarded as the founder of the Wu School, although he was only the chief of a long line of landscape painters in Wu that we could trace back to the T'ang Dynasty. Shen Chou never took office, living in comfortable retirement, a benevolent landlord and member of a circle of scholars and collectors. Under his scholarly teacher Liu Chüeh, he early mastered a wide range of styles from those of the Southern Sung academicians to those of the Yüan recluses. His well-known landscapes in the manner of Ni Tsan are extremely revealing of the change that was coming over the literary man's art during the Ming Dynasty; for while Ni Tsan is almost forbiddingly plain and austere, Shen Chou is something of an extrovert who cannot help infusing a human warmth into his paintings. As he said of himself, "Ni Tsan is simple; I am complex," and whenever he painted in the manner of that difficult master his teacher would shout at him "Overdone! Overdone!"

For Shen Chou was no mere copyist. He distilled a style that is uniquely his own. Whether in long panoramic landscapes, tall mountain scrolls, or small album paintings, his brushwork, seemingly so casual, is in fact firm and confident, his detail crystal-clear yet never obtrusive, his figures—like those of Canaletto—reduced to a kind of shorthand yet full of character, his composition open and informal yet perfectly integrated; and when he used colour he did so with an exquisite freshness and restraint. It is not surprising that he became so popular, not only with the literati of his own time but also with modern connoisseurs. His debt to Huang Kung-wang is subtly evoked both in the style of the album-leaf illustrated here and in the subject, a self-portrait, *Returning Home from the Land of the Immortals*, with, as his companion, a crane who might be the spirit of crazy old Huang himself. Above it Shen Chou writes:

> With crane and lute aboard, I am homeward bound across the lake;
> White clouds and red leaves are flying together.
> My home lies in the very depths of the mountains,
> Among the bamboo, the sound of reading, a tiny couch and a humble gate.[2]

Such album-leaves are full of a natural charm, and it is only when we compare Shen Chou with Huang Kung-wang or Wu Chen that we realise that something of their grandeur and breadth of vision is lost. But it was Shen Chou who transformed their lofty style into a language which other, less gifted, painters could draw upon.

248 Shen Chou (1427–1509), *Landscape in the Manner of Ni Tsan*. Hanging scroll dated equivalent to 1484. Ink on paper. Ming Dynasty.

249 Shen Chou, *Returning Home from the Land of the Immortals*. Album-leaf mounted as a handscroll. Ink and colour on paper. Ming Dynasty.

250 Wen Cheng-ming (1470–1559), *Cypress and Rock*. Handscroll dated equivalent to 1550. Ink on paper. Ming Dynasty.

251 T'ang Yin (1479–1523), *Gentleman Playing the Lute in a Landscape*. Detail of a handscroll. Ink and colour on paper. Ming Dynasty.

As Shen Chou dominated the Wu district in the fifteenth century, so did his follower Wen Cheng-ming (1470–1559) in the sixteenth. Ten times Wen Cheng-ming sat for the civil service examinations, and ten times he failed; but he was called to the capital where he spent a few unhappy years as an official before returning in 1527 to Soochow, to devote the rest of his life to art and scholarship. There he systematically collected and studied the works of the old masters, not only the Yüan literati but such classical and academic figures as Li Ch'eng and Chao Po-chü. His studio became an informal academy through which he passed on his high standards and encyclopaedic knowledge of the history and technique of painting to his many pupils, who included not only his son Wen

Chia and his nephew Wen Po-jen, but the flower painter Ch'en Shun (Ch'en Tao-fu, 1483–1544) and the fastidious landscapist Lu Chih (1496–1576). Although much of his own work is refined and sensitive, in his last years Wen Cheng-ming painted a series of remarkable scrolls of old juniper trees in pure monochrome ink which in their rugged, twisted forms seem to symbolise the noble spirit of the old scholar-painter himself.

T'ANG YIN AND CH'IU YING

Two painters active in the first half of the sixteenth century cannot be classified as belonging either to the Che or to the Wu School. T'ang Yin (1479–1523) ruined a promising career when he became involved in a scandal over the civil service examinations; he could thus no longer be considered a gentleman, and spent the rest of his life between the brothels and wine shops of Soochow on the one hand and the seclusion of a Buddhist temple on the other, painting for a living. He was a pupil of Chou Ch'en, but his true teachers were Li T'ang, Liu Sung-nien, Ma Yüan, and the great Yüan masters. He was also a friend of Shen Chou and Wen Cheng-ming, and because of this is often classed with the Wu School. But his towering mountains painted in monochrome ink on silk are a re-creation of the forms and conventions of the Sung landscapists, though with a hint of mannerism and exaggeration. *Gentleman Playing the Lute in a Landscape* (Palace Museum, Taipei) is a good example of his work at its most refined—scholarly in content, yet highly professional in technique. It is these conflicting qualities in his style and social position that make him so hard to place and have caused a Japanese scholar to label him "neo-academic."

Into the same class falls Ch'iu Ying (c. 1494–c. 1552), a man born also in Wu-hsien, but of lowly origins, who was neither court painter nor scholar but a humble professional, idealising in his pictures the leisurely life of the gentry whose equal he could never be, and happiest if one of the great literati condescended to write a eulogy on one of his paintings. He is also famous for his long handscrolls on silk depicting with exquisite detail and delicate colour such popular themes as the "Lute Song," life at the court of Ming Huang, or the multifarious activities of the ladies of the palace. As a landscapist he was the last great exponent of the green-and-blue style (Fig. 252), though he worked also in the ink-washes of the Wu School. His delightful pictures are widely appreciated both in China and in the West, and next to Wang Hui he is probably the most-forged painter in the history of Chinese art.

TUNG CH'I-CH'ANG AND THE NORTHERN AND SOUTHERN SCHOOLS

In the later development of the literary school no man played a more significant part than the scholar-painter Tung Ch'i-ch'ang (1555–1636), who rose to high office under Wan-li. Not only did he embody, in his paintings, the aesthetic ideals of his class, but he also gave them theoretical formulation through his critical writings. Tung Ch'i-ch'ang was himself a noted calligrapher and a painter of landscapes in monochrome ink, but though he worked freely in the manner of the great masters of the past he was not content merely to paraphrase. His creative reinterpretations of earlier styles are animated by a passion for pure form, an expressive distortion, which few of his followers understood. They preferred to take his theories more literally, to the detriment of scholarly painting during the ensuing three centuries.

For it is as a critic that Tung Ch'i-ch'ang is most famous. It was he, borrowing an idea first put forward by the poet-painter Tu Ch'iung in the fifteenth century, who formulated the theory of the Northern and Southern schools for the express purpose of demonstrating the superiority of the *wen-jen* tradition above all others. It was primarily through landscape painting, he maintained, that the scholar and gentleman expressed his understanding of the working of the moral law in nature, and hence his own moral worth. The *wen-jen*, indeed, was the only kind of man who *could* do this successfully, for only he was free from both the control of the academy on the one hand and the necessity to make a living on the other; moreover, being a scholar, his wide reading in poetry and the classics gave him an understanding of the nature of things combined with an epicurean nobility of taste which the lower orders of professional painters could never hope to acquire. In the spontaneous play of ink and brush, in his freedom to select, omit, suggest, the *wen-jen* had at his command a language capable of conveying the loftiest and subtlest concepts.

The tradition of the independent scholar-painter, Tung Ch'i-ch'ang called the Southern School, because he saw in it an analogy to the southern school of Ch'an Buddhism in the T'ang Dynasty, which had held that enlightenment came of itself, spontaneously and suddenly, as opposed to the Northern or gradual school, which had maintained that it could only be attained by degrees, after a lifetime of preparation and training. To Tung Ch'i-ch'ang,

252 Ch'iu Ying (c. 1494–1552+), *Saying Farewell at Hsün-yang*. Detail of a handscroll. Ink and colour on paper. Ming Dynasty.

all the great gentleman-painters were members of the Southern School, beginning in the T'ang Dynasty with his hero Wang Wei—for a genuine work from whose hand he spent a lifetime in searching—and passing down through the great Northern Sung masters Tung Yüan, Chü-jan, Li Ch'eng, and Fan K'uan, via Mi Fu (another ideal Southern type) to the four great masters of Yüan, ending in his own time with Shen Chou and Wen Cheng-ming. To the Northern School he relegated all academic and court painters, beginning with Li Ssu-hsün and his followers in the green-and-blue style, including among them Li T'ang and Liu Sung-nien, Ma Yüan and Hsia Kuei. He had some difficulty over Chao Meng-fu. As a scholar, calligrapher, and landscapist Tung admired him greatly, but he could never bring himself to include Chao among the Southern painters, because Chao had compromised himself in the eyes of the literati by taking office under the Mongols.

This arbitrary scheme has dominated, and bedevilled, Chinese art criticism for three centuries, while its obvious inconsistencies have caused endless confusion. We may discount Tung Ch'i-ch'ang's prejudices and refuse to accept his classification in individual cases, but his division into Northern and Southern schools does in fact represent a just division between two kinds of painting—the one in its purest manifestations academic, eclectic, precise, and decorative; the other free, calligraphic, personal, subjective. At the same time, the doctrine of the two schools is a reflection of the feelings of the scholars themselves at this time. The corrupt Ming Dynasty was approaching its downfall, and men of integrity were once again withdrawing from public service into obscurity. Amateur painters found comfort and reassurance in the belief that they were the élite, upholding the Confucian virtues, while painters and scholars in the service of the emperor were prostituting their talents. However vague or inaccurate it might be as an interpretation of the history of Chinese painting,

253 Tung Ch'i-ch'ang (1555–1636), *Dwelling in the Ch'ing-pien Mountains*. Hanging scroll. Ink and colour on paper. Ming Dynasty.

254 Shao Mi (active 1620–1640). Leaf from an album of landscapes dated equivalent to 1638. Ink and colour on paper. Ming Dynasty.

255 Ch'en Hung-shou (1599–1652),
Portrait of the Poet Po Chü-i, in the
manner of Li Lung-mien. Detail of a
handscroll dated equivalent to 1649. Ink
and colour on paper. Ch'ing Dynasty.

256 Wu Pin (c. 1568–1626), *Fantastic
Landscape*. Hanging scroll dated
equivalent to 1616. Ink and colour on
paper. Ming Dynasty.

the doctrine is important as a symptom of the predicament of the
late Ming literati—a predicament that is also reflected in their own
painting.

The court by now was hopelessly corrupt and no longer the focus of loyalty and enlightened patronage. Intellectuals withdrew
in despair, a few courageous spirits forming semi-secret protest
groups such as the Tung-lin Society, with which Tung Ch'i-
ch'ang was loosely connected. Yet the decay of the dynasty produced no real closing of the ranks, and the literati were often divided and isolated. Soochow, Sung-chiang, and Nanking were
only the chief among many centres of artistic activity, and it has
been said that there were now as many schools as there were
painters.

But, to compensate, the breakdown also loosened traditional
restraints upon originality. While many artists still followed in the
footsteps of Shen Chou and Wen Cheng-ming, others broke free,
even if their new direction was only into a highly individualistic,
if not willfully perverse, reinterpretation of some aspect of the
tradition itself. In Soochow, for example, Shao Mi and Chao Tso
turned back to the Northern Sung for inspiration, Ch'en Hung-
shou gave an ironic twist to the ancient figure-painting style that
derived from Ku K'ai-chih, Wu Pin produced fantastic distortions
of the classic styles of Li Ch'eng and Fan K'uan whose realism and
chiaroscuro effects were for a time influenced by European engravings brought by the first Jesuit missionaries. Some artists defended the Ma-Hsia School, and one even went so far as to deni-
grate the immaculate Ni Tsan. In such a chaotic and crumbling
world, in which a painter's search for a style, an attitude, a place in
the tradition was at the same time a search for his own identity, it
is easy to see how a dominating personality such as Tung Ch'i-
ch'ang could take command of all but the most independent painters and sweep them along behind him down the path to a new
orthodoxy.

SCULPTURE

To many people "Ming" means not painting—for it is only recently that Ming painting has come to be appreciated outside
China—but the decorative arts. Before we discuss them, however, we should say a word about sculpture. As, during the Sung

and Yüan dynasties, Buddhism gradually loosened its hold over the mind and heart of China, so did Buddhist sculpture decline. Under the Ming revival, what sculpture lacks in spiritual content it makes up for in vigour—a vigour shown, for example, in the colossal guardian figures of officials, warriors, and animals which line the "spirit way" leading to the tombs of the Ming emperors outside Nanking and Peking. The casting of large figures in iron had developed during the Sung Dynasty as a substitute for the more precious bronze. The finest of these figures have a simplicity and compactness of modelling that makes them extremely impressive. Far greater freedom of movement was possible in ceramic sculpture, which now lent an air of gaiety and splendour to the roof ridges of palaces and temples, already glittering with yellow, blue, and green tiles. The boldy conceived figure of a man in green-and-brown-glazed terracotta (*liu-li*) inscribed "Made by Master Ma" and dated equivalent to 1524, is a splendid example of the confident manner in which Ming craftsmen revived and transformed the style of the T'ang Dynasty.

257 Yen-lo-wang (Yama). Pottery decorated with coloured glazes, *liu-li* ware. Inscribed "Made by Master Ma" and dated equivalent to 1524. Ming Dynasty.

The Ming love of colour and of all that made for luxurious living was satisfied by the cloisonné enamel, the lacquer, and the richly woven textiles that were worn both by officials and by the wealthier members of the middle class. Figured silks, embroideries, and brocades have a long history in China: examples of all types going back to the T'ang Dynasty and earlier have been found in the dry desert sand of Chinese Turkestan, and are more perfectly preserved in the Shōsōin Repository at Nara. Many T'ang motifs were still in use in the Sung Dynasty, to be revived once again in the Ming and continued, with some modifications, in the Ch'ing.

The great achievement of the Sung weavers had been the perfecting of *k'o-ssu*, a form of tapestry woven from silk, using a needle as a shuttle. This technique had been invented in central Asia, possibly by the Sogdians, improved by the Uighurs, and finally passed on to the Chinese early in the eleventh century. The term *k'o-ssu*, translatable as "cut silk," is descriptive of the vertical gaps between adjacent areas of colour visible when it is held up to the light, but other variants suggest that *k'o-ssu* is probably a transliteration of the Persian *gazz* or Arabic *khazz* referring to silk and silk products. After the debacle of 1125–1127, the art was taken to the Southern Sung court at Hangchow, where an historian records that *k'o-ssu* was used for mounting paintings and binding books in the Imperial Collection. It was also used for robes, decorative panels, and, most astonishingly, for translating paintings and calligraphy into the weaver's art. We can form some idea of its microscopic fineness when we realise that whereas the finest Gobelins tapestry has 8 to 11 warp threads to the centimetre, Sung *k'o-ssu* has up to 24, and 116 weft threads per centimetre of warp as against the 22 of Gobelins. In the Yüan Dynasty, when trade across central Asia was probably easier than at any other period in history, panels of *k'o-ssu* were exported at enormous expense to Europe,

TEXTILES

258 *Magician Changing a Bamboo Walking-Stick into a Dragon. K'o-ssu* silk tapestry. Ming Dynasty.

213

259 Imperial dragon robe. Woven silk tapestry. Ch'ing Dynasty.

where they were incorporated into the vestments of the cathedrals in Danzig, Vienna, Perugia, and Regensburg, while splendid examples have also been found in Egypt. Hung-wu, the spartan and ferocious first emperor of the Ming, forbade its manufacture, but it was revived early in the fifteenth century under Hsüan-te.

Little Sung *k'o-ssu* has survived until today, but we may get an impression of the splendour of the weaver's art from the court robes of the Ming Dynasty. These include both the ceremonial robes made for the imperial sacrifices and decorated with the "twelve emblems"—sacred symbols which go back to hallowed antiquity and are described in the early Chou *Classic of History* (*Shu-ching*)—and the so-called *dragon robes*, a term used to describe a long semiformal robe worn by courtiers and officials from Ming times onward, embroidered with a number of motifs of which the chief, and most conspicuous, is the dragon. If we are to judge from surviving paintings, dragons with three claws had been a principal motif on T'ang robes and became an established institution under the Yüan. Strict sumptuary laws introduced in the fourteenth century permitted a robe with four-clawed dragons (*mang-p'ao*) to lesser nobles and officials, while restricting to the emperor and royal princes dragons with five claws. The Ming emperors wore robes decorated with both the dragons and the twelve symbols. Dragon robes became extremely popular under the Ch'ing, when the regulations of 1759 confined the twelve symbols, at least in theory, to the emperor's personal use.

The Ming and Ch'ing official robes were further embellished with "Mandarin squares," badges of rank which had already been used decoratively in the Yüan Dynasty and were first prescribed for official dress in the sumptuary laws of 1391. The Ming squares were broad and made in one piece, generally from *k'o-ssu* tapestry. The Manchus, who were content with embroidery, used them in pairs back and front, splitting the front panel down the centre to fit the open riding jacket. Official regulations prescribed bird motifs (symbolising literary elegance) for civilian officials, animals (suggesting fierce courage) for the military; the emblems were precisely graded from the fabulous monster *ch'i-lin* (for dukes, marquesses, and imperial sons-in-law), through white crane or golden pheasant (for civil officials of the first and second ranks), down to the silver pheasant for the fifth to ninth. Military ranks had a corresponding animal scale. Though these woven and embroidered robes vanished from the official world with the passing of the Manchus in 1912, they may still be seen today lending their glitter and pageantry to the traditional theatre.

LACQUER

Lacquer, as we have seen, was already a highly developed craft in the Warring States and Han. At that time, decoration was restricted to painting on a ground of solid colour or incising through one colour to expose another beneath it. In the T'ang Dynasty there started the practice of applying lacquer in many layers—to mirror backs, for example—and then, before it had completely hardened, inlaying it with mother-of-pearl. Sung taste preferred simple unadorned shapes in plain dark red, brown, or black. By the Yüan, lacquer was again being inlaid or engraved, while a new technique, invented in the Sung and known by its Japanese name of *guri*, involved cutting scroll patterns in V-shaped channels that revealed the multiple layers of contrasting colour.

The typical Chinese lacquer of the Ming period was carved in red with rich floral or pictorial designs (*t'i-hung*); either these were modelled in full relief or the background was cut away leaving the design in flat relief as on many Han engraved stones. By the Chia-ching period, two styles, one sharp-edged, the other more rounded, can be identified. The cup stand illustrated here is a richly carved example of Ming *t'i-hung*; it was evidently a palace piece through two dynasties, for in addition to the reign mark of Yung-lo (1403–1424) it carries around the inside an inscription by Ch'ien-lung, dated 1781. The polychrome tray is typical of the more elaborate and intricate taste of the seventeenth century. The names of several master craftsmen of the early Ming period are recorded. Nevertheless, lacquer is easy to imitate, and many of the signed pieces of the fifteenth century, and those bearing Ming reign titles (*nien-hao*), may well be later Chinese or Japanese forgeries. Indeed, by the fifteenth century the Japanese had become so expert in lacquerwork that Chinese craftsmen were journeying to Japan to learn the art.

260 Cup stand. Carved lacquer. Yung-lo (1403–1424) reign mark and Ch'ien-lung inscription dated equivalent to 1781. Ming Dynasty.

261 Rectangular dish. Red, greenish-black, and yellow lacquer carved with a design of dragons amid clouds and waves. Ming Dynasty, Wan-li period (1573–1620).

The earliest known reference to cloisonné enamel in China occurs in the *Ko-ku yao-lun*, a collectors' and connoisseurs' miscellany first published in 1388, where it is referred to as Ta-shih ("Moslem") ware. No authentic examples of fourteenth-century Chinese enamel work have yet been identified, though it is quite possible that pieces were being made for ritual use in the Lama temples of Peking during the latter part of the Yüan Dynasty.[3]

This art, which permits such rich and vibrant colour effects, came into its own in the Ming Dynasty, and the oldest positively dateable pieces have the Hsüan-te reign mark (1426–1435). They

CLOISONNÉ ENAMEL

262 Incense burner. Cloisonné enamel.
Ming Dynasty, sixteenth century.

include incense burners in archaic shapes, dishes and boxes, animals and birds, and pieces for the scholar's desk. In the early Ming pieces the *cloisons* are not perfectly filled and the surface has a certain roughness; but the designs are bold, vigorous, and endlessly varied. Unfortunately, as the technique improved these qualities were lost, till we come to the technically perfect yet lifeless and mechanical enamelware of the time of Ch'ien-lung. Identical shapes and designs were produced through the nineteenth century, while today the reappearance of these same designs bears eloquent witness to the archaistic revival of traditional arts under the People's Republic.

CERAMICS

Porcelain collectors are generally agreed that a climax of refinement combined with freedom of drawing was reached in the blue and white of the Hsüan-te period (1426–1435), to which belong the earliest pieces bearing genuine reign marks. In addition to

263 Wine vessel, *tsun*, in the form of a phoenix. Cloisonné enamel. Ch'ing Dynasty, eighteenth century.

dishes there are stem cups, jars, and flattened pilgrim flasks, in which an earlier tendency to crowd the surface with flowers, waves, tendrils, and other motifs set in ogival panels has given way to a delicate play of lotus scrolls, vines, or chrysanthemums over a white surface. The influence of courtly flower painting on porcelain decoration is very evident in the lovely blue-and-white flask illustrated here.

The blue and white of each reign has its own character, which the connoisseur can readily recognise. The Hsüan-te style continued in the Ch'eng-hua era, though beside it there now appeared in the so-called *palace bowls* a new style more delicate and less sure in its drawing and consequently easier for the eighteenth-century potter to imitate. In the Cheng-te period (1506–1521) there was a great demand among the Moslem eunuchs at court for the so-called *Mohammedan wares*, consisting mostly of brush rests, lamps, boxes, and other articles for the writing-table, whose decoration incorporated inscriptions in Persian or Arabic. The pieces of the reign of Chia-ching (1522–1566) and Wan-li (1573–1620) show a change from the old floral decoration to more naturalistic scenes, while in the former reign the Taoist leanings of the court made popular such auspicious subjects as pine trees, immortals, cranes, and deer.

The imperial wares of the Wan-li period closely follow those of Chia-ching; but there now begins a general decline in quality, the result of mass production, rigidity in the requirements of the palace, and the exhaustion of the fine-quality clay-beds at Ching-te-chen. The most pleasing and vigorous blue and whites of the last hundred years of the Ming are wares made in the numerous commercial kilns. These are of two kinds: those made for domestic

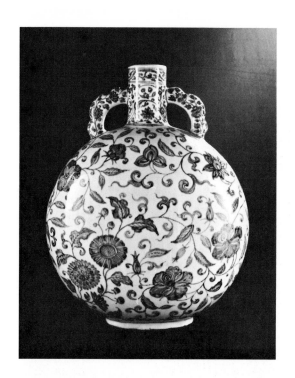

264 Flask. Porcelain decorated in underglaze blue. Ming Dynasty, Yung-lo period (1403–1424).

265 Bowl. Porcelain decorated in underglaze blue. Ming Dynasty, Ch'eng-hua period (1465–1487).

consumption (*min*: literally, "people's"), and the even more roughly modelled and painted export wares, made for sale or barter to the countries of Southeast Asia, to which I shall refer again. Soon after 1600 a particular type of thin, brittle Wan-li export blue and white began to reach Europe. This ware, called *kraak* porcelain because it had formed part of the cargo of two Portuguese carracks captured on the high seas by the Dutch, caused a sensation when it appeared on the market in Holland, and was soon being imitated in the painted faience of Delft and Lowestoft. In spite of intense efforts on the part of European potters, however, it was not until 1709 that the Dresden potter Johann Böttger, an alchemist in the service of Augustus the Strong of Saxony, succeeded for the first time in making true porcelain—more than a thousand years after it had been perfected in China.

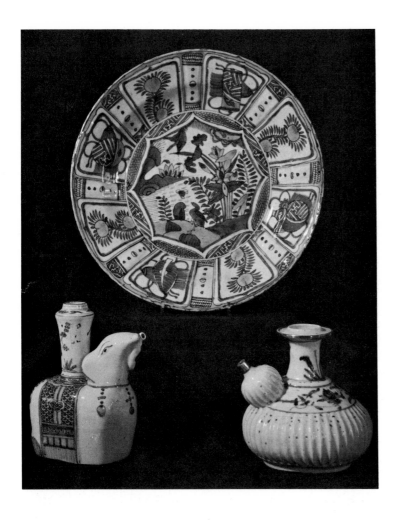

266 Kraak ware dish and two *kendi*
(drinking flasks), export ware. Porcelain
decorated in underglaze blue. Late Ming
period.

By the middle of the fifteenth century, Ching-te-chen had become
the greatest ceramic centre in China. It was ideally situated near
the Poyang Lake, whence its products could go by lake and river
to Nanking and by the Grand Canal to Peking. An apparently
inexhaustible supply of china clay lay in the Ma-ch'ang hills
nearby, while just across the river at Hu-t'ien was to be found the
other essential ingredient in the manufacture of porcelain,
namely, "china stone" (*tz'u-shih*, often called *pai tun-tzu* when in
its prepared form). By this time there had evolved out of the
nearly white *ch'ing-pai* and *shu-fu* wares of Sung and Yüan a true
white porcelain, which was perhaps already being made at the imperial factory for the Hung-wu emperor. The most beautiful
pieces, however, were those made in the Yung-lo period, most of
which are decorated with motifs incised or painted in white slip
under the glaze—a technique aptly called *an-hua* ("secret decoration"), for it is scarcely visible unless the vessel is held up to the
light. From the technical point of view, the eighteenth-century
white glaze is perhaps more perfect, but it lacks the luminous
warmth of the Ming surface. In some Yung-lo bowls the porcelain
body is pared down to paper-thinness so that the vessel appears to

CHING-TE-CHEN

267 "Monk's hat" jug. Porcelain
covered with *pao-shih-hung*, "precious
stone red," glaze. Ch'ien-lung
inscription of 1775 engraved on the
base. Ming Dynasty, Hsüan-te period
(1424–1435).

consist of nothing but glaze: these are the so-called "bodiless" (*t'o-t'ai*) pieces. Almost as beautiful are the monochromes produced at Ching-te-chen, notably the dishes, stem cups, and bowls decorated in "sacrificial red" (*chi-hung*) or with imperial dragons under a yellow or blue glaze.

268 Kuanyin, Fukien Te-hua ware. White porcelain. Early Ch'ing Dynasty.

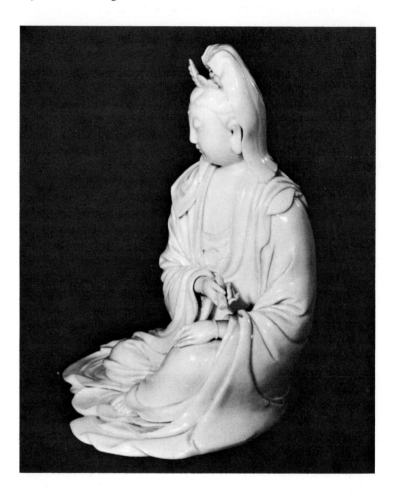

TE-HUA WARES

Ching-te-chen, though the largest, was by no means the only Ming factory producing monochrome wares. A white porcelain was being made at Te-hua in Fukien as early as the Sung Dynasty. The Fukien wares, indeed, form a race apart. They never bear reign marks and are extremely difficult to date accurately, while they range in quality from the finest porcelain with a luminous, warm, and lustrous glaze with a brownish tint where it runs thick, to the more metallic products of the last hundred years. In addition to vessels, boxes, and ceremonial objects such as incense burners and other bronze shapes, the Te-hua potters modelled figurines in white porcelain, a lovely example being the Kuanyin from the Barlow Collection at the University of Sussex. Here the subtle turn of the body and the liquid flow of the drapery show how much ceramic modelling was influenced by the sweeping linear rhythms of figure painting. From the seventeenth century onward, Te-hua ware was shipped from Amoy to Europe where, as "blanc-de-Chine," it had a considerable vogue and was widely imitated.

Robust Ming taste is more typically expressed in the so-called *san-ts'ai*, "three-colour" wares. The exact origin of this family is not known, though there is reason to believe that it may have been produced in stoneware at Chün-chou in Honan, where the kilns were still active in the sixteenth century, while it was also, and more perfectly, made in porcelain at Ching-te-chen. The colours are generally more than three in number, but the ware takes its name from the rich turquoise, dark blue, and aubergine that predominate. They are thickly applied in bold floral motifs and separated by raised ridges which perform the same function as the *cloisons* on Ming enamels. Occasionally the turquoise glaze was used alone, as on a magnificent vase in the Percival David Foundation inscribed on the shoulder "For general use in the Inner Palace." Although this ware follows the range of shapes earlier made in Chün ware—storage jars, flowerpots, and bulb bowls—the vigour of the shapes and the strong, rich-coloured glazes show how much closer in feeling Ming art often comes to that of the T'ang Dynasty than to that of the Sung.

Another important Ming family comprises the five-colour wares (*wu-ts'ai*), a name given to the white porcelain painted with enamel colours, an art which was perfected by Chinese potters, possibly in the reign of Hsüan-te or slightly earlier. The colours were prepared from the material of lead glaze, applied over the glaze or directly on the biscuit, and the vessel fired again at a lower temperature. These pieces are generally small and often of the bodiless variety, the painting—chiefly vines, flower sprays, and flowering branches—disposed with perfect taste and a subtle balance over the white ground. Sometimes, as in the *tou-ts'ai* ware, the enamels were combined with underglaze blue, but this phrase, which means "contesting colours," hardly does justice to their delicate harmony. The five-colour enamels of the Ch'eng-hua period were never surpassed for their purity of form and decoration; they were already being copied in the Wan-li period, while even to the expert the finest of eighteenth-century copies are almost indistinguishable from them.

Besides these exquisite enamels the sixteenth century saw the appearance of a more full-blooded style, often decorated with genre scenes, chiefly in red and yellow; this style was to be echoed in the *wu-ts'ai* wares made for export in the South China kilns—known generally by the misleading term "Swatow" ware. No pottery was made at Swatow itself, but some of these rough and vigorous porcelains (both blue and white and five-colour enamels) were made up-river at Ch'ao-chou and probably at Shih-ma in Fukien, while a kiln producing blue and white export ware has recently

ENAMELLED WARES

269 Vase. Stoneware decorated in *san-ts'ai* (three-colour) enamels. Ming Dynasty.

270 "Fish jar." Porcelain decorated in *wu-ts'ai* (five-colour) enamels. Ming Dynasty, Chia-ching period (1522–1566).

EXPORT WARES

been found in Ch'üan-chou. Swatow, however, was most probably the main port of dispatch.

China's export trade to the *Nan-hai* ("South Seas") was already flourishing in the Sung and Yüan dynasties. Early Ming wares, including celadon, Ching-te-chen white porcelain, Tz'u-chou, *ch'ing-pai*, and Te-hua have been found in huge quantities over an area extending from the Philippines to East Africa. These export wares had a profound influence on the native pottery of Southeast Asia. Blue and white was not only successfully imitated in Japan (Imari ware), but also in Annam and, less successfully because they lacked the cobalt, by the Thai potters at Sawankalok, although the Siamese kilns succeeded in producing a beautiful celadon of their own. Before the end of the Ming Dynasty, the Chinese factories were also making porcelain on order for European customers, notably through the Dutch "factory" established at Batavia (Jakarta) in 1602; but this trade, which was to play so great a part in the contacts between Europe and China, we must leave to Chapter 11.

271 Dish, "Swatow" ware. Porcelain decorated in underglaze blue and enamel red. Probably from Shih-ma, Fukien. Late Ming period.

11
The Ch'ing Dynasty

The Ming Dynasty was brought down by the same inexorable laws of decay that had operated on previous occasions in Chinese history: corruption and the power of the eunuchs at court, leading to breakdown of the administration, large-scale banditry in the provinces, and an enemy on the northern frontier patiently awaiting their opportunity to pounce. In 1618 the Manchu nation had been founded on the banks of the bleak Sungari River. Seven years later the Great Khan, Nurhachi, set up his capital in Mukden, calling his new dynasty Ch'ing ("pure") to parallel the Chinese Ming ("bright"). Their moment came when in 1644 the Chinese general Wu San-kuei appealed to them for help to expel the rebel leader Li Tzu-ch'eng, who had forced his way into Peking. The Manchus promptly accepted, drove Li out of the city and, while Wu San-kuei was pursuing him into the west, quietly occupied the capital and proclaimed the rule of the Ch'ing Dynasty. Their unexpected success left the Manchus momentarily exposed, but Wu San-kuei waited ten years before attempting to dislodge them, and then it was too late. But for nearly four decades he and his successors held South China, which was not finally secured for the Manchus until the capture of Kunming in 1682. As a result of this long civil war there grew up a bitter hostility between north and south; Peking became increasingly remote and suspicious, the south ever more rebellious and independent.

It would be wrong, however, to picture the Manchus as barbarous and destructive. On the contrary, they felt an intense admiration for Chinese culture and leaned heavily on the Chinese official class; but the more independent-minded of the Chinese intelligentsia remained, as under the Mongols, a potential source of danger to the régime, and the Manchu trust of the literati did not extend to a sympathetic consideration for the "new thought" of the eighteenth century. They clung to the most reactionary forms of Confucianism, becoming more Chinese than the Chinese themselves and strenuously resisting up to the end every one of the attempts at reform which were made by the literati, some of whom were responsible and far-seeing men. This hide-bound refusal to recognise the inevitability of change eventually brought about the collapse of the dynasty. But for the first century and a half, China basked in the sunlight of her restored power and prosperity, which was due largely to the work of the second emperor, K'ang-hsi (Sheng-tsu), who ruled from 1662 to 1722. It was he who pacified all China and restored her to a paramount position in Asia.

During the seventeenth century and the first half of the eighteenth, China was treated with enormous respect by the European powers; admiration for her principles of government filled the writers of the Enlightenment, while her arts gave birth to two waves of *chinoiserie*, the first late in the seventeenth century, the second at the height of the eighteenth. During this period, indeed, China had far more influence upon the thought, art, and material life of Europe than had Europe on China. Western influence was confined to court, where, ever since the arrival of the Jesuit missionary Matteo Ricci in 1601, the emperors and their immediate entourage of officials and savants had been in close touch with Western art and learning. But apart from Adam Schall's reform of the calendar and Verbiest's ordnance factory, the arts and techniques brought by the Jesuits were treated by all but a tiny minority of scholars as mere curiosities. This was not entirely true of painting, however: although the literati generally ignored European art, some academicians at court made strenuous efforts to master Western shading and perspective in the interest of greater realism.

The most characteristic intellectual achievement of the Ch'ing Dynasty was, like that of the Ming, not creative so much as synthetic and analytical; indeed, in the production of such works as the huge anthology *Ku-chin t'u-shu chi-ch'eng* (1729) and the *Ssu-k'u ch'üan-shu*, an encyclopaedia in 36,000 volumes begun in 1773 and completed nine years later, the Ch'ing scholars far surpassed their Ming forebears in sheer industry. Characteristically, also, the latter work was compiled not primarily in the interest of scholarship but as a means of seeking out all books whose contents might reflect upon the legitimacy of the Manchu Dynasty. Nevertheless this enormous compilation contains many otherwise unknown texts and the fruits of much scholarly research. For this was an antiquarian age when, as never before, men looked back into the past, burrowing into the classics, dabbling in archaeology, forming huge collections of books and manuscripts, paintings, porcelain, and archaic bronzes. Most famous among the collectors of paintings were Liang Ch'ing-piao, to whom we have already referred, and the salt magnate An I-chou (c. 1683–c. 1740), many of whose treasures were later acquired by the Ch'ien-lung emperor. Ch'ien-lung, who had succeeded the able but ruthless Yung-cheng in 1736, possessed a prodigious enthusiasm for works of art, and in his hands the imperial collection grew to a size and importance it had not seen since the days of Hui-tsung.[1] His taste, however, was not always equal to his enthusiasm, and he

272 Peking, the Forbidden City, looking north from the Wu-men to the T'ai-ho-men.
A corner of the T'ai-ho-tien is visible beyond. Ming and early Ch'ing dynasties.

273 Yüan-ming-yüan. Ruins of the Belvedere (Fang-wai-kuan), designed by Giuseppe Castiglione (Lang Shih-ning, 1688–1766).

could not resist the temptation to write indifferent poems all over his most treasured paintings and stamp them with large and conspicuous seals. His abdication in 1796 (because he considered it unfilial to occupy the throne longer than his illustrious grandfather) marks the end of the great days of the Ch'ing Dynasty. To the familiar story of internal dissolution was added the aggressive advance of the European powers, whose original admiration had now given way to hostility, provoked by impatience at irksome trade restrictions. We need not linger over the tragic history of the nineteenth century, the shameful Opium Wars, the failure of the Taiping rebels to regenerate China, and her final abasement after 1900. This was not a time for greatness either in politics or in the arts. Though a few of the literati maintained a certain independence of spirit, the educated class as a whole took its lead more and more from the reactionary attitude of the Manchus.

ARCHITECTURE

The architecture of the Ch'ing Dynasty was, in the main, a tame and cautious continuation of the style of the Ming—with one notable exception. To the northwest of the capital, the K'ang-hsi emperor laid out an extensive summer palace, in emulation of the great hunting parks of the Han and Liang emperors. It was enlarged by Yung-cheng, who gave it the name Yüan-ming-yüan, and again by Ch'ien-lung, who added to the many palaces already built in it an assembly of pleasure pavilions designed by the Italian Jesuit missionary and court painter Giuseppe Castiglione (1688–1766) in a somewhat Chinesified version of Italian eighteenth-century Baroque. These extraordinary buildings were set about with fountains and waterworks devised by Father Benoît, a French Jesuit who had familiarized himself with the fountains at Versailles and Saint-Cloud. Every detail down to the furniture was specially designed (much of it copied from French engravings) and the walls hung with mirrors and Gobelins tapestries sent out by the French court in 1767. The total effect must have been bizarre in the extreme.

The heyday of the Yüan-ming-yüan was brief. Before the end of the eighteenth century the fountains had long ceased to play, and Ch'ien-lung's successors so neglected their transplanted Versailles that by the time the Western allies destroyed the foreign-style buildings and looted their treasures in 1860, the Yüan-ming-yüan had already fallen into a sad autumnal state of disrepair. But we can obtain some idea of what it looked like in its prime from the engravings made by Castiglione's Chinese assistants in 1786. The last great architectural achievement—if indeed it deserves the name—of the Manchus was the Summer Palace built by the dowager empress Tz'u-hsi on the shore of the Po-hai to the west of the Forbidden City with funds raised by public subscription to construct a navy. Although she was condemned at the time for her extravagance, it has since been observed that had she built a fleet it would certainly have been sunk by the Japanese in the war of 1895, while the Summer Palace will endure for centuries. Less pretentious and far more appealing among the late Ch'ing ceremonial

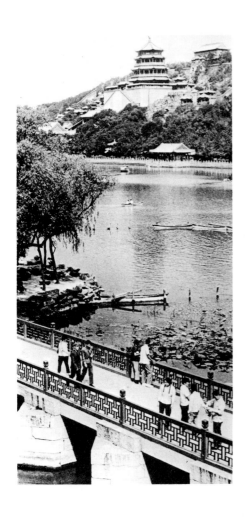

274 The Po-hai and the Summer Palace, Peking. Late Ch'ing Dynasty.

275 The Hall of Annual Prayers, Ch'i-nien-tien, in the Precinct of the Altar of Heaven, Peking. Late Ch'ing Dynasty.

buildings is the Ch'i-nien-tien (Hall of Annual Prayers), erected near the Altar of Heaven in the southern quarter of the city late in the nineteenth century. Its gleaming marble terraces, its richly painted woodwork, and the deep blue of its tiles dazzle the eye. But we need only to glance at the poverty of its detail, its reliance upon paint rather than functional carpentry, to realise that, fairy-like as is its total effect, the Hall of Annual Prayers marks the final exhaustion of a great tradition.

276 Chiao Ping-chen (active c. 1670–1710), *Country Pursuits*. Detail of a hanging scroll. Ink and colour on silk. Ch'ing Dynasty.

EUROPEAN INFLUENCE ON COURTLY ART

In a corner of the Forbidden City, K'ang-hsi set aside a courtyard known as the Ch'i-hsiang-kung as a studio and repair shop where Chinese and Jesuit artists and mechanics worked side-by-side, painting, engraving, repairing clocks and musical instruments. The court painter Chiao Ping-chen studied perspective there under the Jesuits and embodied what he learned in forty-six illustrations to the famous agricultural work *Keng-chih-t'u*, while his pupil Leng Mei was noted for delightful but over-elegant paintings of court ladies, generally in a garden setting and showing some knowledge of Western perspective.[2] Castiglione, who had arrived in Peking in 1715, was already an accomplished painter. He soon mastered the academic manner of his Chinese colleagues, and proceeded to create a synthetic style in which a Chinese medium and technique are blended with Western naturalism, aided by a subtle use of shading. He was a favourite at court, where his still-life paintings, portraits, and long handscrolls depicting

277 Giuseppe Castiglione, *A Hundred Horses in a Landscape*. Detail of a handscroll. Ink and colour on silk. Ch'ing Dynasty.

horses in a landscape or scenes of court life signed, very carefully, with his Chinese name, Lang Shih-ning, were greatly admired. He had numerous pupils and imitators, for the decorative realism of his style was particularly suited to the kind of "furniture paint-ing" the palace required in such quantities to decorate its endless apartments. Castiglione, however, no more affected the general trend of Chinese painting in his time than did the Chinese artists working for the Europeans in Canton and Hongkong. Tsou I-kuei (1686–1772), a court artist to Ch'ien-lung noted for the painstak-ing realism of his flower paintings (an art in which he probably in-fluenced the style of his colleague Castiglione), much admired Western perspective and shading. "If they paint a palace or a man-sion on a wall," he wrote, "one would almost feel induced to enter it." But he makes it clear that these are mere technicalities, to be kept in their proper place. "The student should learn something of their achievements so as to improve his own method. But their technique of strokes is negligible. Even if they attain perfection it is merely craftsmanship. Thus, foreign painting cannot be called art."[3]

The most interesting and neglected of the Ch'ing professional painters, however, was the group around Li Yin and Yüan Chiang, both of whom were working in prosperous Yangchow between about 1690 and 1725, after which the latter, like his son(?) Yüan Yao, became a court painter. They are chiefly noted for hav-ing given a violent twist to the long-moribund Northern tradition by applying to the style and composition of early Sung masters such as Kuo Hsi the fantastic distortions of the late Ming expres-sionists. The blend of fantasy and mannerism in their work can be seen in the meticulously painted landscape by Yüan Chiang illus-trated here.

278 Yüan Chiang (early eighteenth century), *Gentlemen Conversing in a Landscape*. Hanging scroll. Ink and colour on silk. Ch'ing Dynasty.

279 Hung-jen (1610–1664), *The Coming of Autumn*. Hanging scroll. Ink on paper. Ch'ing Dynasty.

WEN-JEN HUA   The literati shared none of the academicians' admiration for European painting, for they now felt themselves to be the custodians of a tradition infinitely more precious than anything the West had to offer. Through the sheer force of his personality, Tung Ch'i-ch'ang had given a new interpretation to the style of Tung Yüan and Chü-jan, but his less-gifted followers in the Ch'ing Dynasty took his injunction to restore the past, *fu ku*, too literally, and in the work of many of the hundreds of painters who now appear on the scene, the free, unfettered art of the leading Ming literati froze into a new academicism in which an obsession with style, and the repetition of hackneyed themes, too often took the place of a direct response to nature. But even if many of the amateur painters played the same tunes over and over again, they played them beautifully, and the enjoyment we derive from this kind of painting comes not from any sudden revelation or strength of feeling but from subtle nuances in the touch of the brush such as we savour in listening to an all-too-familiar piano sonata interpreted by different hands.

But to give the impression that all Ch'ing painting is conventional would be utterly misleading. For the story of the seventeenth century—of the decay and death of the Ming, the Manchu invasion, the civil war and the decades of uncertainty that followed it, and the return to stability under K'ang-hsi—can all be read in the painting of the period, which for this reason is one of the most fascinating, and intensely studied, in the history of Chinese art. The Ming loyalists, called *I-min* (literally, "people left over"), suffered acutely, for their code forbade their taking or holding office under a new dynasty, most of all an alien one. Some committed suicide, some became destitute, some turned wanderer, monk, recluse, or eccentric, while some even lived to become loyal and contented servants of that remarkable Manchu ruler K'ang-hsi.

Thus, the *I-min* responded to the crisis in a number of ways, and there can be no greater contrast than that between, say, the two masters Hung-jen and Kung Hsien. The Anhui monk Hung-jen (1610–1664) faced his predicament by transcending it, expressing

280 Kung Hsien (1620–1689), *A Thousand Peaks and Myriad Ravines*. Hanging scroll. Ink on paper. Ch'ing Dynasty.

281 Chu Ta (Pa-ta Shan-jen, 1626–c. 1705), *Landscape in the Manner of Tung Yüan*. Hanging scroll. Ink on paper.

282 Chu Ta, *Two Birds*. Album-leaf. Ink on paper. Ch'ing Dynasty.

an inner serenity of spirit through his sparse, dry landscapes, fragile yet incredibly solid, sensitive yet monumental, that exude an atmosphere of almost unearthly purity very close to that of Ni Tsan. By contrast, the Nanking painter Kung Hsien (1620–1689) seems to have been "on the run" for some years after the fall of the Ming, harried by political enemies and private anxieties. His desolate, prisonlike landscape in the Rietberg Museum, Zürich, in which no life seems possible, nothing stirs, may owe something to the expressive distortions of Tung Ch'i-ch'ang, but like other pictures of his middle years it is also symbolic, both of the condition of his native land raped by the Manchus and of his own desperate sense of having, literally, nowhere to turn. Yet, his whole career cannot have been so turbulent, for he was also a noted poet, calligrapher, publisher, and art teacher—his pupil Wang Kai was the chief compiler of the *Painting Manual of the Mustard Seed Garden* referred to in Chapter 10—while the calm, monumental landscapes of his later years seem to suggest that he had found peace at last.

These masters were certainly individualists, but that label is often, and arbitrarily, reserved for three great painters who dominated the art of early Ch'ing as Hung-jen and Kung Hsien never did. These men are Chu Ta (1626–c. 1705), K'un-ts'an (Shih-ch'i, c. 1610–c. 1670), and Tao-chi (Shih-t'ao, 1641–c. 1710). Chu Ta, or Pa-ta Shan-jen as he signed himself in his later years, was a distant descendant of the Ming imperial house who on the advent of the Manchus became a monk. When his father died, so the story goes, he was struck dumb and would only shout and laugh, the butt of the children who ran after his ragged figure in the streets. He turned his back not only upon the world but upon the art of painting as practised in his time. His brush style appears careless and slapdash, and yet, like that of the Ch'an eccentrics who were his spiritual ancestors, it is incredibly sure and confident. His landscapes executed in a dashing shorthand carry Tung Ch'i-ch'ang's creative distortion of the Southern tradition to a pitch that must have shocked the orthodox disciples of the late Ming master. Perhaps his peculiar genius shows best in his swift album-sketches, in which a small angry-looking bird perches upon a rock in an infinity of space, or in his studies of fishlike rocks and rocklike fishes, drawn in a few brilliant sweeping lines of the brush. This is "ink-play" at its most unrestrained; yet it is no mere empty virtuosity, for Pa-ta's deceptively simple style captures the very essence of the flowers, plants, and creatures he portrays.

Shih-t'ao and Shih-ch'i are linked together by Chinese art historians as the Two Stones (*Erh Shih*), yet there is no positive evidence that they were close friends. Shih-ch'i was a devout Buddhist who spent all his life as a monk, his later years as abbot of a monastery at Nanking, an austere and unapproachable recluse. The texture of his landscapes, painted with a dry, scrubby brush, has the groping, almost fumbling, quality that we find in Cézanne, and as in Cézanne this very awkwardness, this refusal to make concessions to the viewer, are witness to the painter's integrity. Yet the final effect—in the beautiful autumn landscape in the British Museum, for example—gives an impression of grandeur and serenity.

Shih-t'ao, whose family name was Chu Jo-chi, was a lineal descendant of the founder of the Ming Dynasty, which fell when he was still a child. He later joined the Buddhist community on Lu-shan, taking the monastic name Tao-chi. But he was no recluse, and never a real monk. In 1657 he went to live in Hangchow, and thereafter spent much of his life wandering about China, visiting sacred mountains in the company of monks, scholars, and painter friends such as Mei Ch'ing. He spent nearly three years in Peking (where he and Wang Yüan-ch'i collaborated on a picture of *Bamboo and Rocks*), and finally settled in Yangchow, where he severed his monastic vows and, because he had no private income, became a professional, though highly respected, painter. A chronicle of Yangchow, a city famous for its gardens, says that one of his favourite hobbies was "piling up stones"—i.e., designing gardens, among which his Garden of Ten Thousand Rocks laid out for the Yü family was considered his masterpiece. It may be that some of his little album landscapes were actually suggestions for garden designs.

Shih-t'ao's aesthetic philosophy is contained in the *Hua yü lu*, a profound and often obscure document that cannot possibly be

283 K'un-ts'an (Shih-ch'i, c. 1610–1693), *Autumn Landscape*. Handscroll dated equivalent to 1666. Ink and colour on paper. Ch'ing Dynasty.

284 Shih-t'ao (Tao-chi, 1641–c. 1710), *The Peach Blossom Spring*, illustrating a story by T'ao Yüan-ming. Detail of a handscroll. Ink and colour on paper. Ch'ing Dynasty.

summarised in a paragraph, for it is not a statement of a coherent aesthetic theory so much as a series of utterances that touch on reality, nature, man, and art at many levels.[4] Central to Shih-t'ao's thinking is the concept of the *i hua* (literally, "one line" or "one painting"); but the very word *i* might mean the transcendent "One," the unity of man and nature, or simply "the single," and *hua* either the art of painting, "delineation," or simply "line." Drawing both upon earlier aesthetic theorists going back as far as Tsung Ping and Hsieh Ho, and upon Buddhist and Taoist metaphysics, and not unaware of his own genius, Shih-t'ao meditates upon the artist's power to express his sense of oneness with living nature in the unified, uninterrupted flow of inspiration through his brush. While we may not be able to analyse Shih-t'ao's thought with any precision, in reading the *Hua yü lu* we become aware of what the art, and the act, of painting could mean to the inspired practitioner.

In his own painting, Shih-t'ao justifies his claim in the *Hua yü lu* that by establishing the one-line method he has created a method out of an absence of method. His concept of the ecstatic union of the artist with nature is by no means new, but nowhere in the whole of later Chinese art will we find it expressed with so much spontaneous charm. Whether in a handscroll such as the delightful illustration to T'ao Yüan-ming's *The Peach Blossom Spring*, or in a towering landscape such as the magnificent view of Mount Lu in the Sumitomo Collection, or in any of his album-leaves, his forms and colours are ever fresh, his spirit light, his inventiveness and wit inexhaustible.

All these masters, although they drew upon the tradition, developed and enriched it and so touched the heights. At a rather lower level we encounter a host of painters who represent the orthodox stream, flowing down from Shen Chou, Wen Chengming, and Tung Ch'i-ch'ang, that survived the upheaval and kept its steady, if seldom adventurous, course, growing ever broader and shallower as the Ch'ing Dynasty settled into its long stagnation. In the seventeenth century, however, the stream still runs

285 Shih-t'ao, *A Man in a House Beneath a Cliff*. Album-leaf. Ink and colour on paper. Ch'ing Dynasty.

286 Wang Hui (1632–1717), *Landscape
in the Manner of Fan K'uan*. Hanging
scroll dated equivalent to 1695. Ink and
colour on paper. Ch'ing Dynasty.

287 Wang Yüan-ch'i (1642–1715),
Landscape in the Manner of Ni Tsan.
Hanging scroll. Ink and colour on silk.
Ch'ing Dynasty.

strong in the work of the "Six Great Masters of the Early Ch'ing
Dynasty," that is, the Four Wangs, Wu Li, and Yün Shou-ping.
The earliest of the four was Wang Shih-min (1592–1680) who had
learned to paint from the hand of Tung Ch'i-ch'ang himself. Like
his master, he deeply admired the broad, relaxed manner of
Huang Kung-wang, and his great series of landscapes in the manner of the Yüan recluse, painted in his seventies, are among the
noblest achievements of the Ch'ing literati. Wang Chien (1598–
1677), his close friend and pupil, was an even more conscientious
follower of the Yüan masters. More gifted was Wang Hui (1632–

1717), who as a poor student had been introduced to Wang Shih-min, whose pupil he became. He devoted much of his talent to the imitation of early masters, and his huge oeuvre consists chiefly of endless variations on the styles of Tung Yüan and Chü-jan as they had been successively reinterpreted by Huang Kung-wang, Tung Ch'i-ch'ang, and Wang Shih-min. The Palace Museum collection also contains a number of clever pastiches of tenth-century and Northern Sung landscapes which are almost certainly his work.

Of the four Wangs, Wang Yüan-ch'i (1642–1715) was the most gifted and original. The grandson of Wang Shih-min, he rose to high office under the Manchus, becoming chancellor of the Han-lin Academy and vice president of the Board of Finance. He was a favourite of K'ang-hsi, who frequently summoned him to paint in his presence, and he was appointed one of the editors of the great anthology of painting and calligraphy, *P'ei-wen-chai shu-hua-p'u*, published on imperial order in 1708. But Wang Yüan-ch'i was no academician. Although he drew his themes from the Yüan masters, notably Ni Tsan, and his curious angular rocks and gaunt trees from Tung Ch'i-ch'ang, he had an obsession with form, unique in a Chinese painter. With deep concentration, he would, as it were, pull apart and reassemble the rocks and mountains in his paintings, like a cubist. These are not landscapes to wander in; they are, rather, semi-abstract creations of the painter's mind, to-tally convincing in their own terms and remote from the man-nered distortions of Yüan Chiang and his school.

Yün Shou-p'ing (commonly known as Yün Nan-t'ien, 1633–1690) was the son of a Ming loyalist and consequently had to live in partial obscurity in the Soochow-Hangchow region far from the capital, where he supported himself by his painting and callig-raphy. There is a widely held belief that he gave up landscape painting because he felt he could not compete with his friend Wang Hui. But although his flower paintings, chiefly fans and al-bum-leaves, show an exquisite mastery of the "boneless" tech-nique, his heart was in the landscape, which he painted with a sen-sitivity often lacking in the work of the brilliant Wang Hui.

Wu Li, born in 1632, is of unusual interest because he came un-der the influence of the Jesuits, was baptised, and spent six years studying theology in Macao where he was ordained in 1688,

288 Yün Shou-p'ing (1633–1690), *Autumn Fragrance: Chrysanthemum and Convolvulus*. Ink and colour on paper. Ch'ing Dynasty.

289 Wu Li (1632–1718), *White Clouds and Green Mountains*. Detail of a handscroll. Ink and colour on silk. Ch'ing Dynasty.

290 Chin Nung (1687–1764), *Plum Blossoms*. Hanging scroll dated equivalent to 1761. Ink on paper. Ch'ing Dynasty.

thereafter devoting the rest of his life to missionary work in Kiangsu. However, his conversion in no way changed his style of painting. A pupil of Wang Chien and an intimate friend of Wang Hui, he called himself Mo-ching Tao-jen, the Taoist of the Ink-well (in the literal sense of Alice's treacle-well), continuing, after an unproductive period following his conversion, to paint in the eclectic manner of the early Ch'ing *wen-jen*, without a hint of European influence, until his death in 1718.

By the eighteenth century the settled state of China had created a great demand for works of art, notably in such prosperous cities as Yangchow, at the juncture of the Grand Canal with the Yangtse River. Here, to bear witness to their newly acquired gentry status, salt merchants and other rich traders built up libraries and art collections, entertained scholars, poets, and painters, and expected to be entertained in return. Among the many artists who competed for their patronage the most talented was a group that came later to be known as the Eight Eccentrics of Yangchow, whose idiosyncrasies of behaviour or technique were, in some cases at least, partly assumed for professional reasons. The hallmark of Chin Nung's art, for instance, was not so much his deft ink paintings of birds, flowers, or bamboo as his heavy square calligraphy, derived from Han stone inscriptions, which offers a teasing contrast to the light touch of the brushwork in his *Plum Blossoms*, illustrated here; his contemporary, Huang Shen (1687–c. 1768), playfully distorted the figure style of Ch'en Hung-shou, which was itself already a playful distortion of ancient models; while the art of the immensely prolific Hua Yen (1682–c. 1755) is often an airy commentary on the styles of the great masters of Sung bird and flower painting. In all the works illustrated there is an appeal to the antique, but the attitude of these painters is much less serious than that of their late Ming and early Ch'ing predecessors, and they carry the burden of tradition more lightly. Their purpose, after all, was to please.

Groupings such as the Four Wangs and the Eight Eccentrics of Yangchow have little foundation in fact. Where, for instance, does

291 Huang Shen (1687–1768+), *The Poet T'ao Yüan-ming Enjoys the Early Chrysanthemums*. Album-leaf. Ink and colour on paper.

individualism stop and eccentricity begin? Were there really eight eccentrics in Yangchow? There were many kinds of eccentricity, natural and assumed. Some of these men were friends, others not; some were outstanding, others obscure. But these traditional groupings are helpful, as much to Chinese as to Western readers, in reducing the bewildering number of Ch'ing painters to some sort of order.

The careers of some of the Yangchow eccentrics point to a change in the status of the so-called amateur painter in China. Ideally, he was a salaried official or a man of means who painted for pleasure in his spare time. But among the Ch'ing gentlemen-painters were many—indeed, a majority—who were not officials and had no private income, and so were forced (although this was not openly acknowledged) to paint for a living. Wang Hui, for example, painted industriously for the patrons in whose mansions he lodged for months on end, Chin Nung for a time was reduced to decorating lanterns, while competition for the patronage of the Yangchow salt merchants forced artists such as Chin Nung and Huang Shen to cultivate a deliberate oddity to attract their attention. The miracle is that the discipline of the brush still held, and that there is still so much sensibility and freshness in their art.

The art of the individualists and eccentrics can be interpreted as their private protest against the academicism of the painting of the time. But as the Ch'ing settled deeper into the stagnation that seems to have been the fate of every long-lived dynasty in Chinese history, the lamp of individualism burned more and more dimly, while a kind of spiritual paralysis seemed to grip the scholar class as a whole. Only in Canton and in the brash new treaty port of Shanghai, grown suddenly rich in the late nineteenth century, was

292 Hua Yen (1682–1755+), *Birds, Tree and Rock*. Hanging scroll dated equivalent to 1745. Ink and colour on paper. Ch'ing Dynasty.

239

patronage to be found. Though not of the kind that a fastidious scholar-painter would have sought, it did breathe new life into one corner of the Chinese art world, just as the onslaught of Western industrial civilisation was about to be unleashed on China.

CERAMICS

The political disasters that so deeply affected the seventeenth-century painters touched all Chinese society. None except perhaps the poorest peasant was unaffected. Confusion, banditry, and civil war, which had begun after the death of Wan-li in 1620 and was not stilled until well into the reign of K'ang-hsi, wreaked havoc on the ceramics industry at Ching-te-chen. Already before the end of the Ming Dynasty the imperial wares had sharply declined both in quality and quantity. The reign of T'ien-chi is noted for a coarse, brittle blue and white prized in Japan as *tenkei* ware, but marked pieces from his successor Ch'ung-cheng's era are very rare and of poor quality. During these years China lost to Japan the great market she had built up in Southeast Asia and Europe, and she did not fully recover it again till Wu San-kuei had been defeated and South China brought once more under the control of the central government. Consequently the so-called transitional wares of the mid-seventeenth century, being for the most part continuations of earlier styles, are not always easy to identify. The most characteristic of them are strongly built blue and white jars, bowls, and vases decorated with figures in landscapes, rocks and flowers (especially the "tulip," possibly based on a European motif) in a thick violet glaze which Chinese collectors call "ghost's-face blue" (*kuei-mien-ch'ing*) and Western connoisseurs "violets in milk." Many of them were made primarily for export and, like the export blue and white of Chia-ching and Wan-li, have a freedom of drawing that gives them considerable appeal.

CHING-TE-CHEN

No abrupt change at Ching-te-chen followed the establishment of the new dynasty. The imperial factory was still functioning, after a fashion, in the 1650s, and pieces produced during these unsettled years represent, as we would expect, a continuation of the style of the Wan-li period. Between 1673 and 1675, Kiangsi was laid waste by Wu San-kuei's rebel horde, and in the latter year the imperial factories at Ching-te-chen were destroyed. They were rebuilt a few years later. In 1682 K'ang-hsi appointed as director of the Imperial Kilns Ts'ang Ying-hsüan, a secretary in the Imperial Parks Department. Ts'ang, who arrived at Ching-te-chen early in the following year, was the first of three great directors whose names are linked to this supreme moment in the history of Ching-te-chen. It is not known precisely when Ts'ang retired. In 1726 Yung-cheng appointed Nien Hsi-yao, who in turn was succeeded in 1736 by his assistant T'ang Ying, who held the office until 1749 or 1753. Thus, Ts'ang's directorship corresponds roughly to the K'ang-hsi period, Nien's to Yung-cheng, and T'ang Ying's to the first years of Ch'ien-lung.

Two Chinese works give us useful information on the Imperial Kilns and their output, though both were written after the factory had begun to decline. Chu Yen published his *T'ao-shuo* in 1774, while the *Ching-te-chen t'ao-lu* written by Lan P'u did not appear till 1815. The most valuable description, however, is that contained in two letters written by the French Jesuit Père d'Entrecolles, who was in China from 1698 to 1741 and not only had influential friends at court but also many converts among the humble artisans in the factories at Ching-te-chen. These letters, dated 1712 and 1722, give a vivid picture of the whole process of manufacture, of which he was an intelligent observer.[5] He recounts how the *petuntse* ("china stone") and *kaolin* ("china clay") are quarried and prepared, and the enormous labour involved in kneading the clay. He describes a degree of specialisation among the decorators so minute that it is a wonder the painting has any life at all: "One workman does nothing but draw the first colour line beneath the rims of the pieces; another traces flowers, while a third one paints. . . . The men who sketch the outlines learn sketching, but not painting; those who paint [i.e., apply the colour] study only painting, but not sketching," all in the interests of absolute uniformity. Elsewhere he says that a single piece might pass through the hands of seventy men. He speaks of the hazards of the kiln and of how a whole firing is often lost by accident or miscalculation. He tells how the emperor would send down Sung Dynasty *kuan*, Ju, Ting, and Ch'ai wares to be copied, and of the gigantic fishbowls ordered by the palace which took nineteen days to fire. The greatest challenge, however, was set by the agents of the European merchants at Canton who demanded openwork lanterns, tabletops, and even musical instruments in porcelain. As early as 1635 the Dutch were forwarding, via Formosa, wooden models of the shapes of vessels required. We can get some idea of the extent of the foreign trade from the fact that in 1643 no fewer than 129,036 pieces of porcelain were sent via Formosa to the Dutch governor-general of Batavia for shipment to Holland. Most of it must have been produced at Ching-te-chen.

The most beautiful K'ang-hsi wares, and those which have been most admired in both China and the West, are the small monochromes, which in their classic perfection of form, surface, and colour recapture something of the subtlety and restraint of the Sung. The *T'ao-lu* says that Ts'ang Ying-hsüan's clays were rich, his glazes brilliant, his porcelain thin-bodied, and that he developed four new colours—eel-skin yellow, spotted yellow, snakeskin green, and turquoise blue. He also perfected a mirror black which was often decorated with gold; an exquisite soft red shading to green known as peach-bloom and used, it seems, for a very small range of vases and vessels for the scholar's desk; an "imperial yellow"; and a clear, powder blue, blown on through a bamboo tube and then often painted with arabesques in gold. The latter were especially admired in France, where it was the fashion to mount them in ormolu. The most splendid effect was a rich red produced from copper, known in Europe as *sang-de-boeuf* ("oxblood") and in China as Lang-yao; several members of the Lang

K'ANG-HSI PERIOD WARES

241

293 Vase, *mei-p'ing*. Porcelain with ox-blood (Lang-yao) glaze. Ch'ing Dynasty, K'ang-hsi period (1662–1722).

294 Bottle. Porcelain decorated with plum blossoms reserved on a ground of underglaze blue. Ch'ing Dynasty, K'ang-hsi period.

family have been suggested as possible candidates for the honour of having this ware named after them—the most likely being Lang T'ing-chi who, as governor of Kiangsi from 1705 to 1712, took an active interest in the kilns at Ching-te-chen. The glaze was probably applied by spraying and ran down the sides of the vase, stopping miraculously short of the foot—a degree of control which was lost in the Ch'ien-lung period and has only recently been recovered; while a beautiful effect appears around the rim where the colour has failed to "develop" and the glaze has a pale greenish tinge. The K'ang-hsi potters also copied the beautiful white "eggshell" bowls of Yung-lo, their versions being more flawless than the Ming originals, and made a fine imitation of the classical Ting ware of the Sung period.

These monochromes appealed chiefly to cultivated taste. Much more widely appreciated were the underglaze blue and enamelled wares, for which there was a huge demand both in China and abroad. Most K'ang-hsi blue and white was produced by the mass-production methods of which Père d'Entrecolles gives so depressing a picture, and as a result has a technical perfection combined with dead uniformity only partly redeemed by the colour of the cobalt itself, which has a vivid, intense luminosity never equalled before or since. It had a great vogue in Europe in the first half of the eighteenth century, particularly popular being the "ginger jars" decorated with blossoming prunus on a blue ground reticulated with lines suggesting ice cracks. Thereafter it was largely replaced in favour by the brightly coloured enamelled wares. Between 1667 and 1670 an imperial edict had been issued forbidding the use of the K'ang-hsi *nien-hao*. It is not known how long the ban remained in force, but there are comparatively few genuine pieces with the K'ang-hsi mark, and a correspondingly large number to which the potters added the fictitious marks of the Ming emperors Hsüan-te and Ch'eng-hua.

The great achievement of the potters working under Ts'ang Ying-hsüan, however, was in the enamels, of which two kinds had been developed by the end of the Ming Dynasty: *wu-ts'ai* (five colours) enamelled over the glaze, and *san-ts'ai* (three colours) applied directly "on the biscuit." In the K'ang-hsi *wu-ts'ai*, overglaze violet-blue replaces the underglaze blue of Wan-li, but the dominating colour is a transparent jewel-like green which led its European admirers in the nineteenth century to christen it *famille verte*. Most of these pieces are vases and bowls, made purely for ornament and decorated with birds or butterflies amid flowering branches, disposed with an exquisite and subtle sense of balance which stongly suggests that these designs were inspired by paintings. The revived *san-ts'ai* enamel-on-biscuit was used chiefly for reproductions of archaic bronzes and for figurines of Buddhist and Taoist divinities, children, birds, and animals. Also enamelled directly "on the biscuit" is the so-called *famille noire*, whose polychrome floral decoration is set off against a background of a rich black made almost iridescent by being washed over with a transparent green glaze. Until recently this spectacular ware had an enormous vogue among foreign collectors, and, like certain other Ch'ing enamels, still commands prices out of all proportion to its aesthetic worth. Examples of both *famille verte* and *famille noir* were sometimes adorned with Ch'eng-hua reign marks to show how highly their makers regarded them. Toward the end of the K'ang-hsi period, the robust vigour of the *famille verte* began to yield to a new style dominated by a delicate rose-pink, which is known in Europe as *famille rose* and which the Chinese call *yang-ts'ai* ("foreign colour"). It had been invented, about 1650, by Andreas Cassius of Leyden, who succeeded in producing a rose-red from gold chloride. A saucer dish in the Percival David Foundation dated 1721 must be one of the earliest Chinese examples of the use of this colour, which was probably introduced by the Jesuits.

The *famille rose* came to its full flowering with the appointment of Nien Hsi-yao as director of the imperial factories in 1726. Nien's directorship is chiefly famous for its "imitation of the antique and invention of novelties." As a typical example of the former we have his exquisite copies of classical Sung wares, so perfect that a Ju ware bottle now in the Percival David Foundation was for many years accepted as a genuine Sung piece by the Palace Museum authorities, until its carefully concealed Yung-cheng mark

295 Teapot. *Famille verte* porcelain with enamels in *Ku-yüeh-hsüan* style. Ch'ing Dynasty, Ch'ien-lung period (1736–1796).

YUNG-CHENG PERIOD WARES

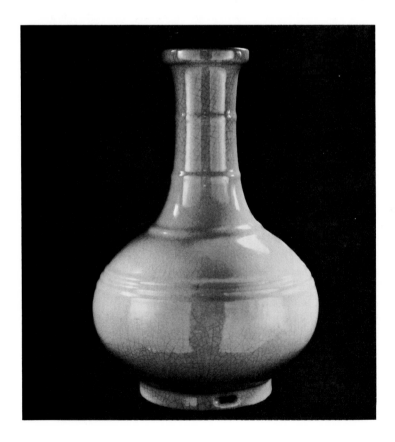

296 Bottle, copy of Ju ware. Porcelain covered with bluish-grey crackled glaze. Ch'ing Dynasty, Yung-cheng period (1723–1735).

297 Double vase, *t'ao-p'ing*. Porcelain, the inner vessel decorated in underglaze blue; the outer, with pierced sides, in *fen-ts'ai* enamels. Ch'ing Dynasty, Ch'ien-lung period.

CH'IEN-LUNG PERIOD WARES

298 Vase. Porcelain decorated with flowers in *famille rose* enamels and a poem by T'ang Ying. Ch'ing Dynasty, Ch'ien-lung period.

was discovered. Indeed, many Yung-cheng pieces had the reign mark ground away so that they might be passed off as Sung when they were illicitly sold out of the Palace Collection. Nien's "novelties" included the "tea-dust" glaze, made by blowing green enamel onto an iron, yellow-brown glaze, an improvement on the exquisite pale blue glaze known in Europe as *clair-de-lune*, and such rococo effects as painting in ink black flecked with gold or in greenish-blue flecked with red. Already in 1712 d'Entrecolles had been asked by the officials at Ching-te-chen for curious European objects which might be copied in porcelain and sent to court, and during the Yung-cheng period—and increasingly under Ch'ien-lung—this taste for extravagant forms and new effects was to absorb the energies of the potters at the cost of real refinement of taste. Its most lamentable results can be seen in the decline of *famille rose*, which early in the Yung-cheng period had had an exquisite delicacy; it was spoilt by the foreign demand for rich and garish decoration, finally degenerating into the livid salmon-pink of the nineteenth century.

In point of sheer craftsmanship the Ch'ien-lung period is supreme, and the finest of the enamelled wares produced under the directorship of T'ang Ying are unsurpassed. T'ang lived and worked with his potters, had complete mastery of their techniques, and was continually experimenting with new effects, reproducing the colour and texture of silver, grained wood, lacquer, bronze, jade, mother-of-pearl, and even cloisonné. He copied Italian faience drug pots, Venetian glass, Limoges enamels, and even Delft painted pottery and Japanese "old Imari" ware which were themselves copies of late Ming blue and white. T'ang Ying also reproduced all the familiar Sung wares (his rather glassy copies of Lung-chüan celadon being particularly fine), while his versions of the robust Canton wares were considered a great improvement on the originals. But the most beautiful of the porcelains produced under his direction are the enamelled eggshell vessels and bowls such as the lovely lavender vase decorated with mallow flowers and chrysanthemums and bearing a poem believed to be by T'ang Ying himself. In recent years, fashion has swung away from these exquisite objects to the more free and vital wares of T'ang and Sung, in which we can see and feel the touch of the craftsman's hand, but nothing can surpass the finest of these Ch'ien-lung pieces for sheer perfection of craftsmanship.

The influence of European taste on the decoration of Ching-te-chen porcelain, which had been growing since the end of the K'ang-hsi period, is nowhere more clearly seen than in a small and choice group of *famille rose* enamelled pieces known as *Ku-yüeh-hsüan*.[6] Indeed, many of them are decorated with European scenes, and even the Chinese flower motifs have a foreign quality in the realistic drawing, shading, and handling of perspective. They generally bear poems followed by red seals, while the *nien-hao* on the base is in embossed enamel.

A few words should be said on the subject of the porcelain made for the European market during the seventeenth and eighteenth centuries. Already in the sixteenth century the South China potters were decorating dishes with Portuguese coats-of-arms, and the Dutch trade vastly increased the demand in the seventeenth century. It was the Dutch who chiefly furnished the "porcelain rooms" in the great houses of France and Germany, of which the unfinished Japanese Palace of Augustus the Strong, King of Poland and Elector of Saxony, was the most ambitious. Augustus is reputed to have bartered a regiment of grenadiers for a set of *famille verte* vases. During the seventeenth century, European enthusiasts had been quite content to receive Chinese shapes decorated in the Chinese taste, but by the end of the century the practice was growing of sending out to Canton not only specimen shapes but also subjects for decoration, in response to which Ching-te-chen sent white porcelain "in the blank" down to Canton, where it was painted under the supervision of the European agents. The motifs included armorial bearings, genre scenes, figure subjects, portraits, hunting scenes, pictures of ships taken chiefly from engravings, and religious subjects such as the Baptism, Crucifixion, and Resurrection—the so-called Jesuit China. Toward the end of the eighteenth century, however, enthusiasm for things Chinese began to wane, as Europe was beginning to supply her needs from her own porcelain factories. The great days of the export trade were over, and the so-called Nankeen ware (enamelled porcelain) of the nineteenth century bears eloquent witness to its decay.

Although the imperial factory continued to flourish until the end of the eighteenth century, its great era ended with the departure of T'ang Ying. Thereafter the decline was slow but steady. At first we see an even greater ingenuity and elaboration in the manufacture of such freakish objects as boxes with porcelain chains and perforated and revolving vases. But after the beginning of the nineteenth century, the decay is more rapid, and though some of the wares of the reign of Tao-kuang (1821–1850) are of fine quality, the industry suffered a crippling blow when Ching-te-chen

PORCELAIN FOR THE EUROPEAN MARKET

299 "Jesuit China" dish. Porcelain decorated in underglaze blue, with a Baptism scene after a European engraving. Ch'ing Dynasty.

NINETEENTH CENTURY AND PROVINCIAL WARES

300 Ch'en Ming-yüan (active 1573–1620), brush-rest, I-hsing ware. Unglazed stoneware. Ming Dynasty.

was sacked by the Taiping rebels in 1853. Thereafter, there was a revival under T'ung-chih (1862–1873), and a further revival has taken place in the twentieth century. Today the factories at Ching-te-chen are run on modern industrial lines, but care is being taken to preserve the skills and techniques of the traditional potters.

While the Imperial Kilns were concentrating on an ever greater technical perfection, it was the provincial factories in the south which most successfully maintained their vigour and vitality. Of the scores of these kilns we can only mention a few. I-hsing in Kiangsu specialised in the production of little vessels, made of red stoneware, for the scholar's table, most ingeniously fashioned in the form of plants, tree trunks, beetles, rats, and other creatures, and in the manufacture of teapots. Te-hua continued to make the fine white porcelain developed in the Ming Dynasty. Other provincial wares were made either for local use or for shipment to regions less exacting in their demands than the Europeans. This applies particularly to the vulgar but vigorous brown stonewares made at Shekwan, near Fatshan in Kwangtung, consisting chiefly of ornamental pieces, figures, and large jars decorated with a thick blue glaze streaked and flecked with grey and green, which since the Ming Dynasty had both gratified local taste and been exported in quantity to the Nan-hai.

DECORATIVE ARTS: JADE, LACQUER, GLASS

About the year 1680, K'ang-hsi set up workshops in the palace precincts for the manufacture of porcelain, lacquer ware, glass, enamel, furniture, jade, and other objects for court use. The porcelain project, intended to replace distant Ching-te-chen, was found impracticable and soon abandoned, but the other workshops turned out a variety of decorative arts of superb quality and continued in production for the rest of the dynasty. The finest pieces of jade carving are often assigned, with very little reason, to the reign of Ch'ien-lung. Carved jade is extremely difficult to date, and work of the highest quality has been produced right up to the present day.

Other factories supplied the needs of the wealthy middle class and of the export market. Peking and Soochow, for example, specialised in carved lacquer, Foochow and Canton in the painted sort. The Canton products were considered inferior both in China and abroad because they were often made hastily to meet the demands of European merchants who were only permitted to reside in Canton for a few months of the year. The Foochow lacquer folding screens and cabinets, with their bold carving and rich colours embellished with powdered gold, were exported not only to Europe but also to Russia, Japan, Mecca, and India. So many were transshipped from the Coromandel Coast of South India that this kind of lacquer became known in eighteenth-century England as Coromandel ware.

K'ang-hsi's glass factory turned out a wide variety of coloured glass bottles and vases, the specialty being an opaque glass laminated in several contrasting colours, through which the designs were carved by the intaglio method. "Snuff bottles" (originally

301 Carp leaping out of the water. Carved green and brownish jade. Ch'ing Dynasty.

302 Taoist paradise. Panel of carved red lacquer inset with jade, lapis lazuli, and gilt metal. Ch'ing Dynasty.

made for medicine in the Sung and Yüan dynasties) were carved in glass and painted with enamel colours. They were also made in an endless variety of semi-precious substances such as lacquer, jade, crystal, coral, agate, and enamel, all of which were imitated in porcelain at Ching-te-chen. In the eighteenth century the art of backpainting on glass was introduced from Europe into China. It was said to have been practised by Castiglione in Peking, and soon became popular for painting delightful genre scenes on the backs of mirrors. The application of this technique to the decoration of the inside surface of transparent snuff bottles, first attempted about 1887, represents the last effort of the dying arts of the Ch'ing Dynasty to venture into new fields.

303 Snuff bottle. Enamelled glass inscribed *Ku-yüeh-hsüan* on the base. Ch'ing Dynasty.

12

The Twentieth Century

It was toward the end of the nineteenth century that China began to stir once more to life, roused by the aggressive penetration of the Western powers. But it was to be decades before her response to Western art was anything more than passive or reluctantly imitative. China's rulers, unlike their Japanese counterparts of the Meiji period, did not see the arts of Europe as an aid to modernisation and reform. If they had any attitude at all to Western culture, as opposed to Western guns and machines, it was one of hostility and contempt, and the problems of the cultural confrontation were left to take care of themselves.

ARCHITECTURE

From the mid-nineteenth century onward, Western-style commercial buildings, schools, and churches were rising wherever the foreigners penetrated. If those put up by the foreigners were bad, the Chinese imitations of them were even worse. A hybrid style combining Chinese and Western elements soon came into being, but until well into the present century, practising architects knew too little about traditional building methods to be able to adapt them successfully to modern materials, and the results were generally disastrous.

In 1930 a group of architects founded the Chinese Architectural Research Society to remedy this defect and to explore new ways of adapting traditional forms to modern needs. It was joined in the following year by Liang Ssu-ch'eng, who became the dominating influence in Chinese architecture for three decades. The results of their work, and that of foreign architects such as Henry K. Murphy, can be seen in government and university buildings put up in Nanking, Shanghai, Peking, and elsewhere during the few peaceful years before the Japanese invasion of 1937. Attractive as some of these are, they are still essentially Western buildings Sinicised with a traditional curved roof and enriched with detail translated from timber into painted concrete. A recent, deplorable example of this style is the National Palace Museum in Taipei, beloved of tourists. These architects had not yet discovered the truth, long since grasped by the Japanese, that the essence of their traditional architecture lies not in the curved roof, lovely as it is, but in the

304 The Great Hall of the People in T'ien-an-men Square, Peking, 1959.

305 Ivory carving, *Ch'ang O Flies to the Moon*. Peking, 1972.

post-and-frame structure which, unlike the roof, is readily adaptable to modern needs and materials.

After liberation in 1949, Chinese official architecture came for a time under the influence of the Soviet wedding-cake style, which left its mark on a group of public buildings put up in the 1950s, notably the Military Museum of the Chinese People's Revolution. This style has since been repudiated on economic no less than ideological grounds. Movement toward acceptance of what is loosely called the international modern style has been slow and cautious. Beginning with the Peking Children's Hospital (1954), it has been most successful where a major structural challenge had to be met, for instance in the Peking Workers' Gymnasium (1961) and the Capital Gymnasium (1971). The Great Hall of the People in Peking, seating ten thousand and completed in 1959 in the astonishingly short time of eleven months, is less remarkable for its style, which is conservative, than for its vast size, the classical dignity of its proportions, and its success as a symbol of the enduring strength of the new China.

DECORATIVE ARTS   The decorative arts of the last hundred years reveal the same unresolved conflict between new alien styles and stagnant traditional ones. Although the level of craftsmanship remained high, the porcelain, lacquer, and carved jade produced before 1950 was derivative and uninspired. Liberation, however, brought with it a vigorous revival of traditional crafts, fostered initially by the Peking Handicrafts Research Institute. To take but one example, in the Peking Jade Studios alone there are today fifteen hundred carvers at work; young apprentices learn secrets once jealously guarded by old master craftsmen, and together they are producing work of a technical quality probably higher than at any time since the reign of Ch'ien-lung.

Much of the output of these workshops is produced for the export market, which demands chiefly traditional designs such as the ivory carving of Ch'ang O flying to the moon (Fig. 305) with the elixir to become a goddess—a technical achievement to match any in the Ch'ing Dynasty. Under Mao we were told that the legendary heroine was "rebelling against feudal oppression and longing for a good life, as she flies skyward." In the post-Mao era these well-loved themes no longer require such a crudely political justification. Ch'ang O can be admired for her own sake—by women especially, who see her as a symbol of their liberation. At the same time some craft industries, such as the great ceramics factory at Ching-te-chen, are being increasingly mechanised, creating the same sort of design problems that faced Europe and America in the nineteenth century.

PAINTING   The painting of the last hundred years presents perhaps the most vivid illustration of the tensions between old ideas and new, native styles and foreign, that are shaping modern China. By the nineteenth century, the court painters, once so highly honoured, had sunk to a status hardly higher than that of palace servants, and

306 Jen Po-nien (1840–1896), *Pine Tree and Mynah Birds*. Hanging scroll. Ink and colour on paper. Ch'ing Dynasty.

307 Wu Ch'ang-shih (1842–1927), *Lychee Nuts*. Hanging scroll. Ink and colour on paper.

308 Chang Dai Chien (1899–1983), *Ten Thousand Miles of the Yangtse*. Detail of a handscroll, showing the Min River at Kuan-hsien, Szechwan. Ink and colour on silk.

even their names are not known. The literati too were victims of the growing paralysis of Ch'ing culture, and there were few outstanding amateur painters. In the first half of the century, Tai Hsi (1801–1860) and T'ang I-fen (1778–1853) were typically orthodox followers of the academic literary style of Wang Hui. But after mid-century there came a gradual change. The style of Jen I (Jen Po-nien, 1840–1896), the most interesting of the late Ch'ing artists, owed part of its vigour to an infusion from popular art, part to the new restless spirit that was then abroad in the prosperous coastal cities such as Shanghai (Fig. 306).

For in Shanghai, where Jen Po-nien lived, the impact of European civilisation was beginning to be felt. It showed itself in painting less in any change of style than in a new energy and boldness, which was perhaps the unconscious answer of the literati to the challenge of Western art. This new spirit burst forth in a handful of late followers of the Wu School such as Chao Chih-ch'ien (1829–1884), a distinguished scholar noted for his paintings of vines and flowers amid rocks, whose compositions and brush techniques were to influence the modern master Ch'i Pai-shih. Chao's follower Wu Ch'ang-shih (1842–1927) was a prolific painter chiefly of bamboo, flowers, and rocks, which he combined with calligraphy in compositions of considerable power (Fig. 307). The heavy, emphatic ink and strong colour these artists employed come as a refreshing contrast to the timid good manners of most of the late Ch'ing painters.

Among the twentieth-century artists who may have been provoked into a reassertion of traditional styles were Huang Pin-hung (1864/65–1955) and Ch'i Pai-shih (1863–1957). Huang Pin-hung was one of the last of the great Wu School landscape painters. He led the busy life of a "professional amateur" between Shanghai and Peking, as painter, teacher, art historian, and connoisseur, developing a style that became more and more daring and expressionistic as he approached old age. From a very different milieu came Ch'i Pai-shih, son of a small tenant-farmer in Hunan who by talent and sheer determination became a dominating figure among painters in Peking, expressing himself with great boldness and simplicity. In his sixties he painted some very original landscapes, but he is best known for his late paintings, chiefly of birds and flowers, crabs and shrimps, which he reduces to essentials while miraculously preserving their inner life. A far more versatile and sophisticated figure is the painter, collector, and connoisseur Chang Dai Chien (Chang Ta-ch'ien), born at Nei-chiang in Szechwan in 1899 and trained in the Ch'ing literary style. While in the landscapes of his later years he made bold experiments in ink-flinging and -splashing that reflect the influence of abstract expressionism—a movement that has stimulated many Far Eastern painters since 1950—he always remained a traditionalist at heart, in his dress and bearing seemingly a survival from another age. The best of his work, such as the great landscape *Ten Thousand Miles of the Yangtse* (Fig. 308) painted in 1968, combines a breadth of conception with a sharpness and clarity of detail that remind us of Sung landscape painting. He died in 1983 in Taipei.

309 Ch'i Pai-shih (1863–1957), *The Thing for Prolonging Life Is Wine!* Hanging scroll. Ink and colour on paper.

THE MODERN MOVEMENT

It might be thought that Westernisation in the first half of the twentieth century would have dealt Chinese traditional art the same crippling blow that had struck Japanese art in the nineteenth. This did not happen, partly because of the overpowering strength of the tradition itself and the cultural self-confidence of the educated class, partly because "fine art" was in the custody of amateurs and kept separate from their professional lives. Their work and milieu might change, but when they took up the brush, it was still to express themselves in the language of Tung Ch'i-ch'ang and Wang Hui. Such was their belief in the validity of the tradition, moreover, that for the most part they could take what they wanted from Western art without surrendering to it. When, much later, Mao Tse-tung exhorted artists to "make foreign things serve China," and to "make the past serve the present," he was pointing a path forward that they found easy to follow, and one indeed that had already been taken by some artists, notably Hsü Pei-hung (Ju Péon, 1895–1953), a decade earlier. In spite of the artistic controversies that enlivened the twenties and thirties, Chinese artists on the whole avoided the violent oscillations between acceptance and rejection of the West that had shaken Japanese art since the Meiji restoration of 1868.

310 Hsü Pei-hung (Ju Péon, 1895–1953), *Magpies on an Old Tree*. Ink on paper. About 1944.

After tentative beginnings here and there in the coastal cities, the modern movement in Chinese art was launched in 1916 by Kao Chien-fu, who had recently returned to Canton from Japan. While in Tokyo, he had come under the influence of the Nihonga movement, dedicated to the revival of the Japanese tradition by introducing Western techniques such as shading and chiaroscuro, and contemporary subject matter: one of Kao Chien-fu's most famous early hanging scrolls depicted a tank and an aeroplane. The work of Kao Chien-fu's *Ling-nan p'ai* (Cantonese School), as it was called, was too Japanese in feeling, and too deliberately synthetic, to command a wide following, but it showed that the traditional medium could be adapted to modern themes. Since 1949, shorn of its somewhat slickly decorative texture, the style created by the *Ling-nan p'ai* has been developed in China as one solution to the problem of expressing realistic, revolutionary content in the traditional medium.

The first modern art school in the Orient had been founded in 1876 in Tokyo. But no developments took place in China until 1906, when Nanking High Normal School and the Peiyang Normal School in Peking each opened a department of fine art on the Western pattern. They were soon followed in Shanghai by several private studios modelled upon romantic notions of the typical Paris atelier which had been acquired, very much at second hand, from Japanese artists who had studied in France. Soon after the end of the First World War, art schools were being opened in Peking and Shanghai, Nanking and Hangchow, while the more fortunate students were flocking to Paris where they came under the influence of the post-impressionists, Picasso and Matisse.

By the middle twenties, Hsü Pei-hung had returned to Nanking, Liu Hai-su to Shanghai, and Lin Feng-mien to Hangchow, and there was beginning to flourish in the big coastal cities an art which was for the most part just as academic as that of the tradi-

311 Li Hua (born 1907), *Refugees: A Contrast*. Woodcut. About 1939.

312 Huang Yung-yü (contemporary), *Mountain Tribespeople*. Woodcut. About 1947.

tional painters, the only difference being that now the medium was not Chinese ink but oil paint. The French Concession in Shanghai became a little Montmartre, the centre of a transplanted bohemianism that was inevitably quite out of touch with the feelings and aspirations of the mass of the Chinese people. In Hangchow, on the other hand, Lin Feng-mien and his pupils were beginning to develop a kind of painting that was both contemporary in feeling and Chinese in medium and technique.

In the early thirties, as the menace of Japanese aggression rose on the horizon, the atmosphere began to change. In Shanghai, the cosmopolitan Société des Deux Mondes founded by the modern painter P'ang Hsün-ch'in was dissolved, and the Storm Society took its place. Artists and writers became involved in bitter debates about their responsibility to society, the bohemians proclaiming a doctrine of art for art's sake, the realists urging a shift to the left and a closer identity with the people.

Finally, all doubts about the place of the artist in modern China were resolved by the Japanese attack on Peking in July 1937. Three years of steady retreat brought the painters and intellectuals close to the heart of the real China; and the later work of P'ang Hsün-ch'in, of the realists such as Hsiao Ting, and of the best of the wood engravers is full of a sense of discovery—not only of their own people but also of their own land. For they had been driven by the war far into the interior, to come for the first time face-to-face with the beauty of the western provinces, as yet untouched by the hybrid culture of the treaty ports. As the war dragged on, however, artists with a social conscience became bitterly disillusioned by the moral decay and corruption on the home front. Some joined the woodcut movement, which had been founded by the great writer Lu Hsün in the 1920s and was now being promoted as a weapon of socialist propaganda; others turned in protest to political cartooning or, to get round the censor, to an elaborate and indirect form of social symbolism.

255

313 Chao Wu-chi (Zao Wou-ki, born 1921), untitled. Oil on canvas.

314 Lin Feng-mien (born 1900), *The Yangtse Gorges*. Ink and colour on paper.

315 Tseng Yu-ho (born 1923), *Hawaiian Village*. Ink on paper. 1955.

The Japanese surrender in 1945 left China exhausted and longing for peace. But hardly had the firing died away when this unhappy land was plunged into civil war and all hopes of peaceful reconstruction were shattered. The art of the last years before the fall of the Kuomintang régime was marked by anger and bitterness on the part of the realist, or an almost defiant lyricism in the work of P'ang Hsün-ch'in, the wood engraver Huang Yung-yü, and Chao Wu-chi (Zao Wou-ki), a young student of Lin Fengmien at the Hangchow Academy who had emerged from the obscurity of the Japanese occupation with a highly sensitive and original style which seemed to point the way to a new direction in Chinese painting. In 1948, Chao Wu-chi went to Paris, where he has since acquired an international reputation. Perhaps the most remarkable metamorphosis occurred in the art of Tseng Yu-ho, who, from being a competent academic painter in the manner of her master P'u Ch'in in postwar Peking, has, since she went to live in Honolulu, come under the influence of some of the most advanced movements in Western art.

For nearly three decades, Chinese artists living outside the People's Republic have been expressing themselves as Chinese on the international scene. While the first Asian response to abstract expressionism took place in Japan in the 1950s, the Chinese painters who embraced the movement in the sixties gave it a new depth, for their response was at the same time a rediscovery of the abstract, calligraphic roots of their own tradition and not merely, as it had been for some Japanese artists, a skillful adoption of yet another new style from abroad. Yet, even when their work appears most abstract it is, like that of the late T'ang expressionists, never entirely divorced from the natural world, and the fact that we can

316 Lü Shou-k'un (1919–1976), *Mountain*. Hanging scroll. Ink on paper. 1962.

257

"read" their abstractions as landscapes gives them an added, and very Chinese, dimension. The pioneers were the Fifth Moon group in Taipei, Lü Shou-k'un (Lui Shou Kwan), and members of the lively Circle and In Tao groups in Hongkong. Notable among Chinese artists in Southeast Asia, Chung Ssu-pin (Cheong Soo-pieng) in Singapore, before he became an abstract painter and worker in metal, was responding to the exotic beauty of the tropics with a style refreshingly free from the obvious influence of Gauguin. The time is now past when the work of the Chinese artists living abroad was unacceptable in socialist China, and it is beginning to be recognised as a uniquely Chinese contribution to the increasingly international character of modern art.

ART IN CHINA
SINCE LIBERATION

Meanwhile within the People's Republic the total mobilisation of hands and minds to the task of creating a modern socialist society out of a backward peasantry put the arts firmly in the service of politics and the state. Inspired by Mao Tse-tung's exhortation to serve the people, artists in the 1950s, with varying degrees of enthusiasm, quit the academies and went down to farm and factory to live with the workers and "learn from them." Modernism and internationalism were forgotten. The art of these years, although coloured by propaganda and anything but avant-garde, became experimental in a purely technical sense when artists were called upon to depict in traditional brush and ink such new themes as oil refineries, construction work, and commune life. A few old masters, notably Ch'i Pai-shih, were left in peace, but more active painters such as Fu Pao-shih, Ch'ien Sung-yen, and Li K'o-jan were expected to infuse some ideological content into their pictures: the figure gazing at the waterfall must be no longer a dreaming poet, but a surveyor or hydraulic engineer.

One might have expected that the dictates of socialist realism would have forced artists to abandon the traditional landscape conventions enshrined in such handbooks as the *Painting Manual of the Mustard Seed Garden* and simply paint what they saw. There is in China today a good deal of realistic art—or, rather, what is called *revolutionary romanticism*; for it illustrates in semi-Westernised techniques not the actual state of society but what it ideally should be. At a more sophisticated level, however, artists are not abandoning their repertoire of conventional brushstrokes so much as checking it against nature itself and making it accord with their own visual experience. By thus "checking his *ts'un*" (the phrase is Ch'ien Sung-yen's), Li K'o-jan in his delightful *Village in the Mountains* gives a new lease of life to the traditional language of landscape painting. In the 1950s and 1960s, Li K'o-jan, Ch'ien Sung-yen, Shih Lu, Ya Ming, and other painters of the older generation thus succeeded in establishing a new traditional style, and their influence on younger artists has been considerable.

Although, by Western standards, the culture of the early 1960s was limited and conformist, it became the target for the Great Proletarian Cultural Revolution of 1966/69, which launched a devastating attack upon current "bourgeois" trends in education, schol-

317 Li K'o-jan (born 1907), *Village in the Mountains*. Hanging scroll. Ink and colour on paper. About 1960.

arship, and the arts. Universities and art schools were closed, museums shut their doors, there were no more art exhibitions, and in June 1966 publication of all the art and archaeology journals abruptly ceased. Almost everyone engaged in these activities was criticised for "revisionist" attitudes, and many were publicly disgraced, sent as virtual slaves to farm or factory, or driven to suicide. The impression formed abroad was that all scholarly and artistic activity had come to an end—an impression which the Chinese authorities themselves did nothing to dispel. To remove all traces of elitism in the arts, the centre of artistic activity was shifted from the cities and art academies to factories and rural communes, while trained artists were urged to identify themselves with the masses. Vast numbers of workers, peasants, and soldiers took up the arts as amateurs, developing new styles and techniques to express their own experience. Much of this new art lacks individuality, but it is bright in colour, sometimes daring in composition, and positive, if not overtly propagandist, in tone. After a slight relaxation in 1972–73, when the archaeological journals reappeared after six years of silence, even tighter control of art and culture was imposed by Chiang Ch'ing (Mme. Mao) and the Gang of Four.

During the turbulent years of the Cultural Revolution, artists and sculptors tended to sink their individuality in anonymous group projects such as *The Rent Collection Courtyard*, which, although completed in 1965, was praised by the leaders of the Cultural Revolution as a model and was widely copied. A dramatic tableau of life-size figures in clay plaster, this much-admired work re-creates around the courtyard of a rapacious former landlord in Szechwan a harrowing scene that had been only too familiar to the local tenant-farmers before liberation.

318 Anonymous team of sculptors, *The Rent Collection Courtyard*. Detail of a life-size tableau in clay-plaster, in a former landlord's mansion at Ta-yi, Szechwan. 1965.

Earlier editions of this book ended with the suggestion that the storms of the years after 1949 were past and that Chinese civilisation had resumed its steady flow into the future. But it is now clear that the storms were more violent and prolonged than had appeared to the outside observer, begining with the wilting of the deceptively liberal Hundred Flowers movement of 1957 and only ending with the arrest of the Gang of Four in October of 1976—a period of almost twenty years during which artists who did not conform were victimised with varying degrees of savagery. In the early years after the Revolution of 1949 creative men and women had generally responded to Mao's appeal to be unselfish, reject elitism, and serve society. By 1976, however, that idealism had long since evaporated. Cultural activities were under the control of the Gang of Four, led by Mao's fanatical wife, Chiang Ch'ing,

319 Wu Kuan-chung (born 1919),
Reflections in the Rice Fields. Chinese ink.
1979.

and a paralysis gripped all forms of artistic expression except those promoted by Chiang Ch'ing herself.

With the death of Mao Tse-tung in September of 1976 and the fall of the Gang of Four a month later, the floodgates began cautiously to open: at first a trickle, then in 1979–80 a great outpouring of pent-up bitterness at the horrors of the recent past and of hope for the future. The painting of these years, depicting not only vividly remembered sufferings but also the great protest demonstration of April 4/5, 1976, at T'ien-an-men Square, was more dramatic, expressive of feelings more widely shared, than any perhaps in the history of Chinese art.

Now the work of old painters who had survived, such as Liu Hai-su, Li K'o-jan, Ch'ien Sung-yen, and Lin Feng-mien, came to life again. Painters in mid-career, among them Huang Yung-yü and Wu Kuan-chung, produced works that blended traditional and modern with great originality and freedom. Wu Kuan-chung, who spent several years in France in the 1950s, has through his writings been a leading influence in the post-Mao era in preparing the reading public for modernism, teaching them not to be intimidated by the abstraction that under Mao had been condemned as "bourgeois formalism." Wu's oil painting is fresh and subtle, while his works in the Chinese medium, such as the landscape of Szechwan illustrated here, show how easily he assimilates the happy influence of Dufy to the language of the Chinese brush.

Behind these masters came the swelling tide of a new generation of artists, often inarticulate yet hopeful, facing the same challenges that had faced Chinese artists in the 1930s: to be contemporary yet Chinese, to be in touch with the feelings and aspirations of the masses yet artistically free. In the art of this new phase, propaganda was conspicuously absent; the nude was no longer forbidden, woodcuts became colourful, even romantic, while artists and students, for years starved of contact with the outside world, showed keen interest in every aspect of Western art, from that of the ancients to Picasso and Jackson Pollock. Some of the work of the early post-Mao years is inevitably amateurish because artists had forgotten—if indeed they ever knew—how to express their true feelings. But in the work of some of the younger artists—of Li Hua-sheng, Yang Yen-p'ing, and Ch'en Tzu-chuang, for example—we see a new assurance that seems to proclaim that a painter need not go far beyond his traditional idiom to express thoroughly contemporary ideas and feelings.

By 1980 the Party had decided that freedom had gone far enough. Democracy Wall in Peking was closed down, and the "dissidents" who in risky unofficial exhibitions were expressing the hopes and frustrations that many felt about contemporary life were being viewed by the authorities with growing hostility. Creative men and women in China now live from day to day, never knowing whether tomorrow will bring new freedom or tighter controls, or both at the same time. In the summer of 1981, for instance, a Party spokesman repudiated Mao's insistence on the supremacy of politics over art, which had been Party dogma for nearly forty years; yet at the same time some artists and writers who had strayed too far from the narrow zigzag path were being forced to confess their errors and told to mend their ways. In spite of uncertainty, however, it seems that the trend that set in after the death of Mao toward a broader and less simplistic view of the role of art and the artist in modern Chinese society is irreversible, and that a new era is slowly, sometimes painfully, dawning.

Yet lest the observer should imagine that the arts in China are now, or could ever be, as free as they are in the Western democracies, it is well to remember that there exists in China a rein on artistic freedom far older than that imposed by Mao and his heirs. The belief that the individual must put his loyalty and responsibility to the group, be it his family or the state, before his personal freedom is deeply rooted in traditional Chinese culture. The overriding purpose is to achieve social harmony. It is only when that harmony breaks down, at the decay of a dynasty or in times of intolerable oppression, that individualism speaks with a strong voice.

We should not, then, expect to find in today's China, except in the case of rarely gifted and often eccentric artists, the anti-establishment stance taken by many artists in the West and considered as the mark of a vital culture. We may expect to see in the years to come some tension between the artist and authority, the artist pressing against, while he partly accepts, the constraints that the régime, or society as a whole, impose upon his personal freedom. But it was within those constraints that most of the great art of the past was produced, and it is from within them also that great art will come in the future.

Notes to the text

CHAPTER 1

1. This is not in fact a very ancient legend, for in early times the Chinese had no creation myths at all, believing, rather, in a self-generating cosmos. Frederick Mote, *Intellectual Foundations of China* (New York, 1971, pp. 17–19) follows Derk Bodde in suggesting that this myth may even be of non-Chinese origin. But the fact that it became so well accepted suggests that it fulfilled a need at least the popular level.

2. Carbon-14 dates cited in this book are corrected according to the chronology of the bristlecone pine, but even these should be treated with some caution.

3. The prehistory of eastern China between the Yellow River and the Yangtse is still the subject of much debate. For years we accepted Kwang-chih Chang's "Lungshanoid" as a convenient label for the pre-Lungshan cultures in this area. Some Chinese scholars now consider the cluster of sites in the Ch'ing-lien-kang area as distinct; others would stress two main areas: Ta-wen-k'ou leading into Lung-shan in Shantung, Ho-mu-tu and its successors in Kiangsu, with Ch'ing-lien-kang sharing features of both. For a convenient summary, see Cho-yun Hsu, "Stepping into Civilisation: The Case of Cultural Development in China," *National Palace Museum Quarterly* XVI, 1 (1981): 1–18.

CHAPTER 2

1. Mizuno Seiichi, *Bronzes and Jades of Ancient China*, pp. 8–9.

2. Bernhard Karlgren, studying the form and decoration of a large number of Shang bronzes, divided them into two styles, A and B, though he could not explain why there should be two styles. Kwang-chih Chang has suggested a simple solution to the problem. He has shown that the Shang rulers had a dualistic system whereby the succession went to two different groups of the royal house alternately; there were two traditions of the oracle-bone scripts, two parallel rows of ancestral halls, two clusters of royal tombs. It is reasonable to suppose, therefore, that the two bronze styles were associated with these two lines of succession in

the royal family. See his *The Archaeology of Ancient China*, p. 255. David Keightley (*Journal of Asian Studies* XLI, 3 [May 1982]: 552), however, believes that this "bold and imaginative hypothesis" needs more evidence before it can be substantiated.

3. S. Howard Hansford, *Chinese Jade Carving*, p. 31.

CHAPTER 3

1. Arthur Waley, *The Book of Songs* (London, 1937), pp. 282–83.

2. Slightly adapted from Bernhard Karlgren, *A Catalogue of the Chinese Bronzes in the Alfred F. Pillsbury Collection*, p. 105. The last sentence makes it clear that the bronzes were made for ritual use rather than for burial.

3. Just how difficult it is to date early Chinese jades is shown by the discovery in a Neolithic grave at Hsi-hsia, Pu-chiang, Kwangtung Province, of two jade *tsung* very similar to the piece illustrated in Figure 49, which has hitherto been dated in the early Chou Dynasty. See *Wen-wu* 1978, p. 15.

CHAPTER 4

1. It was Arthur Waley in *An Introduction to the Study of Chinese Painting* (London, 1923, pp. 21–23) who first pointed out the importance of Ch'u in the emergence in ancient China both of creative art and of a consciousness of the power of the artistic imagination. More recently, David Hawkes discussed the contribution of Ch'u in his *Ch'u Tz'u, the Songs of the South* (Oxford, 1959). This has since been amply confirmed by excavations not only in Changsha, which was a relatively unimportant town, but in Chiang-ling, the Ch'u capital, and Hsin-yang. The discovery in 1980 near Chengtu in Szechwan of a timber tomb very similar to those at Changsha shows how far the influence of Ch'u had spread by the Western Han period.

2. David Hawkes, op. cit., p. 108. The phrase *hsi-pi*, indicating the Western origin of these buckles, may be derived from the Turkic-Mongol word *särbe*.

3. See Su T'ien-chun, "Report on the Excavation of a Warring States Tomb at Sung-yüan-ts'un, Ch'ang-p'ing

District, Peking," *Wen-wu* 1959, 9. My remarks, written in 1966, are borne out by a thermoluminescence test on twenty-two typical "Hui-hsien" pieces from well-known English and American collections, all of which turned out to be modern. See S. J. Fleming and E. H. Sampson, "The Authenticity of Figurines, Animals, and Pottery Facsimiles of Bronze in the Hui Hsien Style," *Archaeometry* 14, 2 (1972): 237–44.

CHAPTER 5

1. David Hawkes, *Ch'u Tz'u*, pp. 105–107. Hawkes suggests that this poem may have been written in 208 or 207 B.C.

2. Translated by Arthur Waley, *An Introduction to the Study of Chinese Painting* (London, 1923), pp. 30–31.

3. B. Karlgren, "Early Chinese Mirror Inscriptions," *BMFEA* 6 (1934): 49. Some private manufacturers put the name of the Shang-fang on their mirrors to increase their value. See Wang Chongshu, *Han Civilisation*, trans. K. C. Chang et al. (New Haven, 1982), p. 107.

4. While it is generally assumed that objects placed in the tomb, including copper cash, were for the use of the deceased, inscribed placques found in some Han tombs show that the food was a tax paid to the earth gods and that the cash was to buy the land from the administration of the underworld.

5. As fresh discoveries increase the number of known kilns—only a few of which are mentioned in this book—the problem of nomenclature becomes more and more acute. But until Chinese ceramics experts produce a new definitive classification, it would not be helpful to the reader to depart too far from accepted names for well-known kilns. For a list of kilns, see Yutaka Mino and Patricia Wilson, *An Index to Chinese Kiln Sites from the Six Dynasties to the Present* (Royal Ontario Museum, Toronto, 1973). For a more up-to-date (though incomplete) list with illustrations of shards in colour, see the *Catalogue of the Exhibition of Ceramic Finds from Ancient Kilns in China* (Fung Ping Shan Museum, Hong Kong, 1981).

CHAPTER 6

1. Beautifully translated by Ch'en Shih-hsiang in *Literature as Light against Darkness*, rev. ed. (Portland, Maine, 1952).

2. William R. B. Acker, *Some T'ang and Pre-T'ang Texts on Chinese Painting* (Leiden, 1954), p. xxx.

3. There are a number of delightful stories about him in his official biography and in that fascinating collection of gossip, *Shih-shuo hsin-yü*. See Arthur Waley's account of him in *An Introduction to the Study of Chinese Painting*, pp. 45–66, and Ch'en Shih-hsiang's translation of the official life, No. 2 in the University of California's translations of Chinese Dynastic Histories biographies (Berkeley, 1953).

4. A Late Sung version of the *Lieh-nü t'u* in Peking is illustrated in *Chung-kuo li-tai ming hua*, vol. 1 (1978), pls. 20–32. The copyist has made effective use of the shading technique for drapery (visible also in the bed hangings of the *Admonitions* scroll), which seems to have been a peculiarity of Ku's style.

5. This motive was frankly admitted in an edict of one of the barbarian rulers of Later Chao (c. A.D. 335): "We were born out of the marches," he declared, "and though We are unworthy, We have complied with our appointed destiny and govern the Chinese as their prince. . . . Buddha being a barbarian god is the very one we should worship." See Arthur Wright, "Fo-t'u-teng, a Biography," *Harvard Journal of Asiatic Studies* II (1948) :356.

6. The caves were first documented by Sir Aurel Stein, who visited them in 1907 and brought away with him a large collection of manuscripts and paintings from a sealed library. In the following year, the great French Sinologue Paul Pelliot systematically photographed and numbered the caves. His numbers, totalling nearly 300, are familiar to Western readers and appear in my text in brackets, preceded by the letter "P." A second system of numbering was used by the noted painter Chang Ta-ch'ien, who with his assistants copied some of the frescoes during the Second World War. A third system was adopted by the National Art Research Institute at Tunhuang, which since 1943 has been actively engaged in preserving, restoring, and copying the paintings under the directorship of Ch'ang Shu-hung. This organisation has now identified 492 caves and niches, and I have used their system in this book.

CHAPTER 7

1. It was probably the demands of Mahāyāna Buddhism for the endless multiplication of icons, diagrams, spells, and texts that brought about the rapid development of block printing during the T'ang Dynasty. The earliest dated printed text yet discovered is a Buddhist charm on paper of A.D. 770, found at Tunhuang by Sir Aurel Stein. It is likely, however, that the Chinese and Tibetans had been experimenting with block printing since the middle of the sixth century, while the use of seals in Shang China and the practice of taking rubbings of inscriptions engraved on stone (made possible by the Han invention of paper) point to the existence of printing of a sort at a far earlier date.

2. Chang Tsao's contribution to the evolution of T'ang landscape style is discussed in my *Chinese Landscape Painting*. Vol. II: *The Sui and T'ang Dynasties*, pp. 65–69.

3. *Ahbār as-Sīn Wa I-Hind*, trans. and ed. Jean Sauvaget (1948), 16, Section 34.

4. The Ting-ware kilns at Chien-tz'u-ts'un in Hopei were in the late T'ang already producing a fine white porcelain, which may have been the elusive Hsing-yao, but no kilns have yet been found in Hsing-chou itself.

5. See *Chinese Tomb Pottery Figurines* (Hong Kong, 1953), p. 9.

6. From the *Compendium of Deities of the Three Religions, San chiao sou shen ta chuan*, quoted in Lu Hsün, *A Brief History of Chinese Fiction*, trans. Yang Hsien-yi and Gladys Yang (Peking, 1959), pp. 21–22.

CHAPTER 8

1. Sickman and Soper, *The Art and Architecture of China*, p. 192.

2. This passage has been slightly adapted from Tsung Pai-hua, "Space-Consciousness in Chinese Painting,"

Sino-Austrian Cultural Association Journal I (1949): 27 (trans. Ernst J. Schwartz). Chinese theorists distinguish three kinds of perspective in Chinese painting: *kao yüan* ("high distance") depicts the mountains as they would be seen by someone who was looking upward from below; *shen yüan* ("deep distance") presents a bird's-eye view over successive ranges to a high and distant horizon; while *p'ing yüan* ("level distance") involves a continuous recession to a rather low horizon, such as we most often encounter in European landscape painting.

3. Yoshikawa Kōjirō, trans. Burton Watson, *Introduction to Sung Poetry* (Cambridge, England, 1967), p. 37.

4. This passage has been slightly adapted from Naitō Tōichirō, *The Wall-Paintings of Hōryūji*, trans. William Acker and Benjamin Rowland (Baltimore, 1943), pp. 205–206. Although the temple in question was burned down at the end of the Liang Dynasty, and the connection with Chang Seng-yu is legendary, there is little doubt that this technique was practised in sixth-century wall painting.

5. Osvald Sirén, *Chinese Painting: Leading Masters and Principles*, vol. 1, p. 175.

6. K. Okakura, *The Awakening of Japan* (1905), p. 77.

Chapter 9

1. See Sir Henry Yule, trans., *The Travels of Marco Polo* (London, 1903).

2. For a discussion of what and why the Chinese write on paintings, see my *Three Perfections: Chinese Painting, Poetry and Calligraphy* (New York, 1979).

3. Chang Yen-yüan in the *Li-tai ming-hua-chi* mentions three bamboo paintings executed before A.D. 600, and bamboo can be seen in the murals in several of the Six Dynasties caves at Tunhuang.

Chapter 10

1. Yung-lo is not, properly speaking, the name of the emperor, but an auspicious title which he gave to his reign period as a whole, thus doing away with the old system of choosing a new era name every few years. The custom continued during the Ch'ing Dynasty. K'ang-hsi, for example, is the title of the reign period of the emperor Sheng-tsu, Ch'ien-lung that of Kao-tsung. But because these reign titles have become so well known in the West, chiefly through their use as marks on Chinese porcelain, I shall continue to use them in this book.

2. Adapted from Richard Edwards, *The Field of Stones:*

A Study of the Art of Shen Chou (Washington, D.C., 1962), p. 40.

3. See Sir Percival David, *Chinese Connoisseurship: The Essential Criteria of Antiquities* (London, 1971), pp. 143–44.

Chapter 11

1. The catalogue of the Ch'ien-lung collection *Shih-ch'ü pao-chi*, was compiled in three volumes between 1745 and 1817. Buddhist and Taoist works were catalogued separately. A survey made by the Palace Museum authorities in 1928–1931 showed the vast scale of the collection: 9,000 paintings, rubbings and specimens of calligraphy, 10,000 pieces of porcelain, over 1,200 bronze objects, and a large quantity of textiles, jades, and minor arts. Some of the finest pieces had been sold or given away by the last Manchu emperor, P'u-yi, during the twenty years following the revolution in 1911. All but a fraction of the remainder were shipped to Taiwan by the Kuomintang in 1948.

2. For a discussion of the European impact on Chinese art, see my *The Meeting of Eastern and Western Art* (London and New York, 1973), and Cecile and Michel Beurdeley, *Giuseppe Castiglione: A Jesuit Painter at the Court of the Chinese Emperors*, trans. Michael Bullock (Rutland, Vermont, 1972).

3. Europe, at this time, felt much the same way about China. "In *Painting*," wrote Alvarez de Semedo in 1641, "they have more curiositie than perfection. They know not how to make use of either *Oyles* or *Shadowing* in the Art. . . . But at present there are some of them, who have been taught by us, that use *Oyles*, and are come to make perfect pictures." Sandrart, in his *Teutsche Akademie* (1675), expressed a similar view. Cf. my article, "Sandrart on Chinese Painting," *Oriental Art* I, 4 (Spring 1949): 159–61.

4. For a translation and commentary on this difficult text, see Pierre Ryckmans, *Les "Propos sur la Peinture" de Shitao* (Brussels, 1970).

5. They were originally published in the Jesuit miscellany *Lettres édifiantes et curieuses*, vols. XII and XVI (1717 and 1724), reprinted in S. W. Bushell, *Description of Chinese Pottery and Porcelain: Being a Translation of the T'ao Shuo*, and translated in part by him in his *Oriental Ceramic Art* (New York, 1899). Some interesting passages are quoted by Soame Jenyns in his *Later Chinese Porcelain* (London, 1951), pp. 6–14.

6. The various theories about the origin and meaning of the name are discussed by Soame Jenyns in Appendix I of his *Later Chinese Porcelain*, pp. 87–95.

Books for Reference and Further Reading

GENERAL WORKS ON CHINA

Raymond Dawson, ed., *The Legacy of China* (Oxford, 1964).
C. P. Fitzgerald, *China: A Short Cultural History*, 3rd rev. ed. (London, 1961).
Charles O. Hucker, *China's Imperial Past: An Introduction to Chinese History and Culture* (Stanford, 1975).
Joseph Needham, *Science and Civilisation in China*, 5 vols. (Cambridge, 1954–).

GENERAL WORKS ON CHINESE ART

S. Howard Hansford, *A Glossary of Chinese Art and Archaeology*, rev. ed. (London, 1961).
Sherman E. Lee, *A History of Far Eastern Art*, rev. ed. (New York, 1973).
Laurence Sickman and A. C. Soper, *The Art and Architecture of China*, rev. ed. (London, 1971).
Michael Sullivan, *Chinese Art in the Twentieth Century* (London, Berkeley, and Los Angeles, 1959); *Chinese and Japanese Art* (London and New York, 1966); *The Meeting of Eastern and Western Art* (London and New York, 1973).
Mary Tregear, *Chinese Art* (London, New York, and Toronto, 1980).

EXHIBITIONS AND GENERAL COLLECTIONS

Wen Fong, ed., *The Great Bronze Age of China: An Exhibition from the People's Republic of China* (New York, 1980).
Jan Fontein and Tung Wu, *Unearthing China's Past* (Boston, 1973).
S. Howard Hansford, *Chinese, Central Asian and Luristan Bronzes and Chinese Jades and Sculptures*, vol. I of *The Seligman Collection of Oriental Art* (London, 1957).
R. L. Hobson and W. P. Yetts, *The George Eumorfopoulos Collection*, 9 vols. (London, 1925–1932).
Sherman E. Lee and Wai-Kam Ho, *Chinese Art under the Mongols: The Yüan Dynasty (1279–1368)* (Cleveland, 1969).
Nelson Gallery–Atkins Museum, Kansas City, and Asian Art Museum of San Francisco, *The Chinese Exhibition: A Pictorial Record of the Exhibition of Archaeological Finds of the People's Republic of China* (Kansas City, Missouri, 1975).
Royal Academy of Arts, *The Chinese Exhibition: A Commemorative Catalogue of the International Exhibition of Chinese Art in 1935–36* (London, 1936).
Michael Sullivan, *Chinese Ceramics, Bronzes and Jades in the Collection of Sir Alan and Lady Barlow* (London, 1963).

ARCHAEOLOGY

Terukazu Akiyama and others, *Arts of China, Neolithic Cultures to the T'ang Dynasty: New Discoveries* (Tokyo and Palo Alto, 1968).
J. G. Anderson, *Children of the Yellow Earth* (London, 1934).
Anon., *Historical Relics Unearthed in New China* (Peking, 1972).
Edmund Capon, *Art and Archaeology in China* (London and Melbourne, 1977).
Kwang-chih Chang, *The Archaeology of Ancient China* (3rd ed. (New Haven and London, 1977); *Shang Civilisation* (New Haven and London, 1980).
Cheng Te-k'un, *Archaeology in China*. Vol. I, *Prehistoric China* (Cambridge, 1959); Vol. II, *Shang China* (Cambridge, 1960); Vol. III, *Chou China* (Cambridge, 1966); *New Light on Prehistoric China* (Cambridge, 1966).
P'ing-ti Ho, *The Cradle of the East* (Chicago, 1976).
Li Chi, *The Beginnings of Chinese Civilisation* (Seattle, 1957); *Anyang* (Seattle, 1977).
Jessica Rawson, *Ancient China: Art and Archaeology* (London, 1980).
Michael Sullivan, *Chinese Art: Recent Discoveries* (London, 1973).

BRONZES

Noel Barnard, *Bronze Casting and Bronze Alloys in Ancient China* (Canberra and Nagoya, 1961).
Bernhard Karlgren, *A Catalogue of the Chinese Bronzes in the Alfred F. Pillsbury Collection* (Minneapolis, 1952), and many important articles in *The Bulletin of the Museum of Far Eastern Antiquities* (Stockholm).

Max Loehr, *Chinese Bronze Age Weapons* (Ann Arbor, Michigan, 1956); *Ritual Vessels of Bronze Age China* (New York, 1968).

J. A. Pope and others, *The Freer Chinese Bronzes*, 2 vols. (Washington, D.C., 1967 and 1969).

Mizuno Seiichi, *Bronzes and Jades of Ancient China* (in Japanese with English summary, Kyoto, 1959).

William Watson, *Ancient Chinese Bronzes* (London, 1962).

PAINTING AND CALLIGRAPHY

James Cahill, *Chinese Painting* (New York, 1960); *Hills Beyond a River: Chinese Painting of the Yüan Dynasty, 1279–1368* (New York and Tokyo, 1976); *Parting at the Shore: Chinese Painting of the Early and Middle Ming Dynasty, 1368–1580* (New York and Tokyo, 1978); *The Compelling Image: Nature and Style in Seventeenth Century Chinese Painting* (Cambridge, Massachusetts and London, 1982).

Chiang Yee, *Chinese Calligraphy* (London, 1954).

Lucy Driscoll and Kenji Toda, *Chinese Calligraphy*, 2nd ed. (New York, 1964).

Richard Edwards, *The Field of Stones: A Study of the Art of Shen Chou* (Washington, D.C., 1962); *The Art of Wen Cheng-ming (1470–1559)* (Ann Arbor, Michigan, 1975).

Marilyn and Shen Fu, *Studies in Connoisseurship: Chinese Paintings from the Arthur M. Sackler Collection in New York and Princeton* (Princeton, New Jersey, 1973).

Shen Fu, *Traces of the Brush: Studies in Chinese Calligraphy* (New Haven, 1977).

R. H. van Gulik, *Chinese Pictorial Art as Viewed by the Connoisseur* (Rome, 1958).

Thomas Lawton, *Chinese Figure Painting* (Washington, D.C., 1973)

Sherman E. Lee, *Chinese Landscape Painting*, rev. ed. (Cleveland, 1962).

Chu-tsing Li, *A Thousand Peaks and Myriad Ravines: Chinese Paintings in the Charles A. Drenowatz Collection*, 2 vols. (Ascona, 1974); *Trends in Modern Chinese Painting* (Ascona, 1979).

Max Loehr, *The Great Painters of China* (Oxford, 1980).

Laurence Sickman, ed., *Chinese Painting and Calligraphy in the Collection of John M. Crawford, Jr.* (New York, 1962); with Waikam Ho, Sherman Lee, and Marc Wilson, *Eight Dynasties of Chinese Painting: The Collections of the Nelson Gallery–Atkins Museum, Kansas City, and the Cleveland Museum of Art* (Cleveland, 1980).

Osvald Sirén, *The Chinese on the Art of Painting* (New York, 1963); *Chinese Painting: Leading Masters and Principles*, 7 vols. (London, 1956 and 1958).

Michael Sullivan, *The Birth of Landscape Painting in China* (Berkeley, Los Angeles, and London, 1961); *The Three Perfections: Chinese Painting, Poetry and Calligraphy* (New York, 1980); *Symbols of Eternity: The Art of Landscape Painting in China* (Stanford and Oxford, 1979); *Chinese Landscape Painting*. Vol. II, *The Sui and T'ang Dynasties* (Berkeley and Los Angeles, 1980).

SCULPTURE

René-Yvon Lefebvre d'Argencé, ed., *Chinese, Korean and Japanese Sculpture in the Avery Brundage Collection* (San Francisco, 1974).

Mizuno Seiichi and Nagahiro Toshio, *Chinese Stone Sculpture* (Tokyo, 1950); *Unko Sekkutsu: Yun-kang, the Buddhist Cave Temples of the Fifth Century A.D. in North China*, 16 vols. in Japanese with English summary (Kyoto, 1952–1955); *Bronze and Stone Sculpture of China: From the Yin to the T'ang Dynasty* (in Japanese and English, Tokyo, 1960).

Alan Priest, *Chinese Sculpture in the Metropolitan Museum of Art* (New York, 1954).

Richard Rudolph, *Han Tomb Art of West China* (Berkeley and Los Angeles, 1951).

Osvald Sirén, *Chinese Sculpture from the Fifth to the Fourteenth Centuries*, 4 vols. (London, 1925).

A. C. Soper, *Literary Evidence for Early Buddhist Art in China* (Ascona, 1959).

Michael Sullivan and Dominique Darbois, *The Cave Temples of Maichishan* (London, Berkeley, and Los Angeles, 1969).

ARCHITECTURE AND GARDENS

Andrew Boyd, *Chinese Architecture and Town Planning* (London, 1962).

Maggie Keswick, *The Chinese Garden: History, Art and Architecture* (London and New York, 1978).

Michèle Pirazzoli-T'Serstevens, *Living Architecture: Chinese* (London, 1972).

J. Prip-Møller, *Chinese Buddhist Monasteries* (Copenhagen and London, 1937).

Osvald Sirén, *The Walls and Gates of Peking* (London, 1924); *The Imperial Palaces of Peking*, 3 vols. (Paris and Brussels, 1926); *Gardens of China* (New York, 1949).

CERAMICS

John Ayers, *Chinese and Korean Pottery and Porcelain:* Vol. II of *The Seligman Collection of Oriental Art* (London, 1964); *The Baur Collection*, 4 vols. (London, 1968–74).

Stephen Bushell, *Description of Chinese Pottery and Porcelain: Being a Translation of the T'ao Shuo* (Oxford, 1910).

Sir Harry Garner, *Oriental Blue and White*, 3rd ed. (London, 1970).

G. St. G. M. Gompertz, *Chinese Celadon Wares* (London, 1958).

R. L. Hobson, *A Catalogue of Chinese Pottery and Porcelain in the Collection of Sir Percival David* (London, 1934).

Soame Jenyns, *Ming Pottery and Porcelain* (London, 1953); *Later Chinese Porcelain*, 4th ed. (London, 1971).

Margaret Medley, *Yüan Porcelain and Stoneware* (London, 1974); *T'ang Pottery and Porcelain* (London, 1981).

John A. Pope, *Chinese Porcelain from the Ardebil Shrine* (Washington, 1956).

Mary Tregear, *Song Ceramics* (London, 1982).

Suzanne G. Valenstein, *A Handbook of Chinese Ceramics* (New York, 1975).

See also Exhibitions and General Collections.

MINOR ARTS

Michel Beurdeley, *Chinese Furniture* (Tokyo, New York, and San Francisco, 1979).

Schuyler Cammann, *China's Dragon Robes* (New York, 1952).

Martin Feddersen, *Chinese Decorative Art* (London, 1961).

Sir Harry Garner, *Chinese and Japanese Cloisonné Enamels* (London, 1962); *Chinese Lacquer* (London, 1979).

S. Howard Hansford, *Chinese Jade Carving* (London, 1950); *Chinese Carved Jades* (London, 1968).

George N. Kates, *Chinese Household Furniture* (London, 1948).

Berthold Laufer, *Jade: A Study in Chinese Archaeology and Religion* (New York, 1912).

Max Loehr, *Ancient Chinese Jades from the Grenville L. Winthrop Collection* (Cambridge, Massachusetts, 1975).

Pauline Simmons, *Chinese Patterned Silks* (New York, 1948).

PERIODICALS

Archives of Asian Art (formerly *Archives of the Chinese Art Society of America*) (New York, 1945–   ).

Artibus Asiae (Dresden, 1925–1940); (Ascona, 1947–   ).

Art Orientalis (Washington, D.C., and Ann Arbor, Michigan, 1954–   ).

Bulletin of the Museum of Far Eastern Antiquities (Stockholm, 1929–   ).

China Reconstructs (Peking, 1950–   ).

Early China (Berkeley, 1975–   ).

Far Eastern Ceramic Bulletin (Boston, 1948–1950; Ann Arbor, Michigan, 1951–1960).

Oriental Art (Oxford, 1948–1951, New Series, 1955–   ).

Transactions of the Oriental Ceramic Society (London, 1921–   ).

Index

liu-po (liubo), 76
Liu Sheng, Han prince, 38, 62
Liu-t'ung-ssu, Hangchow (Liu-
tongsi, Hangzhou), 170
Loehr, Max, cited, 25
Lohan, 145
Lolang, Korea, 69
Loyang, Honan (Louyang, He-
nan), 35, 57, 59, 74, 86
Lu Chi (Lu Ji), 87
Lü Chi (Lü Ji), 205
Lu Chih (Lu Zhi), 209
Lu Hsün (Lu Xun), 255
Lu Yü (Lu Yu), author of Tea Clas-
sic, 138
Lü Shou-k'un (Lü Shoukun), 258
Lung-ch'üan (Longquan) ware,
176–178, 195
Lungmen, Honan (Longmen,
Henan), 103–104, 122
Lung-shan, Shantung (Longshan,
Shandong), 7, 8, 9, 14

Ma-chia-yao, Kansu (Majiayao,
Gansu), 7
Ma-wang-tui, Changsha, Hunan
(Mawangdui, Changsha,
Hunan), 50, 71
Ma Yüan (Ma Yuan), 168–169
Mai-chi-shan, Kansu (Maijishan,
Gansu), 100, 104–105
Man-ch'eng, Hopei (Mancheng,
Hebei), 38
Manchus, 223–224
Mao Tse-tung (Mao Zedong), 1,
253, 258, 261
Mei Ch'ing (Mei Qing), 233
Meng-ch'i pi-t'an (Mengqi bitan),
quoted, 155–156
metal-working, early evidence for,
10, 14–15
Mi Fu, 161–163
Mi Yu-jen (Mi Youren), 163
microlithic culture, 3
ming-ch'i (mingqi) "spirit utensils,"
49
Ming Huang. See Hsüan-tsung
(Xuanzong) T'ang Emperor
(713–756)
Ming-t'ang (Mingtang), 34
mirrors, 52–53, 74–76, 135–136
Mizuno Sei-ichi, quoted, 26
mo-ku-hua (moguhua), "boneless
painting," 132, 237
Mongols, 179–180
Mu-ch'i (Muqi), 170–171
Mu Wang, Chou (Zhou) king, 32,
49
music, 43, 45–46, 117

"Nankeen ware," 245

Nanking (Nanjing), 85, 92, 103,
198, 232
Nanyang, Honan (Nanyang,
Henan), 29, 66
Nara, Japan, 98
Neo-Confucianism, 143, 202
neolithic culture, 3–11
Ni Tsan (Ni Zan), 189, 190–191,
195, 206
Ni Tuan (Ni Duan), 205
Nien Hsi-yao (Nian Xiyao), 240,
243
Noin-Ula, Mongolia, 79–80
Northern and Southern Schools of
landscape painting, 131, 210–
212

O-p'ang Kung (Epang Gong),
Ch'in (Qin) palace, 54
oracle bones, 12, 14, 16–17, 185
Ordos art, 46–47

pagoda, 98, 118, 144
pa kua (bagua), eight trigrams, 13,
90
Pa-ta Shan-jen (Bada Shanren). See
Chu Ta (Zhu Da)
painted pottery, Neolithic, 5–9
painting: Ch'u (Chu), 50–51; Han,
67–71; Six Dynasties, 87–95;
T'ang (Tang), 124–133; Five
Dynasties, 148–150; Sung
(Song), 151–172; Yüan (Yuan),
183–185, 188–195; Ming, 204–
212; Ch'ing (Qing), 228–240;
twentieth century, 250–262. See
also bamboo painting; bird-and-
flower painting; dragon painting; landscape painting; realism
in painting; wall-painting
pan-chu (banzhu) building technique, 17
P'an-lung, Hupei (Panlong, Hu-
bei), 16
Pan-p'o, Shensi (Banpo, Shaansi),
5–7, 79
Pan-shan, Kansu (Banshan,
Gansu), 5, 7
P'an-keng (Pangeng), King, 13
P'an Ku (Pan Gu), 1
P'ang Hsün-ch'in (Pang Xunqin),
255
paper, invention of, 70–71
Pei-yao-ts'un, Honan (Beiyaocun,
Henan), 39
P'ei Wen-chung (Pei Wenzhong),
Dr., 3
Peking (Beijing), 179–182, 223,
226–228, 250
Peking man, 3
perspective, 155–156

pi (bi), jade, 10, 53
Pien Wen-chin (Bien Wenjin), 204
Pin-yang-tung, Lungmen, Honan
(Binyangdong, Longmen,
Henan), 104
Ping-ling-ssu, Kansu (Bing-lingsi,
Gansu), 100
po-shan hsiang-lu (boshan xianglu)
incense burner, 73
Polo, Marco, 180
porcelain: definition of, 39; per-
fecting of, 137
pottery, definition of, 39
printing, 143, 266 (Ch. 7n. 1); col-
our, 203–204
P'u Ch'in (Pu Qin), 257
P'u-tu-ts'un, Shensi (Puducun,
Shaansi), 39

realism in painting, 158–160
Rent Collection Courtyard, 260
Ricci, Matteo, 203, 224
Rome, Chinese silk in, 79
roof curve, origin of, 119

San Ta Tien (San Da Dien), Three
Great Halls, Peking (Beijing),
181–182
san ts'ai (sancai), three colour
wares, 140, 221
screen painting, 92, 151
sculpture: Shang, 19–20; Chou
(Zhou), 34; Ch'u (Chu), 50;
Han, 62–67; Six Dynasties, 100–
107, 110–111; T'ang (Tang),
121–123; Sung (Song), 145–156;
Ming, 212–213; twentieth cen-
tury, 260
Shan-hai-ching (Shanhaijing), 56
Shang-fang (Shangfang), Imperial
Workshop, 70, 76
Shang-lin-hu, Chekiang (Shang-
linhu, Zhejiang), kilns at, 84,
113, 137
Shang-ts'un-ling, Honan (Shang-
cunling, Henan), 36
Shang-yü-hsien, Chekiang
(Shangyuxian, Zhejiang), kilns
in, 113
Shao Mi, 212
Shen Chou (Shen Zhou), 206–209,
211
Shen Kua (Shen Gua), cited, 155–
156, 160, 166
Shih-chai-shan, Yunnan (Shizhai-
shan, Yunnan), 73–74
Shih-ch'i (Shiqi), 233
Shih-ching (Shijing), Book of Songs,
33–34, 79
Shih-chu-chai shu-hua p'u (Shizhu-
zhai shuhua pu), 204

Designer: Eric Jungerman
Compositor: Wilsted & Taylor
Printer: Kingsport Press
Binder: Kingsport Press
Text: 10/12 Bembo
Display: Bembo